D1283248

1/20/73

THE NEW APOCALYPSE:

THE RADICAL CHRISTIAN VISION

OF WILLIAM BLAKE

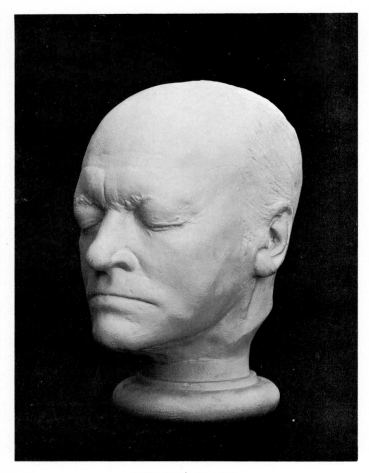

WILLIAM BLAKE.
Plaster Cast from a Life-Mask by J. S. Deville, 1823.
Courtesy of the National Portrait Gallery, London.

THE NEW APOCALYPSE:
THE RADICAL CHRISTIAN VISION
OF WILLIAM BLAKE

by Thomas J. J. Altizer

MICHIGAN STATE UNIVERSITY PRESS

1967

★
★
★
★
★

Credit is given to the Westminster Press for material originally
appearing in *The Gospel of Christian Atheism* (1966).

For Jane and Nell

CONTENTS

CONTENTS

ABBREVIATIONS

FOR WORKS OF WILLIAM BLAKE

NOTE: Citations from the engraved works of Blake contain references first to the number of the plate and then to the line or lines on the plate (e.g., J. 10:10); citations from the manuscripts of Blake are either to the line of the manuscript (e.g., F.Z. I, 10) or to the original page number of Blake's notebook (e.g., V.L.J. p. 70). All of this material may be found in Sir Geoffrey Keynes edition of the *Complete Writings of William Blake* (Nonesuch and Random House, 1957). The dates of composition given below are taken from *A Blake Bibliography* by G. E. Bentley, Jr., and Martin K. Nurmi (University of Minnesota Press, 1964).

A.	*America* (engraved), 1793
B.U.	*The First Book of Urizen* (engraved), 1794
E.	*Europe* (engraved), 1794
E.G.	"The Everlasting Gospel" (manuscript), 1818 (probably)
F.Z.	"Vala" or "The Four Zoas" (manuscript), 1795–1808 (probably)
J.	*Jerusalem* (engraved), 1804–1807–1820 (probably)
M.	*Milton* (engraved), 1804–1808 (probably)
M.H.H.	*The Marriage of Heaven and Hell* (engraved), 1790–1793
S.E.	*Songs of Experience* (engraved), 1794
S.I.	*Songs of Innocence* (engraved), 1789
V.D.A.	*Visions of the Daughters of Albion* (engraved), 1793
V.L.J.	"Vision of the Last Judgement" (manuscript), 1810

INTRODUCTION

IT IS the thesis of this book that William Blake is the most original prophet and seer in the history of Christendom, that he created a whole new form of vision embodying a modern radical and spiritual expression of Christianity, and that an understanding of his revolutionary work demands a new form of theological understanding. Although radical Christianity was given a genuine mystical expression by Meister Eckhart and his followers, to say nothing of the radical Protestant mystics of the sixteenth and seventeenth centuries, it has never made a real impact upon Christian theology, and not until Blake was it given a full visionary form. Unlike the epic poetry of Dante and Milton, Blake's prophetic poetry both transcends and negates its roots in the Christian tradition: it unveils a Jesus who is the totality of both God and man, envisions a cosmic history reflecting a movement from Fall to Apocalypse, and records an ecstatic immersion in the joy and the horror of concrete experience. To enter the world of Blake's vision is to be initiated into a new and radical form of faith, a paradoxical but deeply modern faith which is both sacred and profane, both mystical and contemporary at once. For Blake was the first Christian atheist, the first visionary who chose the kenotic or self-emptying path of immersing himself in the profane reality of experience as the way to the God who is all in all in Jesus.

If a Heidegger can speak of the poet as the shepherd of Being, then the Christian theologian must learn to treat the artist as a prophetic seer, a visionary whose work records a new epiphany of the Spirit. So long as theology and the Christian community maintain the priestly conviction that revelation is a once-and-for-all event of the past, it will be closed to the prophetic faith that revelation continues in history, and continues in such a way as to challenge the most deeply cherished certainties of faith. That Blake's vision is still in effect unknown to the theologian is mute testimony to theology's reluctance to open itself to a prophetic or revolutionary vocation. True, it was not until almost a hundred years after his death in 1827 that a genuine appreciation and understanding of Blake arose; but surely there can no longer be an excuse for theology's refusal at this date to encounter the most original visionary produced by the Christian world. The present study represents an initial theological attempt to enter the world of Blake's vision, to appropriate from that vision a theological form that will be relevant to our situation, and to do so on the basis of a dialectical understanding of theology. Inasmuch as Christian theology has never yet given expression to a consistent dialectical method, this study has chosen Hegel as a guide to the dialectical ground and meaning of Blake's vision: for Hegel is the only thinker in the West who has created a comprehensive mode of dialectical thinking. While Calvinism or medieval scholasticism can provide the basis for a conceptual understanding of the visions of Milton and Dante, no comparable source exists to give such a mode of entry into Blake's vision, and it is a thesis of this study that Hegel's dialectical "system" is a far more effective guide to Blake's visionary world than are the traditional forms of Christian theology and mysticism.

Literary critics often pretend that no conceptual key is needed to the meaning of a work of literature. Yet even Blake's ablest interpreters again and again fall back upon a simple allegorical translation of Blake's symbols—despite the fact that Blake violently attacked such allegorical thinking and insisted that it represents the antithesis of "Vision"—thus demonstrating that the "non-philosophical" critic will only engage in bad philosophical thinking. Many critics also protest against a theological interpretation of Blake's work, but it is idle to pretend that his vision is non-theological; we have only to recognize that it proceeds out of an inversion of the Christian thelogical tradition in order to realize how profoundly theological it is, and thereby we will also come to see that his vision is inseparable from a dialectical ground. It is precisely at this point that Blake's work has such profound relevance to the contemporary theologian; and he should also rejoice to discover that Blake celebrated the death of God as providing the path to a total union with Jesus. Indeed, the Blake who went beyond even Nietzsche in the violence and comprehensiveness of his attack upon the Christian God, was also the Blake who arrived at a totally Christocentric vision of faith.

However, ours is a time in which both the theologian and the profane thinker are united in their opposition to the reality of "Vision." Not only is the theologian closed to vision, but he has also increasingly attacked both myth and religion, finding them to be either sinful expressions of idolatry and self-righteousness, or joining the positivistic temper of the age by ascribing them to pre-scientific fantasy. Such judgments have little critical weight if only because their conception of religion is invariably drawn from the debased piety of a dying Christendom; but they can have tragic effects, such as the Barthian school's search for a biblical but non-religious language of revelation, or the Bultmannian school's seemingly unquestioned assumption that early Christian mythical symbols can be translated into modern existential categories without in any way affecting their ultimate meaning. Despite the remarkable expressions of vision in contemporary art and literature, it would seem to be a common assumption of our time that vision is confined to a pre-modern culture, that it cannot survive in the presence of scientific thinking, and that it has no integral relation to the true or purer meaning of faith. Tempting as it would be simply to assign such an assumption to the province of ignorance, a deeper problem is at hand. For faith and vision are now dissociated: as the imagination and faith have increasingly become alienated from one another, each can exist only by dissolving, negating, or transforming the other.

To speak in our time of the mutual alienation of faith and the imagination is to speak in fact of the death of God in the modern world. Lament as we may its vanished glory, the whole world of Christendom is eroding about us; as its foundations disappear into the dark ocean of our historical past, we can experience only the receding ripples of its dying waves. Twentieth century theology has met this challenge by an heroic if futile effort to establish an island of faith, an impregnable fortress fully shielded from the dangers about it, but a fortress containing a lighthouse that would direct a saving beacon to the darkness without. Faith is then declared to be either *a priori* or autonomous; transcending a human or an historical ground, it is open to no experience whatsoever. At last the time has come when the waters of destiny have swallowed up this celestial island; or, at least, it is no longer present to view; it has vanished from our historical horizon, as its beacon has become a mirror reflecting the vacuity of a faith attempting to stand upon thin air. Wholly isolated from contemporary history and experience, the traditional Word of faith is now silent; and, linger as we may with its vanishing echo, we are nevertheless confronted with the necessity of either desperately clinging to a past moment of the Christian Word or of opening ourselves to a radically new form of faith.

As the waters of a profane darkness converge upon the island of faith, theology has an inevitable temptation to return to a past moment of faith, and more particularly to exalt a priestly theology of salvation history, a celebration of a series of events that are past and irreversible as the source of salvation. Grave dangers already beset this theological choice: either the events of salvation history are isolated and hidden from the events of profane history, as in the Bultmannian school; or the meaning and reality of salvation history is transformed into the mass currents of our profane history, if only in response to the overwhelming power of the profane consciousness in our time. The contemporary reader of the Bible almost invariably discovers that he reads its priestly epics either as recounting a series of isolated and legendary events or as narrating a sequence of a profane and all-too-human history. Not only do we inherit the historical revolution of the nineteenth century, a revolution which stripped all historical events of a transcendent ground; but we also live in an epoch which has effected what Marx termed the reification of human consciousness, an alienated state of self-consciousness in which external objects and events have become the measure of man. Today a priestly theology of salvation history all too quickly assumes a positivistic form. Theology may avoid this danger by retreating from history and understanding salvation as subjective, solitary, and "existential." Or, insofar as it employs a language retaining any meaning, it must allow the past events of salvation history to pass into an archaic world that is wholly isolated and irrecoverable in the present. Consequently, we must recognize that a priestly form of biblical theology is not possible for us: such events as the Exodus and the Resurrection cannot appear to us in both an historical and a sacred form, just as Jesus can no longer appear to faith as the eternal Word of God who is simultaneously the historical Jesus of Nazareth.

Christian theology, in our situation, can continue to maintain its traditional form only by becoming the depository of a Word that has no relevance and therefore no meaning in our world. While such a vocation may well be essential to the preservation of the existing community of faith, it must be complemented and challenged by a radical theology that dares to encounter the new world which is dawning in our era, even if such a confrontation condemns theology to pass through a revolutionary process of rebirth. Moreover, now that the Second Vatican Council gives promise of a reformation of the Catholic Church which will both absorb the positive gains of the Protestant Reformation and make possible an entrance of Catholicism into the modern world, it is also time for theology to return to the call of the radical reformers with their promise of a spiritual Christianity which will usher in the third age of the Spirit. From the time of the early Franciscan movement such radical reformers have attacked the institutional Church as the embodiment of the repressive authority of the past; and they have called for a total compassion and self-giving which is the consequence of a true participation in the new age of the Spirit, an eschatological time marking the full coming together of God and man. Radical Christian movements have always been either mystical or apocalyptic, and often they have been both: for in opposing a given form of religious meaning and moral law, they have sought a total convergence of flesh and Spirit making possible an immediate actualization of the eschatological promise of Jesus.

William Blake is not only the most original but he is also the most daring and most radical of all Christian visionaries. It was not for nothing that after his death one of his friends destroyed many of his manuscripts—which, alas, are now irretrievably lost!—because of a conviction that they were inspired by Satan. Nor is it accidental that it took so long for Blake's work to gain a hearing. While his lyric poetry is overwhelming in its simple power and sheer immediacy, his prophetic poetry poses innumerable problems for his reader if only because it records a vision that is not susceptible to expression in traditional poetic forms. Blake was forced to create not only a new imagery and a new symbolism but also a new literary genre, the poetic apocalypse. We must also note that his poetry cannot be separated from his illustrations and designs; for his prophetic poems are not simply poetry, inasmuch as each poem is integrally related to the etchings or drawings which accompany it, whether in the actual engravings or in his notebook. Likewise it is essential to know that Blake was a self-educated man. Without a single day of what we know as formal schooling, he was spared the artificial learning which is so dominant in the West, and came to believe that education is a fundamental error insofar as it substitutes instruction for experience. He deeply shocked Crabb Robinson by declaring education to be "the great sin." No doubt there is a significant relation between Blake's escape from a formal education and his ability to enter a state of vision; nevertheless, his visions are not those of an ignorant man, they are saturated with references to a wide variety of data and often show an uncanny understanding of the imaginative tradition which preceded him. We will only understand Blake as a revolutionary seer by realizing that he passed through an interior reversal and transformation of the Western Christian tradition.

A major source of confusion in the study of Blake is the repeated attempt to discover an exact conceptual or mythical system in his vision, with the underlying assumption that the center of his vision is capable of being translated into a precise and fully coherent scheme. When one remembers the passion with which Blake attacked a pure reason or "Ratio," it seems incredible that a responsible critic could believe that a rational or systematic thinking lies at the foundation of his work, to say nothing of the fact that Blake chose the worst possible vehicle for the expression of this kind of system. It is true, of course, that in his greatest work, *Jerusalem*, he declared:

"I must Create a System or be enslav'd by another Man's.
I will not Reason & Compare: my business is to Create."
(J. 10:20 f.)

Yet Blake's is a "system" which is not the product of a rational analysis and it cannot be translated into rational terms. Blake profoundly opposed all of the established forms of conceptual coherence and we must never lose sight of this fact. Thus it is wholly misleading to speak about the exact meaning of Blake's mythical figures, or the precise route of his "Circle of Destiny," or even about his pantheon or his psychological or metaphysical system. It must be stated unequivocally that to find such meaning in Blake's vision is to abandon both its imaginative form and its revolutionary achievement.

Too many critics continue to believe that Blake's vision is yet another expression of an ancient mystical tradition; but not the least of the accomplishments of recent Blake scholarship is to have completely shattered this illusion. From the perspective of the discipline of the history of religions, the most startling thing about Blake's work is the way in which it so fully integrates a mystical and a prophetic vision. True, Blake attempted to recreate the prophetic visions of the Bible in the language of modern poetry. But he went beyond his biblical predecessors in the manner in which he integrated the burning social and intellectual problems of the modern West into the body of his visions, just as he created a unique form of vision capturing the immediacy of concrete experience. Blake ever sought a total form of vision, a vision embodying the totality and comprehensiveness of the mystical tradition, but one which was directed to the actuality of what he called "Experience." In his mature work he created a new apocalyptic form comprehending the realms of heaven, paradise, earth, and death; but the very reality of this vision depends upon a continual and dialectical movement between its fourfold components, a movement whose ground and goal is an apocalyptic union of the seemingly separate worlds of vision.

While both the proclamation of Jesus and the faith of primitive Christianity were fully apocalyptic, as Christianity evolved into its established or orthodox form it progressively abandoned and dissolved its original apocalyptic foundation. A wide variety of sectarian and heretical movements have repeatedly attempted to return to Christianity's original apocalyptic faith, but the movement of Christian history would seem to be irreversible, as the goal of recovering the primitive Christian faith has ever remained elusive. We can sense the depth of Christianity's estrangement from its original ground by noting that until the work of Blake it was only in the non-verbal arts that Christendom produced an apocalyptic imagery, to say nothing of the fact that Christian theology has never assumed an apocalyptic form, nor has the theologian even made the attempt to think through the full meaning of Jesus' apocalyptic or eschatological proclamation. Blake was, of course, an apocalyptic seer; but we must not imagine that he simply recovered the apocalyptic vision of Jesus, for he re-created that vision in a new and more comprehensive and universal form. One has only to compare Blake's *Jerusalem* with ancient apocalyptic writings to realize the magnitude of Blake's achievement, and to note that Swedenborg is his greatest modern rival as an apocalyptic seer is to speak wondrously of Blake. Perhaps soon we shall even come to understand that Blake's revolutionary transformation of apocalyptic vision made possible a whole new world of literature, a world extending from the symbolist poetry and drama of the nineteenth century to such apparently diverse descendents as *Finnegans Wake* and *The Castle*.

The greatest problem posed for Blake's reader is that of entering his vision; for his is a visionary world, and we can comprehend its meaning only to the extent that we ourselves become open to "Vision." We must be prepared to enter a world of total vision, a vision intending to embrace all reality whatsoever, and calling upon its participant to engage all his faculties in a new and unified mode of vision. Thus the central figure of *Jerusalem* is Albion, a cosmic and primordial Man whose fall and redemption is celebrated on the plates of this epic. Albion, however, is both a human and a cosmic figure, and his movements are a symbolic reflection of the totality of both history and the cosmos. Furthermore, Albion is simultaneously both human and divine, and his fall and redemption embody a movement in the Godhead, as the transcendent God comes into existence through a fall, then dies, and is finally resurrected as Jerusalem or "The Great Humanity Divine." Neither the poetry nor the designs of *Jerusalem* move forward in a consistent or consecutive sense; nor do we find a plot, a theological argument, or even distinct characters and events. Everything flows together in this apocalyptic epic, as both the mythical and the human figures are transformed into one another, and each event is repeated and reenacted in the multiple cosmic and historical worlds which are here unveiled. *Jerusalem* leads its reader through a total range of experience, moving back and forth between the poles of an orderless chaos and a fully integrated mode of vision, as we ourselves are summoned to become what we behold. In one sense, reading *Milton* or *Jerusalem* is like reading a Buddhist sutra, which is to say that it is not "reading" at all, but rather an interior repetition of a mystical Totality. Yet unlike their mystical counterparts these epics are genuine works of literature which are directed to the imaginative faculties of every man. Indeed, these works confront us with the call to a new Totality, a Totality which is both sacred and profane, while simultaneously being both human, cosmic, and divine.

We cannot hope within the limits of this study to comprehend the whole world of Blake's vision, nor can we hope to assess its full theological meaning. Inevitably, distortion and error will enter this analysis, and not simply because of the obvious limitations of the author, but also because we must in large part enter uncharted ground. Recognizing the barriers to the contemporary reader which are posed by Blake's vision, we shall only gradually enter the strange new world which is present in his work, at first inquiring into its intrinsic foundations, and then pursuing its ultimate theological implications. Our study will revolve about the major Blakean motifs of Fall, Redemption, History, and Apocalypse. But it must not be presumed that these motifs are related to one another in a rationally consistent sense: each can and does dialectically pass into the other, and it is only in a highly artificial and misleading sense that we can conceive of them as representing the progressive stages of the evolution and involution of Spirit.

All of the quotations from the Bible will be from the King James translation; for while Blake taught himself Hebrew and Greek, he was deeply influenced by the King James version. A word of warning is also in order about the punctuation to be found in this book. Blake himself employed little punctuation in his major works, and the punctuation to be found in the citations here is simply taken verbatim from Sir Geoffrey Keynes' 1957 edition of the *Complete Writings of William Blake* (Nonesuch Press and Random House). Readers who wish to consult an authoritative version of the original texts should employ David V. Erdman's edition of *The Poetry and Prose of William Blake* (Doubleday, 1965). I have also been forced in my own analysis to make use of capitalization in a seemingly arbitrary manner (e.g., Creation is distinguished from creation); but almost invariably my intention was to capture by this means a meaning which otherwise could not be expressed.

Speaking both as a lover of Blake and as a theologian, I take pleasure in acknowledging my great debt to those pioneering studies of Blake which have made his work available to today's reader, and most particularly so to those of Joseph Wicksteed, F. Foster Damon, Milton O. Percival, and Northrop Frye. I must also confess that I have largely approached Blake by way of Nietzsche, not that Nietzsche has been directly employed in this study, but I know that it was only through Nietzsche that I became open to Blake. Those readers who would prefer a conservative approach to the theological meaning of Blake can find one in J. G. Davies' *The Theology of William Blake* (The Clarendon Press, Oxford, 1948), where Blake's vision is for the most part understood as an expression of the orthodox Christian tradition. I would like to think that my study of Blake is the product of a new theological mood in America, a mood that is expressing itself in a theological movement resting upon a positive acceptance of the death of God, and I hope that Blake will prove to be a major prophet for the contemporary radical Christian. The present book is also in part a continuation of my previous book, *Mircea Eliade and the Dialectic of the Sacred* (The Westminster Press, 1963); it certainly is dependent upon Eliade's understanding of the *coincidentia oppositorum,* and while writing the major portion of this book I received the constant encouragement and support of Professor Eliade.

My wife, Gayle, has not only given me her devoted support but has also played an invaluable role by her response to the thinking and writing that went into these pages. I am grateful for a grant received from the Research Committee of Emory University that paid for many of the expenses incurred in the preparation of the book; and I am once again grateful to Barbara Harkins who performed many of the duties of an editor in typing the manuscript.

INTRODUCTION

The book is dedicated to my sisters if only because they embody so many of the qualities which Blake envisioned in the female. Finally, I would be the first to acknowledge that this book only faintly and inadequately does justice to its theme; but if it serves in any way to lead the contemporary Christian to the living waters of William Blake, it will have more than fulfilled its purpose.

I
FALL

---

1. Dialectic and Fall

ONE CRY is ever upon Blake's lips as he sings one song in myriad forms: "Awake! Awake O sleeper of the land of shadows, wake! expand!" (J. 4:6). Man, the cosmos, reality itself—having fallen into division, generation, and decay—now sleeps the sleep of eternal death; and, the fall is not a once-and-for-all event, it is an eternal process, an eternal round of darkness and horror, even though that horror has assumed the illusory light of a fallen sun. Poets and prophets must name the horror: but the very act of naming stills its power, unveils its darkness, bringing light to darkness itself. Blake reveals that finally the poet and the prophet are one; the piper whose song brings joy to the child is the lamb whose pain both challenges and defies the tyrannic wheels of experience. If Innocence and Experience, the two contrary states of the human soul, must culminate in a common Vision, then that Vision must act upon that which it portrays; it must affect that which it reflects, and this must be because Vision is only possible by means of a transfiguration of its matter, a loosening of the stones that bind fallen man to his divided state. Hence the poet and the prophet must pronounce and act a No upon the world about and within them. Only on the basis of this No can Vision appear, and the power and scope of Vision depend inevitably upon the comprehensiveness of its rejection and reversal of experience. Blake, like his Old Testament prophetic forebears, would appear to have spent his life and work in final No-saying; but that No-saying is dialectical; on its ground, and only on its ground, appears the Yes-saying of Apocalypse.

Hegel, too, created a dialectical mode of vision, a vision reflecting a continual movement of negation; but dialectical negation is the source of life and movement, of comprehensive understanding (*Vernunft*) and forward-moving process. True conceptual understanding, as Hegel conceives it, is identical with religion insofar as it must negate the given: "for religion equally with philosophy refuses to recognize in finitude a veritable being, or something ultimate and absolute, or non-posited, uncreated, and eternal."[1] The philosopher who believed that Essence is the absolute negativity of Being, who maintained that the Essence of anything is the antithesis to that which it presents to immediate experience, was an Idealist only in the sense that he identified reality with the negativity of that which appears and directed the deepest thrust of his Dialectic against the sheer "isness" of immediate being. The given, simple immediacy or finitude, is not simply the veil of the Absolute. For the Absolute can only appear, can only exist, in the reversal or negation of the immediately given. Therefore the process of negating the given in all its forms is the one and only means by which the Absolute exists; and the Dialectic must not simply identify the immediately given world as a fallen world, but must unveil the alienation and brokenness of fallenness as the very arena and process in which Spirit appears and is real.

Just as Blake, the purest lyricist of English poetry, was destined by his very vision to become the greatest prophetic seer in Christendom, so Innocence must become Experience, and the imagery of Experience must reflect a night which has become all-encompassing, allowing no residue of light or purity to escape or transcend its awesome totality. Albion's fall into division and decay is not only the fall of man but also of all reality whatsoever; no God or Heaven remains above or beyond this round of suffering and chaos; no realm of goodness or truth is immune to this universal process of descent; no primordial paradise or Eden remains open to ecstatic entry. In the light of Vision, the Fall is all, and, dialectically, the very fullness of Vision derives from the totality of its fallen ground: Vision cannot reverse all things unless it initially knows them in a fallen form. An eschatological End can only follow a primordial Beginning, but that Beginning is not Creation, it is Fall; and not Fall as a primordial and distant event but as a continual and present process, a process that has become identical with the very reality of existence itself. Consequently, we must not be appalled at the centrality of the image of the Fall in

Blake's work, we must not be dismayed that he very nearly succeeded in inverting all of the established categories of Western thought and experience; we must rather recognize that it is precisely this act of dialectical inversion which prepares the way for the apocalyptic vision of genuine faith. Faith is Vision, proclaims Blake, and every seer. But Vision can neither arise nor be consummated apart from a transformation of the totality of Experience. If Faith is to become real in this final sense, it must ground itself in a dialectical inversion of everything which has passed through the "dark Satanic Mills" of history and the cosmos.

II. God

WHILE Blake is the one poet who has in a very real sense created a whole mythology, it is clear upon analysis that he derived the majority of his mythical figures and symbols from various historical traditions, the great exceptions being his symbol of the Web or Wheel of Religion and his figure of Nobodaddy or Urizen. Blake's vision was ever circular and fluid: characters and images move within and without his range in a perplexing manner. No real "system" is present in his work; instead we find a poetic or prophetic consistency arising from a series of dominant, if evasive, motifs. From the beginning he rebelled against God, or against the God then present in Christendom, ironically disguising his attack by presenting Him under the guise of a number of simple though powerful symbols, the most successful of which is surely the Tiger. The God of Blake's manuscript poem "To Nobodaddy" is a silent and invisible Father of jealousy, the author of the tyrannically harsh but obscure laws of revelation. In one sense, as Joseph Wicksteed suggests,[2] "The Tyger" is an answer to Nobodaddy, but it is an answer which deepens the horror of the silent Deity.

> Tyger! Tyger! burning bright
> In the forests of the night,
> What immortal hand or eye,
> Dare frame thy fearful symmetry?

Much has been made of the fact that Blake has changed the "Could" of the first stanza to the "Dare" of the last stanza, while leaving the stanza otherwise intact. But this change was necessitated by the penultimate stanza which contains the real meaning of the poem:

> When the stars threw down their spears,
> And water'd heaven with their tears,
> Did he smile his work to see?
> Did he who made the Lamb make thee?

Not only did the Creator make both the Lamb and the Tiger; he is also manifest in each. Yet in Experience he is truly present only in the fearful symmetry of the Tiger.

For the early Blake, the passionate rebel, God is the primary product and agent of repression, His law, the deepest obstacle to liberty and joy. Yet the transcendent and wholly other God is not eternal; only when "Thought chang'd the infinite to a serpent" did God become "a tyrant crown'd" (E. 10:16–23). The first chapter of *The Book of Urizen* opens with these lines:

> Lo, a shadow of horror is risen
> In Eternity! Unknown, unprolific,
> Self-clos'd, all-repelling: what Demon
> Hath form'd this abominable void,
> This soul-shudd'ring vacuum? Some said
> "It is Urizen." But unknown, abstracted,
> Brooding, secret, the dark power hid.

Here, Urizen appears as the Creator, who, unseen and unknown, divides and measures space by space in his "ninefold darkness." Thus Urizen is a product of the Fall, His very holiness, His *mysterium tremendum*, is created out of his dark solitude, where as He proclaims, "Here alone I" have written:

> "Laws of peace, of love, of unity,
> Of pity, compassion, forgiveness;
> Let each chuse one habitation,
> His ancient infinite mansion,

> One command, one joy, one desire,
> One curse, one weight, one measure,
> One King, one God, one Law."
>   (B.U. 4:34–40)

The figure of Urizen undergoes many transitions and transformations as Blake's vision unfolds until he finally disappears in *Jerusalem*. Always, however, He is associated with the iron laws of the present creation, the repressive laws of morality, and the tyranny of governments and history. His realm is the shadowy north but His true abode is a solitary void, for the God who alone is God can only be evolved out of absolute solitude.

Urizen is a peculiarly Blakean creation and, while He may initially have been little more than a parody of the Christian God, He gradually but surely brings to expression much of the fullness of Blake's pathos. Finally Urizen must be judged to be both an artistic and a prophetic failure but, by examining His role in Blake's manuscript epic, *The Four Zoas,* we may be led more deeply into a vision of the Fall and be prepared for its ultimate transfiguration. Urizen first appears in this epic, and we may surmise first comes into existence Himself, when He descends from eternity and announces: "Now I am God from Eternity to Eternity" (I, 319). But Urizen is evolved out of the fall of Albion, the "Universal Man,"; it is man's sense of guilt which makes him imagine a God of purity.[3]

> "Then Man ascended mourning into the splendors of his palace,
> Above him rose a Shadow from his wearied intellect
> Of living gold, pure, perfect, holy; in white linen pure he hover'd,
> A sweet entrancing self delusion, a wat'ry vision of Man
> Soft exulting in existence, all the Man absorbing.
>
> Man fell upon his face prostrate before the wat'ry shadow,
> Saying, 'O Lord, whence is this change? thou knowest I am nothing.' "
>   (III, 49–55)

The voice of the "Slumberous Man" speaks idolatrously to his own Shadow, humbling himself before his God and confessing that he is nothing (Blake then makes him speak the second and seventh verses of the 143rd Psalm). However, the reader must not be misled into believing that God or Urizen is simply a product of delusion in the ordinary sense. Man's "self-delusion" is the inevitable consequence of a fallen cosmos; his Shadow is fully and brutally real in fallen time. So long as man lives in guilt and impotence he can never escape the repressive power of his fearful opposite. Nor did Blake himself abandon this vision; he included this whole section of *The Four Zoas* in the 29th plate of *Jerusalem,* merely omitting the name of Urizen. Significantly, most of the manuscript epic revolves about the acts of Urizen although Blake's frequent and disorderly revisions have obscured whatever pattern these may once have possessed. Urizen is the Creator not of one but of two worlds, the second arising from the ruins of the first; He Himself falls continually and is bound to a fallen world; He creates and then becomes entangled in his own Web of Religion, finally condemning the Lamb of God to death (although this is a very late addition to the epic); then, in the apocalyptic finale (again a late addition) Urizen is resurrected by the Eternal Man, He repents, and then rises to meet the Lord Jesus.

By the conclusion of the epic, Urizen has been transposed into Satan, the Spectre or Selfhood of the mature Blake. At this point we must fully recognize that Blake committed the blasphemy of blasphemies by identifying the biblical God as Satan. Not only did Blake leave numerous personal statements to this effect but in his supreme pictorial creation, his illustrations to the book of Job (and Blake like Kierkegaard ever identified himself with Job), he depicted God as Satan on the magnificient eleventh plate, and did so in fulfillment of his own vision in this work that redemption can only take place after the transcendent and numinous God has been recognized as Satan or Selfhood.[4] Blake concludes *The Gates of Paradise* by addressing these words to Satan:

> Tho' thou art Worship'd by the Names Divine
> Of Jesus & Jehovah, thou art still
> The Son of Morn in weary Night's decline,
> The lost Traveller's Dream under the Hill.

This identification is a consistent motif throughout Blake's later work and as we shall see it underlies his whole prophetic vision of

Apocalypse. In *Milton* Satan has taken on all of the former functions of Urizen, only here Satan does not declare "I am God Alone" until He establishes the Law of repression (9:25). Now Satan is the Spectre of Albion who made Himself a God and destroyed the "Human Form Divine" (32:13); as such He is the Chaos dwelling beyond the skies (20:33). This vision of God as Satan is consummated in *Jerusalem* where the Spectrous Chaos says to Albion, "that Human Form you call Divine is but a Worm," and then reveals that God is the "Great Selfhood, Satan" (33:1–24).

When we reflect that this identification of God and Satan was reached by no ordinary atheist, that it was achieved only after a long and bitter struggle, and was a consequence of a reborn faith and a newly found sense of ultimate regeneration, and above all was integrally a product, as we shall see, of Blake's revolutionary identification with Jesus, then we must be prepared to search out its positive Christian meaning. Fortunately, a clear parallel is present in Hegel's understanding of the "Bad Infinite," and his formulation of this concept in his *Logic* is one of his most luminous expositions. As we have seen, the Dialectic is rooted in the pervasive reality of finitude, but the truth of finitude lies in its end. This end is neither literal nor allegorical for finitude perishes eternally. Accordingly, the true finite and the true infinite reciprocally determine one another, neither can be true nor real apart from the other, and each has its immediate origin in the other, as together they form a dialectical unity. The finite is finite only with reference to the infinite, just as the infinite is infinite only with reference to the finite: "They are inseparable and, at the same time, absolutely, in the relation of Other to each other: each has its Other in itself; thus each is the unity of itself and its Other . . ."[5] The true infinite is known by the conceptual or dialectical understanding (*Vernunft*) which knows that the finite must pass beyond itself and become infinite just as the infinite must pass beyond itself and become finite. But abstract or non-dialectical reason (*Verstand*) cannot think the truth of contradiction and must dualistically separate or isolate the finite from the infinite: "Each is set in a different place: the finite is Determinate Being 'on this side'; the infinite, although it is the in-itself of the finite, is yet placed on the far side, in a dim and inaccessible distance, outside of which the finite is supposed to be and remain."[6]

Thereby the "Bad Infinite" comes into existence, but its ground is not a mere abstract one; it is bound to a "perpetual Ought," it labors under repression insofar as it is nothing more than the bare negation of the finite, and it must be "beyond" if only because it can have no positive relation to the finite. Yet because bad infinity arises as the non-dialectical negation of the finite, it cannot truly rid itself of finitude; the latter reappears within it as its Other: "The progress to infinity is therefore only a recurring monotony, one and the same wearisome alternation of this finite and infinite."[7] True infinity is the infinity of the finite but bad infinity is the infinity of the infinite; the true infinite is already finite but the "Bad Infinite" is wholly other, the God who alone is God.

... infinite, in the sense in which it is taken by this reflection (namely, as opposed to the finite), has in it its Other just because it is opposed to it; that, therefore, it is limited and itself finite. Therefore, if it is asked how the infinite becomes finite, the answer is that there is no infinite which first is infinite and then must become finite or pass on to finitude, but that for itself it is already finite as much as infinite. . . . Or, rather, this should be said, that the infinite has ever passed out to finitude; that absolutely, it does not exist, by itself and without having its Other in itself . . .[8]

Precisely because the "Bad Infinite" is simply opposed to the finite, it is itself both limited and created by this very opposition. An infinite which can become finite only by ceasing to be itself is an infinite that is doomed to be perpetually estranged from finitude. In Blake's terms, this "Bad Infinite" is Satan or Selfhood; it can exist only in an isolated solitude, it can be no more than the simple negation of humanity, and therefore it is the inevitable product of a fallen world.

III. Nature

SHORTLY before Blake's death, Crabb Robinson, who has supplied us with our most accurate portrait of Blake the man, wrote to Dorothy Wordsworth: "Now, according to Blake, Atheism consists in worshipping the natural world, which same natural world, properly speaking, is nothing real, but a mere illusion produced by Satan."[9] Remarkably enough, by this criterion, Blake judged Dante to be an "Atheist," and his own illustrations to *The Divine Comedy* are a virtually unique artistic achievement if only because of their success in transmuting Dante's vision into his own.[10] In his notes to these illustrations, he wrote:

Every thing in Dante's Comedia shews That for Tyrannical Purposes he has made This World the Foundation of All, & the Goddess Nature Mistress; Nature is his Inspirer & not . . . the Holy Ghost. As Poor Shakspeare said: "Nature, thou art my Goddess."

. . . .

Swedenborg does the same thing in saying that in this World is the Ultimate of Heaven. This is the most damnable Falshood of Satan & his Antichrist.

Blake's crucial distinction between Imagination or Vision and Fable or Allegory is that Vision is a representation of what eternally exists whereas Allegory (or that common allegory which is not addressed to the "Intellectual powers" but rather to the mere "Corporeal Understanding") is formed by the "daughters of Memory" (V.L.J. p. 68); such memory can do no more than record the brute actuality of the natural world, hence it is but another prison of fallen man. Thus, in his "Address to the Christians" in *Jerusalem*, Blake speaks of: "Imagination, the real & eternal World of which this Vegetable Universe is but a faint shadow, & in which we shall live in our Eternal or Imaginative Bodies when these Vegetable Mortal Bodies are no more" (J. 77:13). Blake's usual term for the "Atheists" who are bound to nature and memory is Deists, for Deists accept the present

9

state of man and the world and refuse to recognize that: "Man is born a Spectre or Satan & is altogether an Evil, & requires a New Selfhood continually, & must continually be changed into his direct Contrary" (J. 52:10).

Blake was the first Christian seer since the author of the book of Revelation to insist that human redemption is inseparable from the total transformation of the natural world, and like Paul he knew all too firmly that the very advent of the New Adam stands awesome witness to the fallen state of the cosmos. Thereby Blake stood opposed to that overwhelming Western tradition which posits a chasm between man and nature and thus he refused to admit the existence of an autonomous nature. Already in *The Marriage of Heaven and Hell*, one of his proverbs of Hell states that: "Where man is not, nature is barren." Nature is barren apart from man because nature does not and cannot exist apart from man, the idea of an autonomous nature ("the delusive Goddess Nature") is the product of a fallen man estranged from his own eternal being. Blake's clearest evocation of his vision of nature is present in the first book of *Milton:*

> The nature of infinity is this: That every thing has its
> Own Vortex, and when once a traveller thro' Eternity
> Has pass'd that Vortex, he percieves it roll backward behind
> His path, into a globe itself infolding like a sun,
> Or like a moon, or like a universe of starry majesty,
> While he keeps onwards in his wondrous journey on the earth,
> Or like a human form, a friend with whom he liv'd benevolent.
> As the eye of man views both the east & west encompassing
> Its vortex, and the north & south with all their starry host,
> Also the rising sun & setting moon he views surrounding
> His corn-fields and his valleys of five hundred acres square,
> Thus is the earth one infinite plane, and not as apparent
> To the weak traveller confin'd beneath the moony shade.
> Thus is the heaven a vortex pass'd already, and the earth
> A vortex not yet pass'd by the traveller thro' Eternity.
>
> (15:21-35)

What we know as natural objects are vortexes, reflections of the past movements of man. Likewise, nature itself is a reflection of the human "traveller"; its form is always a response to a particular human state;

hence, the vast distances of the starry heavens give witness to the vast time separating us from our ancient human form, just as the compelling immediacy of the earth arises from a particular and present human condition, a condition not yet "pass'd."

First let us note that this startling and fantastic view is not peculiar to Blake; it is found in one form or another in all the great prophets and seers, particularly in the East where mysticism has not been so repressed and inhibited. What is noteworthy is that Blake reached this idea in eighteenth-century England, after having been nourished in radical political circles (although, also, of course, in Swedenborgianism), and quite naturally he ever thereafter looked upon Bacon, Newton, and Locke as his "spiritual" enemies. In a very real sense, Blake's understanding of nature was reached by a dialectical inversion of the idea of nature in Western science, or, at least of that science present upon Blake's horizon. As Milton O. Percival has aptly remarked, for Blake: "It is not the mind, but the world which is 'conditioned.' "[11] Furthermore, the world is conditioned by man; that which we know as external or objective nature is a projection of fallen man. If finally nature is the scattered and broken body of a fallen Albion, then, as Northrop Frye observes: "What we see in nature is our own body turned inside out."[12] But Frye dilutes this insight when he says:

When a fallen human body is created, the physical universe takes the form in which that body must necessarily perceive it. The physical universe thereby becomes the objective counterpart of the fallen human body.[13]

The macrocosm is not simply in harmony with the microcosm: the universe is but a mask of man; its "infinity" testifies to man's original and eternal state; the barrier that separates nature from man is but a sign of man's present alienation. Just as the Oriental mystic attempts to take into himself the cosmos as a whole, Blake's visionary work was directed to the humanization of nature, to the transfiguration of a dead and alien cosmos into the life and joy of the human Imagination. For Blake came not simply to know but also to *see* that it is not only God but likewise nature that only "Acts & Is in existing beings or Men."

Yet unlike the Oriental mystic and the ancient seer, Blake was compelled to encounter an absolutely autonomous nature, an idea and a reality created by modern Western man, wherein nature assumes its most powerful and its most terrible form. Imagination has all but been destroyed by "imitation of Nature's Images drawn from Remembrance" (M. 41:24) as man now sleeps the sleep of eternal death. However, the deepest darkness is an apocalyptic sign of the imminence of the coming Day:

"Will you suffer this Satan, this Body of Doubt that Seems but Is Not,
To occupy the very threshold of Eternal Life? if Bacon, Newton, Locke
Deny a Conscience in Man & the Communion of Saints & Angels,
Contemning the Divine Vision & Fruition, Worshiping the Deus
Of the Heathen, The God of This World, & the Goddess Nature,
Mystery, Babylon the Great, The Druid Dragon & hidden Harlot,
Is it not that Signal of the Morning which was told us in the Beginning?"
(J. 93:20–26)

Moreover, the full meaning of the fallen cosmos cannot arise until the cosmos has become most deeply alienated from man and can finally appear as the apocalyptic "Mystery." The poet's vocation is to make that alienation incarnate in his imagery, to unveil a world of Experience which is an epiphany of Hell, and to pipe a song that will recreate in an audible form the silent horror of its hearer. Through the poet's Vision, the world is present once more in a human form; albeit it can now become manifest only under the forms of pain and auguish. But a suffering world is a human world; if a poet can create a pathos that draws all life, all form, all meaning into its boundaries, then the "Goddess Nature" will cease to be distant and divine and will reveal itself instead to be that Satan who does not "exist."

IV. Perception and the Senses

IN A poem included in a letter written to his friend and patron, Thomas Butts, in 1800, Blake wrote of his first "Vision of Light," a vision of the glorious beams of an unfallen "Sun":

> For each was a Man
> Human-form'd. Swift I ran,
> For they beckon'd to me
> Remote by the Sea,
> Saying: Each grain of Sand,
> Every Stone on the Land,
> Each rock & each hill,
> Each fountain & rill,
> Each herb & each tree,
> Mountain, hill, earth & sea,
> Cloud, Meteor & Star,
> Are Men seen Afar.

Standing in the streams of "Heaven's bright beams," the poet's "Eyes"

> Like a Sea without shore
> Continue Expanding,
> The Heavens commanding,
> Till the Jewels of Light,
> Heavenly Men beaming bright,
> Appear'd as One Man.

A little over a year earlier, in his now famous letter to The Rev. Dr. Trusler, Blake had defended his work against this clerical detractor, insisting that "This World Is a World of imagination & Vision," but it is so only to the eye of Vision, for a miser sees a guinea as being far more beautiful than the sun:

Some See Nature all Ridicule & Deformity, & by these I shall not regulate my proportions; & Some Scarce see Nature at all. But to the Eyes of the Man of Imagination, Nature is Imagination itself. As a man is, So he Sees. As the Eye is formed, such are its Powers.

Or, as Blake was later to write in his annotations to Sir Joshua Reynold's *Discourses:* "Every Eye sees differently. As the Eye, Such the Object."

Only a Deist or a worshipper of the "Goddess Nature" could believe that our senses do no more than reflect a reality that lies beyond and apart from them.[14] We *see* that we *are*, proclaims the seer; the forms of existence create the forms of perception. Yet the Fall inverts the original harmony of the senses, shattering their initial unity, so that the senses become isolated and estranged from one another, with the result that man actually perceives the alien "Goddess Nature." In the eternal cycle of the fallen cosmos, men perceive themselves as an alien other, yet so likewise do they themselves become that other; hence, the haunting refrain of *Jerusalem,* "they became what they beheld." A fallen existence is an expression of its own alienation; bound to a disordered state of its own organs, it now perceives "with" rather than "through" the senses:

> This Life's dim Windows of the Soul
> Distorts the Heavens from Pole to Pole
> And leads you to Believe a Lie
> When you see with, not thro', the Eye
> That was born in a night to perish in a night,
> When the Soul slept in the beams of Light.
> (E.G. d, 103 ff.)

Perception "with" the senses is a perception that is an expression of the senses in their individual and mutually isolated form; such perception creates what we know as nature, and therefore it is confined to what Blake condemned as the "natural man." In his first didactic work, *There Is No Natural Religion* (1788), Blake argued that "naturally" man is only a natural organ subject to sense. While subject to sense, he not only believes a "Lie," but also actually *is* a lie in his own being; apart from that lie his perceptions would not be "bounded by organs of perception."

Blake's insight into the nature of perception could easily be duplicated from the philosophical literature of India, but it also finds a strange if partial parallel in contemporary Western philosophy. Alfred North Whitehead's philosophy of organism is in large measure directed against the dominant subjectivism and sensationalism of the Western philosophic tradition. In attacking this tradition in *Process and Reality,* he defines the "subjectivist" and the "sensationalist" principles as follows:

The subjectivist principle is, that the datum in the act of experience can be adequately analysed purely in terms of universals.
The sensationalist principle is, that the primary activity in the act of

experience is the bare subjective entertainment of the datum, devoid of any subjective form of reception. This is the doctrine of *mere* sensation.[15]

Blake also attacked the idea that there is a "General Knowledge," insisting that all knowledge is "Particular."[16] But Whitehead was more truly Blakean than he was aware when he adopted a reformed subjectivist principle (which he believed was merely an alternative statement of the principle of relativity): "This principle states that it belongs to the nature of a 'being' that it is a potential for every 'becoming.' "[17] Moreover, the *being* of an existing being is constituted by its 'becoming': "*how* an actual entity becomes constitutes *what* that actual entity is."[18] Whitehead's philosophy of organism knows the whole universe as consisting of elements disclosed in the analysis of the experiences of subjects. Process is the becoming of experience in the actual world, and being itself is identified with process: "Finally, the reformed subjectivist principle must be repeated: that apart from the experiences of subjects there is nothing, nothing, nothing, bare nothingness."[19]

Yet another attack upon the idea of mere sensation with all its larger implications may be found in the "phenomenological positivism" of Maurice Merleau-Ponty. In his *Phenomenology of Perception*, Merleau-Ponty understands perception as the background from which all human acts stand out, and it is a background presupposed by these acts. But perception is an interpretation of the world and it is by no means to be understood as secondary to and derivative from an unconscious and prior sensation:

We arrive at sensation when we think about perceptions and try to make it clear that they are not completely our work. Pure sensation, defined as the action of *stimuli* on our body, is the "last effect" of knowledge, particularly of scientific knowledge, and it is an illusion (a not unnatural one, moreover) that causes us to put it at the beginning and to believe that it precedes knowledge. It is the necessary, and necessarily misleading way in which a mind sees its own history. It belongs to the domain of the constituted and not to the constituting mind.[20]

To perceive, in the full sense of the word (which for Merleau-Ponty is the antithesis of imagining), is not to judge but rather to apprehend an immanent meaning in the sensible before judgment begins. True

15

perception is in fact an act of creation: "perception is just that act which creates at a stroke, along with the cluster of data, the meaning which unites them—indeed which not only discovers the meaning *which they* have, but moreover *causes them to have a meaning.*"[21] When perception is understood in this sense, the world can only be known as being inseparable from the subject, but so likewise the subject must be understood as being "destined to be in the world";[22] such a subject can be "nothing but a project of the world,"[23] but this world is a world which the subject projects from itself.

Like all profane thinkers, neither Whitehead nor Merleau-Ponty has any awareness of a world apart from the Fall; thus they identify the whole of reality with either the process of experience or with the world which is projected by the self. Nevertheless, the very totality of their visions inevitably brings them to an apprehension of a natural world which is inseparable from a human world of experience and intention. What their visons lack is the very fluidity of Blake's "fourfold vision" that can comprehend a virtually infinite series of varying relations between humanity and the world. When the four eternal senses of the primordial Man (the four Zoas) became "Four Elements separating from the Limbs of Albion" (J. 36:32), a new world dawned, a world in which humanity is divided and estranged from its original "nature." But the fullness of Blake's vision reveals that this world comes into existence through the contraction of the senses, and, as the senses contract and expand, wholly different worlds arise and pass away, as the "conversations" of the Zoas in Eternity makes manifest:

And they conversed together in Visionary forms dramatic which bright
Redounded from their Tongues in thunderous majesty, in Visions
In new Expanses, creating exemplars of Memory and of Intellect,
Creating Space, Creating Time according to the wonders Divine
Of Human Imagination throughout all the Three Regions immense
Of Childhood, Manhood & Old Age; & the all tremendous unfathomable
    Non Ens
Of Death was seen in regenerations terrific or complacent, varying
According to the subject of discourse; & every Word & Every Character
Was Human according to the Expansion or Contraction, the Translucence
    or
Opakeness of Nervous fibres: such was the variation of Time & Space

Which vary according as the Organs of Perception vary; & they walked
To & fro in Eternity as One Man, reflecting each in each & clearly
Seen and seeing, according to fitness & order.

(J. 98:28–40)

Cryptic, gross, and disordered as these words may appear, they are
bursting with a symbolic portrait of a cosmic totality varying with the
organs of human perception. This totality appears and exists in innumerable worlds; each world is real, and each world is created by
perception. Terrible as the fallen worlds may appear and be to a
disordered perception, they can pose no ultimate threat to humanity,
for a world that is created by the contraction of the senses can be
wholly transformed when these senses expand.

How do you know but ev'ry Bird that cuts the airy way,
Is an immense world of delight, clos'd by your senses five?

(M.H.H. 6–7)

v. Sex and the Body

THERE can be no doubt that Blake was a mystical poet and seer, but
in what sense remains unclear. We know little about Blake's own reading in the mystical tradition, but we do know that he carefully read at
least two works of Swedenborg, that he read in William Law's transla-
tions of the works of Jacob Boehme, that he studied certain of the
eighteenth-century English mythologists such as Jacob Bryant, who
attempted to resurrect the hermetic and Gnostic traditions in a modern
historical form,[24] and that he was at least indirectly acquainted with
the Kabbalah. The critical studies of Damon and Percival have
demonstrated that Blake's poems are pervaded with an immense
number of mystical images and symbols, although neither Damon nor
Percival has recognized that Blake's vision effected a radical transformation of the mystical tradition itself. In his address, "To the
Jews," in *Jerusalem*, Blake declares:

17

Your Ancestors derived their origin from Abraham, Heber, Shem and Noah, who were Druids, as the Druid Temples (which are the Patriarchal Pillars & Oak Groves) over the whole Earth witness to this day.

You have a tradition, that Man anciently contain'd in his mighty limbs all things in Heaven & Earth: this you recieved from the Druids. "But now the Starry Heavens are fled from the mighty limbs of Albion."

Albion was the Parent of the Druids, & in his Chaotic State of Sleep, Satan & Adam & the whole World was Created by the Elohim.

(J. 27:10–17)

That the Fall preceded the Creation is a universal mystical motif, so likewise there are numerous mystical symbols of a primordial Man who contained all things, but this symbol reached its most powerful Western form in the medieval Kabbalah.

Blake's symbolical hero, Albion, is obviously an English appropriation of the Jewish, Adam Kadmon, whose fall both preceded and initiated the fall of the material world. However, two striking differences exist between these primordial figures. First, Blake's deepest vision refuses to allow any difference of nature or being between Man and God whereas the Kabbalah understands the primordial Man as a lower manifestation of the Godhead or the En-Sof; and, second, the Kabbalists, despite their repudiation of sexual asceticism, refrained from employing sexual imagery in describing the relation between Man and God. As Gershom G. Scholem analyzes the Kabbalah:

The Biblical Word that man was created in the image of God means two things to the Kabbalist: first, that the power of the Sefiroth, the paradigm of divine life, exists and is active also in man. Secondly, that the world of the Sefiroth, that is to say the world of God the Creator, is capable of being visualized under the image of man the created. From this it follows that the limbs of the human body . . . are nothing but images of a certain mode of spiritual existence which manifests itself in the symbolic figure of Adam Kadmon, the primordial man. For, to repeat, the Divine Being Himself cannot be expressed. All that can be expressed are His symbols. The relation between En-Sof and its mystical qualities, the Sefiroth, is comparable to that between the soul and the body, but with the difference that the human body and soul differ in nature, one being material and the other spiritual, while in the organic whole of God all spheres are substantially the same.[25]

18

In this perspective, we may surmise that Blake's passionate refusal of any distinction between body and soul was integrally related to his refusal of a divine transcendence. Both Blake and the Kabbalists chose sexual imagery as the language most truly reflecting the mystery of life in the Godhead, but while the Kabbalists only employ sex as a symbol of the love between the Godhead and Its emanation, the Shekhinah, the divine "I" and the divine "You,"[26] Blake knows the very reality of sex as the deepest epiphany of the Divine Man, and thus he can identify the actual passion of sex as the radiant presence of an energy either demonic or divine.

It is precisely because sex in its truest form is the portal to the paradise of Eden, the apocalyptic union of Man and God, that Blake responds with such a shudder of horror to the fallen form of sex. This horror is most clearly, if most simply, present in his early prophetic poems, *Thel* and the *Visions of the Daughters of Albion,* only to become a recurrent theme in the *Songs of Experience,* as witness "The Sick Rose":

> O Rose, thou art sick!
> The invisible worm
> That flies in the night,
> In the howling storm,
>
> Has found out thy bed
> Of crimson joy:
> And his dark secret love
> Does thy life destroy.

The poignancy of these lines if not deepened is nevertheless extended to a broader horizon by the fairy's words on the first plate of *Europe:*

> "Five windows light the cavern'd Man: thro' one he breathes the air
> Thro' one hears music of the spheres; thro' one the eternal vine
> Flourishes, that he may receive the grapes; thro' one can look
> And see small portions of the eternal world that ever groweth;
> Thro' one himself pass out what time he please; but he will not,
> For stolen joys are sweet & bread eaten in secret pleasant."

Of all the now isolated and disordered senses, only touch or sex can find a passageway that offers a way out of a fallen time, for this is the one sense that is capable of both an immediate and a reciprocal union with its object; only sex can bridge the chasm lying between the disparate fragments of a fallen Albion. Yet the Fall has inverted the direction and form of sexual energy. In its fallen form, "Energy" has become enclosed within itself, no longer passing immediately and spontaneously to the other; it takes narcissistic delight in its own circular and solitary movement, and each expression of its now perverted power binds fallen man all the more securely to his alienated form. Nevertheless, even a fallen sex brings joy, and not only the spontaneous joy of Innocence, but also a joy deriving from the life and movement of Experience, for narrow and confined as this movement may be, and perverse as it certainly is in its actual form, it remains an expression of life itself and therefore *all* sex is Holy: "For every thing that lives is Holy" (*A Song of Liberty*).

Blake, as we shall see, directed his bitterest scorn upon religion, and he did this because he believed that the laws of religion were laws of sexual repression, and such repression was the source of the cruelty and death that rules man's life in history.

"Are not these the places of religion, the rewards of continence,
The self enjoyings of self denial? why dost thou seek religion?
Is it because acts are not lovely that thou seekest solitude
Where the horrible darkness is impressed with reflections of desire?"
(V.D.A. 7:8–11)

Hence the Blake who passionately identified himself with Jesus came to look upon the doctrine of the virgin birth as blasphemous and insisted in *The Everlasting Gospel* that Jesus himself neither was chaste nor taught chastity, for the sexual organs are "Love's temple that God dwelleth in," and the sexual act of the "Naked Human form divine" is that on which "the Soul Expands its wing" (E.G. e, 64–68). Sexual imagery dominates Blake's work from beginning to end; he succeeded in discovering a sexual theme and meaning wherever he cast his prophetic light. Perhaps nowhere else can one so fully uncover the underlying unity of Blake's work as a whole. Although he would later come to move beyond its simplicity and one-sidedness, nothing in Blake's later work led him to repudiate the teaching of the voice of the Devil in *The Marriage of Heaven and Hell:*

All Bibles or sacred codes have been the causes of the following Errors:

1. That Man has two real existing principles: Viz: a Body & a Soul.
2. That Energy, call'd Evil, is alone from the Body; & that Reason, call'd Good, is alone from the Soul.
3. That God will torment Man in Eternity for following his Energies.

But the following Contraries to these are True:

1. Man has no Body distinct from his Soul; for that call'd Body is a portion of Soul discern'd by the five Senses, the chief inlets of Soul in this age.
2. Energy is the only life, and is from the Body; and Reason is the bound or outward circumference of Energy.
3. Energy is Eternal Delight.

That which we know as "Body" is in fact the "Soul" as perceived by the isolated and shrunken senses, therefore "Energy" (or sex) is the fallen form of the "Soul," and the eternal delight of "Energy" stands witness to its embodiment of the redemptive life of the Holy. From the little apocalypse on the 14th plate of *The Marriage of Heaven and Hell,* we learn that the end of the world will come by an improvement of "sensual enjoyment," for:

If the doors of perception were cleansed every thing would appear to man as it is, infinite.

For man has closed himself up, till he sees all things thro' narrow chinks of his cavern.

If sex marks the presence of the Holy and is itself eternal delight, it might well be asked wherein lies the sign of its fallen form. First, Blake follows the Kabbalah and Jacob Boehme, as well as many mystical and mythical traditions of a far earlier time, in believing that man's original and primordial state was androgynous:

The Feminine separates from the Masculine & both from Man,
Ceasing to be His Emanations, Life to Themselves assuming:
. . . . that no more the Masculine mingles
With the Feminine, but the Sublime is shut out from the Pathos

In howling torment, to build stone walls of separation, compelling
The Pathos to weave curtains of hiding secresy from the torment.
                    (J. 90:1–13)

Sex, as we know it, is polarized by the division of the sexes; no longer
does sexual energy flow freely between Albion's "Emanations," as
their fallen estrangement compels the masculine and the feminine to
exist in isolation and secrecy. Now the "Bodies in which all Animals &
Vegetations, the Earth & Heaven" were contained in the primordial
Imagination are "wither'd & darken'd" (J. 49:13 f.). These dark
bodies are evolved by the contraction of the senses and the division of
the Eternal Man, and sexual bliss can only be consummated in this
world of mutual isolation by becoming "a Generated Mortal, a
Vegetating Death."

> And now the Spectres of the Dead awake in Beulah; all
> The Jealousies become Murderous, uniting together in Rahab
> A Religion of Chastity, forming a Commerce to sell Loves,
> With Moral Law an Equal Balance not going down with decision.
> Therefore the Male severe & cruel, fill'd with stern Revenge,
> Mutual Hate returns & mutual Deceit & mutual Fear.
>   (J. 69:31–37)

War itself is "energy Enslav'd" (F.Z. IX, 152), for the "Veil" which
Satan puts between Adam and Eve (J. 55:11) is an impenetrable
fortress separating man from man, forcing men to live in mutual
hostility and fear, and inevitably inverting bodily energy so that
"Sexual Love" now springs from "Spiritual Hate" (J. 54:12).

Consequently, the one certain sign that sex in our world is a fallen
sex is its inseparability from death. Our sex is not only bound to a
cycle of generation, an eternal movement from life to death to life
again, but it also necessarily expresses itself in hatred and revenge,
such hatred being a consequence of the repressed state of our alienated
and withered bodies. While bound to a condition of isolated and
fragmented "Selfhood," our bodily energy must be particularized and
directed to fleeting fragments of the life about us. Such a fragmenta-
tion and particularization of energy can provide no true outlet for the
shrunken bodily form of the "Soul"; hence it spends itself hopelessly

in a futile attempt to escape its narrow bounds and in the process creates "Spiritual Hate." Blake fully anticipated Nietzsche and Freud in his understanding of repression, and he surpassed both in the simplicity and power with which he portrayed the living reality of repressed bodies in his "Proverbs of Hell" (M.H.H. 7–9):

> He who desires but acts not, breeds pestilence.
> The cistern contains: the fountain overflows.
> Expect poison from the standing water.
> Damn braces: Bless relaxes.
> Sooner murder an infant in its cradle than nurse unacted desires.

But Blake invariably speaks prophetically; his condemnation flows swiftly into affirmation, for his imagery is dialectical and thus his very portrait of fallen bodies contains the seeds of their apocalyptic transfiguration.

> The road of excess leads to the palace of wisdom.
> Prudence is a rich, ugly old maid courted by Incapacity.
> The busy bee has no time for sorrow.
> All wholesom food is caught without a net or a trap.
> The roaring of lions, the howling of wolves, the raging of the stormy sea, and the destructive sword, are portions of eternity, too great for the eye of man.
> The tygers of wrath are wiser than the horses of instruction.
> Exuberance is Beauty.

The exuberance to which Blake points is one that must break all the bounds that history and the cosmos have imposed upon fallen man; not only must religion and the moral law be shattered, but also the actual form and structure of our repressed and shrunken bodies must pass away. A genital and bisexual energy is simply a repressed product of the contraction of the senses; it is bound to separation and death and can find no outlet to the totality of exuberance; hence: "Sexes must vanish & cease To be when Albion arises from his dread repose" (J. 92:13 f.).

VI. Reason

THE more radical expressions of mysticism in the West from Orphism
to Hellenistic Gnosticism to the Kabbalah and to Jacob Boehme have
either arisen in opposition to the dominance of reason or have assumed
the function of opposing its sovereignty. No mystic has ever attacked
reason with greater passion than does Blake, nor has any mystical
thinker in East or West discovered the demonic presence of a destructive reason throughout such a comprehensive range of experience.
"Reason," Blake declared to Crabb Robinson, "is the only sin." Nor
need we look far to ascertain the ground of Blake's hatred of reason:

> The Spectre is the Reasoning Power in Man, & when separated
> From Imagination and closing itself as in steel, in a Ratio
> Of the Things of Memory, It thence frames Laws & moralities
> To destroy Imagination, the Divine Body, by Martyrdoms & Wars.
> (J. 74:10–13)

Note that when reason is separated from imagination, it becomes a
"Ratio of the Things of Memory"; thereby reason becomes the author
of a rational and a moral law that destroys the imagination, and these
laws of repression are responsible for all the suffering and the chaos
in history.

> But Albion fell down, a Rocky fragment from Eternity hurl'd
> By his own Spectre, who is the Reasoning Power in every Man,
> Into his own Chaos, which is the Memory between Man & Man.
> (J. 54:6–8)

An autonomous reason or "Ratio" is accordingly a product of the
Fall; moreover, its very activity reflects a fallen state in which the
senses are isolated from one another and man is separated from man.
Such reason manifests itself in the "Memory between Man & Man,"
for memory can merely reflect the given; it simply records the brute
factuality of the fallen order of time and space, and is itself the only
mental activity of a fully shrunken body. Reason is the forbidden

fruit, "the Atheistical Epicurean Philosophy of Albion's Tree," and it appears only when the feminine and the masculine are separated from Man (J. 67:13 f.).

Two extremely important judgments about ratio are already made in *There Is No Natural Religion:*

If it were not for the Poetic or Prophetic character the Philosophic & Experimental would soon be at the ratio of all things, & stand still, unable to do other than repeat the same dull round over again.

. . . .

He who sees the Infinite in all things, sees God. He who sees the Ratio only, sees himself only.

The first judgment is an anticipation of Blake's mature understanding of the identification of reason and memory; pure reason is a negative power in the non-dialectical sense; it cannot create, it can only reflect and record: thus it is a dead, lifeless power, a law enclosing the energy of life. This judgment also anticipates Nietzsche's metaphysical doctrine of the eternal recurrence of all things: when God or the Imagination is dead, there can be no ultimate meaning or order in the world; all things revolve in a perpetual and chaotic flux. This flux is the arena of an autonomous "Selfhood," and therefore the first judgment passes naturally into the second and anticipates Blake's identification of "Ratio" and Satan.

But the Spectre, like a hoar frost & a Mildew, rose over Albion,
Saying, "I am God, O Sons of Men! I am your Rational Power!
Am I not Bacon & Newton & Locke who teach Humility to Man,
Who teach Doubt & Experiment? & my two Wings, Voltaire, Rousseau?
Where is that Friend of Sinners? that Rebel against my Laws
Who teaches Belief to the Nations & an unknown Eternal Life?
Come hither into the Desart & turn these stones to bread.
Vain Foolish Man! wilt thou believe without Experiement
And build a World of Phantasy upon my Great Abyss,
A World of Shapes in craving lust & devouring appetite?"
(J. 54:15–24)

Satan is the pride of "Selfhood," building a world in which man is by his nature the enemy of man, a world "unwieldy stretching out into

Non Entity, Generalizing Art & Science till Art & Science is lost"
(J. 43:53 f.).

We have already seen in a passage from *Europe,* that "Thought
chang'd the infinite to a serpent," and "man became an Angel, Heaven
a mighty circle turning, God a tyrant crown'd" (10:16–23). And we
have also noted that Blake, like every apocalyptic seer, identifies the
advent of the lowest and most terrible form of the world as a sign of
the coming end; accordingly, *Europe* also contains a mocking
apocalyptic reference to Newton:

> A mighty Spirit leap'd from the land of Albion,
> Nam'd Newton: he siez'd the trump & blow'd the enormous blast!
> Yellow as leaves of Autumn, the myriads of Angelic hosts
> Fell thro' the wintry skies seeking their graves,
> Rattling their hollow bones in howling and lamentation.
> (13:4–8)

Newton, the foremost representative to Blake of "Generalizing
Science," is a form of the Antichrist, and, with the appearance of
Newton and the rise of "Deism," Satan himself becomes manifest in
his most powerful form, a form revealing that Satan's deepest epiphany
does not occur until the triumph of modern science. Thus in *Milton,*
Satan becomes Newton's "Pantocrator":

> "O Satan, my youngest born, art thou not Prince of the Starry Hosts
> And of the Wheels of Heaven, to turn the Mills day & night?
> Art thou not Newton's Pantocrator, weaving the Woof of Locke?
> To Mortals thy Mills seem every thing, & the Harrow of Shaddai
> A Scheme of Human conduct invisible & incomprehensible."
> (4:9–13)

Shaddai is the Hebrew name of the solitary and almighty Creator in
the Book of Job, a God whose sheer existence crushes the spirit of
man, and we find that the same abject humility and human nothingness which the solitary Lord imposes upon His subjects is repeated
once more in the new reign of "Generalizing Science." Even the starry
heavens are now infinitely removed from man, as man becomes reduced
to the state of a dull round of lifeless matter.

REASON

The new tyrant God, "Ratio," is the most terrible abstract deity of all; its reign is universal, encompassing all thought and experience, and the very universality of its power reduces the human individual, Blake's "minute particular" (who originally was not intermeasurable by anything else), to a state wherein the thou becomes an it, and all individuals become intermeasurable by one another. In the dreadful present of the time of pure reason, past and future collapse into a vacuous present, for a dead reason rules over all:

> I see the Four-fold Man, The Humanity in deadly sleep
> And its fallen Emanation, The Spectre & its cruel Shadow.
> I see the Past, Present & Future existing all at once
> Before me. O Divine Spirit sustain me on thy wings,
> That I may awake Albion from his long & cold repose;
> For Bacon & Newton, sheath'd in dismal steel, their terrors hang
> Like iron scourges over Albion: Reasonings like vast Serpents
> Infold around my limbs, bruising my minute articulations.
> (J. 15:6–13)

The original infinity of the human Imagination has become the false infinity of the serpent; this serpent "Ratio" is a contraction of the imagination, a contraction which can "view a small portion & think that All, And call it demonstration, blind to all the simple rules of life" (F.Z. VII b, 185 f.). Demonstration inverts the true infinite which "alone resides in Definite & Determinate Identity"; the generalizing demonstrations of the rational power must consequently destroy the minutely organized particulars, as individual men are "pounded to dust & melted in the Furnaces of Affliction" (J. 55:56–64). All of the fury of Dostoevski's "underground man" against the Euclidean reason of abstract mind is also present in Blake, but Blake not only sees that the existing individual is annihilated by abstract reason, but that so likewise humanity itself is destroyed when it is understood as a series of atomic monads operating in accordance with a rational law, and this destruction lies behind the present power of the "Goddess Nature" and the deathlike sleep of the eternal Man.

Underlying Blake's prophetic vision of reason is a dialectical mode of understanding, and in the West pure dialectical thinking like the radical mysticism to which it is so intimately related has ever been

27

directed against the sovereignty of reason. In *The Marriage of Heaven and Hell,* Blake declares that without "Contraries" there is no progression: "Attraction and Repulsion, Reason and Energy, Love and Hate, are necessary to Human existence." When reason is isolated from energy, it becomes a lifeless and destructive power, reducing definite and determinable identities to intermeasurable entities, and enslaving man to the alien state of the natural powers. A solitary and autonomous reason is what Blake came to call a "Negation," but its rise to power is not wholly a calamity; it comes into existence to make possible a yet deeper union of the "Contraries":

> "All that can be annihilated must be annihilated
> That the Children of Jerusalem may be saved from slavery.
> There is a Negation, & there is a Contrary:
> The Negation must be destroy'd to redeem the Contraries.
> The Negation is the Spectre, the Reasoning Power in Man:
> This is a false Body, in Incrustation over my Immortal
> Spirit, a Selfhood which must be put off & annihilated alway."
> (M. 40:30–36)

The Blake who was persuaded that "Truth can never be told so as to be understood, and not be believ'd" (M.H.H. 10), knew that finally the reasoning Spectre must itself be destroyed, that the "mathematic power" that has given a body to falsehood will be cast off forever (J. 12:12 f.); but dialectically this destruction is creation; the very process by which reason rises to the zenith of absolute power is a process by which the "Negations" will ultimately and finally be annihilated, and, when "Ratio" has been totally inverted, then "sweet Science" will reign.

Let us openly acknowledge that no real philosophical thinking is present in Blake's poetry, nor should we expect it to be in the work of a poet and seer, but it does not follow that his vision has no philosophical ground; we have only to recognize that it is an integral expression of the Western dialectical tradition. Blake's contemporary, Hegel, was likewise hostile to Newtonian science and Enlightenment rationalism. He was deeply influenced by the dialectical ground of Boehme's mysticism, and Hegel created a dialectical logic, the only fully dialectical logic ever produced in the West. Hegel's *Logic* contains a systematic attack upon all of the major laws and categories of formal logic; moreover, such an attack is necessary if only to establish the ground of dialectical understanding, for dialectical thinking thinks in and through contradiction. As Hegel announces in the introduction to his *Logic*.

The one and only thing *for securing scientific progress* (and for quite *simple* insight into which, it is essential to strive)—is knowledge of the logical precept that negation is just as much affirmation as negation, or that what is self-contradictory resolves itself not into nullity, into abstract nothingness, but essentially only into the negation of its *particular* content, that such negation is not an all-embracing negation, but is *the negation of a definite somewhat* which abolishes itself, and thus is a definite negation; and that thus the result contains in essence that from which it results— which is indeed a tautology, for otherwise it would be something immediate and not a result. Since what results, the negation, is a *definite* negation, it has a *content*. It is a new concept, but a higher, richer concept than that which preceded; for it has been enriched by the negation or opposite of that preceding concept, and thus contains it, but contains also more than it, and is the unity of it and its opposite.[27]

Dialectical negation is a process of simultaneously cancelling and transcending (*aufheben*); by this process it dissolves the abstract and static laws of formal thinking, and is itself a method that is identical with its object and content: "for it is the content in itself, the *Dialectic* which *it has in itself*, that moves it on."[28]

A purely formal thinking abstracts itself from all content, establishing a chasm between subject and object, or between a subjective and conscious entity existing for itself and an objective entity existing in itself. This chasm not only makes necessary an acceptance of the given, or whatever happens to appear or to be present, but it also establishes the given as alien to the thinker, wholly isolating consciousness from its ground. Hegel's term for the abstract reason or ratio that is the product of formal thinking is *Verstand,* but *Verstand* is antithetically related to the higher dialectical and conceptual mode of understanding which Hegel terms *Vernunft. Verstand* is "positive" because it makes determinations and maintains them while *Vernunft* is "negative" because it dissolves these determinations.[29] When *Verstand* or ratio operates apart from *Vernunft*, it separates the content from the form of knowledge, isolating the object from the subject of consciousness, and thus reflects a world of alienation. Dialectic arises to oppose this world, for dialectic is the higher movement of *Vernunft* "where terms appearing absolutely distinct pass into one another because they are what they are, where the assumption of their separateness cancels itself."[30] But a term is dialectically cancelled or transcended only in so far as it has come into unity with its opposite, and such a process can allow for no barriers or ultimate dichotomies whatsoever, such as the traditional Western dichotomies between subject and object, body and soul, man and nature, or man and God. Hegel's attack upon "Ratio's" idea of God illuminates his understanding of dialectic:

God was defined as the Sum-total of all Realities; and of this sum-total it was said that it contained no contradiction, none of the realities cancelling the other; for a reality was to be taken merely as something complete and affirmative, containing no negation. Thus the realities were neither opposed nor contradictory to one another.[31]

However, such an idea of God reveals its ground in "Ratio" by finally becoming manifest as a wholly abstract Being: "God as the purely Real in all Reals, or as the Sum-total of all Realities, is that same indeterminate and nebulous something as the empty Absolute where everything is one."[32]

Obviously the God of pure reason is the "False Infinite," a God that can appear either as a distant Heavenly Father or as a tyrannical "Generalizing Science"; in either case the God of rational demonstration is the product of alienation; it must necessarily reflect a chasm between the thinker and the known, between consciousness and the given, or between thought and actuality; and Hegel declares that such an abstract and formal "One" is the highest and most stubborn error, which nevertheless takes itself for the highest truth.[33] Formal or "logical" thought makes contradiction unthinkable; it holds contradictory terms apart in spatial and temporal juxtaposition, and thus no way can be found for them to come into contact in consciousness. The inevitable result is that the infinite is isolated from the finite, the eternal from the temporal, the beyond from the here and now, thus dooming the "higher" contradictory term to the status of being indifferent and passive to the "lower" realm of movement and life. Spinoza was ever for Hegel (as Plato was for Blake) the philosopher who epitomized these disastrous pitfalls of abstract thinking. Spinoza's Substance is an inseparable totality; there are no determinations of thought which are not both contained and dissolved in this Absolute. But his Substance is reached by an external cognition or reflection that takes up the determinations of "Ratio" as given, reducing them into the Absolute rather than reaching them from the Absolute. Consequently, finitude can neither be comprehended by nor illuminated from the Absolute; it exists only as "vanishing" and not as "becoming," and this vanishing can only take its positive beginning from without.[34] In other words, there is no integral relationship between finitude and the Absolute, no necessary transition between Spinoza's Absolute Substance and its inessential modes. Both finitude and the Absolute remain locked in isolation, no real path lies between them, and this is so because his Absolute is solitary and inactive, having neither the necessity nor the path to move to finitude. Spinoza's Substance is absolute indifference, and finally this is so because it is reached by an external and non-dialectical thinking, a thinking that remains frozen in the categories of abstract thought, and hence remains closed to the actual processes of finitude and to the complexity and the richness of individual modes of life.

Spinoza is richly illustrative of the demonic dangers of pure thinking in the highest rational sense; his very demand of thought that it is to consider everything under the form of eternity, *sub specie aeterni,* is finally positivistic, for the abstract thinking demanded by his method can only know an eternity that is an unmoved identity, and such an identity must remain estranged from the actual concretions of living process, merely recording the static forms of a movement which here ceases to flow. So long as the mind remains bound to purely rational thinking, it must reflect and know a static and lifeless world, for it can do no more than react to a world that is isolated from and alien to its own activity, and it can find no path by which to establish a reciprocal relationship between the thinker and the known. Only a contradiction which dissolves the abstract and static categories of

31

reason can establish the ground for the appearance of dialectical understanding; but such understanding is not an arbitrary negation of these inevitable determinations of thought, for the necessity of contradiction is inherent in the very nature of rational thinking. To think with the deepest purity is to think *to* contradiction for "*all things are contradictory in themselves*"; yet this very contradiction is the source of all movement and life, and it is only insofar as it contains a contradiction that "anything moves and has impulse and activity."[35] Abstract self-identity has no life; but the fact that the "positive" in itself is negativity causes it to pass outside itself and to change.

Something comes to life only insofar as it contains contradiction, and is that force which can both comprehend and endure contradiction. But if an existent something cannot in its positive determination also encroach on its negative, cannot hold fast the one in the other and contain contradiction within itself, then it is not living unity, or ground, but perishes in contradiction.[36]

The full movement of ratio must then succeed in dissolving itself, but such a dissolution is no more than a fulfillment of the negativity already implicit in ratio, and this very negativity is a reflection of the actual processes of life which finally become resurrected in such a way as to both cancel and transcend the static forms of thought. Ultimately the categories of pure reason are their own negation but this ultimate negation will only be reached when that final barrier is dissolved between the thinker and the known, consciousness and its object, or being-for-itself and being-in-itself: when this deepest of all negations occurs, then the Absolute will reach its fullest epiphany, and the Hegelian apocalypse will dawn.

VII. Space and Ulro

BLAKE's reputation for madness is not wholly unwarranted; he refused to believe that the world was round, declared in a letter in 1804 that "distance is a phantasy," denied the reality of natural causation (M. 26:45), continually asserted that he lived in a world of spirits and only wrote when he was commanded by the spirits. One of these spirits, the dead poet, Cowper, came to Blake and said: "You retain health and yet are as mad as any of us all—over us all—mad as a refuge from unbelief—from Bacon, Newton and Locke."[37] When Satan announced in *Milton*, "I am God alone: There is no other!," his bosom grew

> Opake against the Divine Vision: the paved terraces of
> His bosom inwards shone with fires, but the stones becoming opake
> Hid him from sight in an extreme blackness and darkness.
> And there a World of deeper Ulro was open'd in the midst
> Of the Assembly. In Satan's bosom, a vast unfathomable Abyss.
>   (9:31-35)

Albion's sleep of eternal death is the sleep of Ulro (J. 4:1); this satanic abyss of Ulro shrinks the organs of the eternal man until they seem finite and Ulro itself seems infinite, and, while "Satanic Space is delusion" (M. 36:20), it is created by a fallen reason and is the anvil upon which Vision arises:

> As to that false appearance which appears to the reasoner
> As of a Globe rolling thro' Voidness, it is a delusion of Ulro.
> The Microscope knows not of this nor the Telescope: they alter
> The ratio of the Spectator's Organs, but leave Objects untouch'd.
> For every Space larger than a red Globule of Man's blood
> Is visionary, and is created by the Hammer of Los:
> And every Space smaller than a Globule of Man's blood opens
> Into Eternity of which this vegetable Earth is but a shadow.
>   (M. 29:15-22)

Los or Blake or any visionary must live and create in a world of Vision, a world that must appear to be madness to the rational mind; but, to the eye of Vision, the world of pure reason is a cold and rocky abyss, a world barely on this side of nothingness and wholly enclosed by the darkness of its own rays.

At this point we cannot hope to do more than touch upon the fullness and complexity of Blake's vision of fallen space. A hint of this vision has already been given in our examination of a fallen nature, but not until we have passed through the fourfold prophetic vision of Fall, Redemption, History, and Apocalypse can we try to understand the real meaning of this dark abyss. First, let us note the imagery that Blake employs to describe Ulro in this passage from *Jerusalem:*

> The Vegetative Universe opens like a flower from the Earth's center
> In which is Eternity. It expands in Stars to the Mundane Shell
> And there it meets Eternity again, both within and without,
> And the abstract Voids between the Stars are the Satanic Wheels.
>
> There is the Cave, the Rock, the Tree, the Lake of Udan Adan,
> The Forest and the Marsh and the Pits of bitumen deadly,
> The Rocks of solid fire, The Ice valleys, the Plains
> Of burning sand, the rivers, cataract & Lakes of Fire,
> The Islands of the fiery Lakes, the Trees of Malice, Revenge
> And black Anxiety, and the Cities of the Salamandrine men,
> (But whatever is visible to the Generated Man
> Is a Creation of mercy & love from the Satanic Void).
>   (13:34–45)

We see that horrible as the emptiness and the terror of this shrunken space is, it remains visible, and precisely for this reason, it is a creation of mercy and love; but nevertheless it is a creation from the "Satanic Void." In the crucial years that Blake spent working upon his manuscript epic, *Vala* or *The Four Zoas,* he underwent a decisive redemptive experience, an experience, as we shall later see, that led him to a vision not only of the necessity of the Fall but also to a realization of its redemptive ground. Thus in *Milton* he writes of the creation of a "New Space" to protect Satan from punishment; and then goes on to say: "The Divine hand found the Two Limits, first of Opacity, then of Contraction" (13:20). Opacity is named "Satan," and contraction "Adam," symbolizing that Satan is the state most impervious to the light of Vision and Adam the fully contracted or shrunken state of the fallen man; accordingly, Satan and Adam are archetypal twins, as Percival says: "You cannot have Satan without shrinking the infinite universe to the stature of the individual, the me—without making of the immortal and sexless Albion the mortal and sexual Adam."[38]

Natural imagery pervades Blake's work but it invariably serves a prophetic purpose as can most clearly be seen by an examination of his illustrations. Joseph Wicksteed's perceptive studies of the Job illustrations and of the illustrations to *Jerusalem* show that in these works Blake's designs of natural bodies both vary in accordance with the particular phase of the vision at hand and in their own form and organization are independent fragments of vision. Throughout these illustrations the heavenly bodies play a primary role, their shapes and movements embodying a complex alchemical and astrological symbolism, and, while the stars symbolize the realms of reason and war, they are nevertheless seen as fragments or remembrances of the divine light. In his study of the *Songs of Innocence and of Experience,* Wicksteed interprets the stars in "The Tyger" as ambivalent symbols of light and darkness:

It is probably not too much to describe the stars as the seeds of Man with which the womb of night is sown, and whose harvest is the Dawn. For the benighted soul these sexual atoms are all that is left of Day, and all that the darkness of a priestly rationalism itself cannot obliterate. They are the symbols at once of man's slavery and his unconquerable soul. And so it is their thrust of light into the great womb of Nature that dissolves the night into tender Pity and fertility, and brings forth the Sun, even as Nature first became the receptacle of, and then gave birth to, Christ.[39]

As fragments of unfallen light, the stars bring into relief the dark abyss of Ulro or Hell, the abode of Satan, the world of abstractions which in aggregate are matter, nature, reason, and memory.[40] We have seen that the abstract voids between the stars are the "Satanic Wheels." *Milton* also contains lines speaking of the "Newtonian Voids between the Substances of Creation":

> For the Chaotic Voids outside of the Stars are measured by
> The Stars, which are the boundaries of Kingdoms, Provinces
> And Empires of Chaos invisible to the Vegetable Man.
> (37:47–49)

These empires of chaos remain invisible to fallen man if only because fallen man remains a generated being and therefore cannot know the total horror of unreality. This horror, it is true, is implicitly present in the world of reason and memory, but that world cannot be wholly pure so long as it assumes a human form; apart from that form it is simply Hell itself.

Blake declared that the most pernicious idea which can enter the human mind is the supposition that before the creation all was "Solitude & Chaos" (V.L.J. pp. 91–92), for a failure to realize that "Chaos" is a product of the Fall is an abject and inhuman submission to sheer nothingness. When chaos is known as a consequence of the Fall, it can be understood as the reflection of a human movement, thereby losing its awesome autonomy and revealing itself in its myriad forms to be the tracks of dark Albion's "dread Wheels":

> . . . stretching out spaces immense between,
> That every little particle of light & air became Opake,
> Black & immense, a Rock of difficulty & a Cliff
> Of black despair, that the immortal Wings labour'd against
> Cliff after cliff & over Valleys of despair & death.
> The narrow Sea between Albion & the Atlantic Continent,
> Its waves of pearl became a boundless Ocean bottomless,
> Of grey obscurity, fill'd with clouds & rocks & whirling waters,
> And Albion's Sons ascending & descending in the horrid Void.
>   (J. 44:9–17)

Let us join Bernard Blackstone and others in affirming that space for Blake is simply the form taken by the internal universe when it is seen as external,[41] and let us concede that at this point Blake's vision of space is at harmony with the perennial philosophy of mysticism, but what is uniquely modern or Blakean is the conjunction of this perennial vision with an openness to and an immersion in the concrete and actual space of the fallen order of time. Caves, rocks, trees, lakes, forests, marshes, pits, valleys, and all the multiple forms of matter in its organic or inorganic state are reborn in Blake's imagery in such a manner as to overwhelm the reader in their stark reality, yet they are invariably present in a symbolic form; we know at once that the cosmos of fallen space is here present in its vast and impersonal power, but in its very fallenness an external space reveals its human ground. We relive in Blake's vision Pascal's shudder at the immensity of space, but in seeing Ulro or

Hell as the ultimate form of space, we know that the infinity of the cosmos discovered by the Renaissance is a Faustian truth reached by a perverse if creative will, and thereby we recognize that our dread in response to the infinite distance of the stars is at bottom a terror inspired by the inverted form of our own bodies.

VIII. Religion

A DISTINCTIVE sign of radical Christianity is a joint protest against the Christian Church and its doctrine of God, this protest arising from the conviction that a perverted form of faith has given expression to a false and tyrannical God, and the protest itself is often found in strange places. In the closing pages of *Process and Reality*, Whitehead condemns the Christian doctrine of God—"the doctrine of an aboriginal, eminently real, transcendent creator, at whose fiat the world came into being, and whose imposed will it obeys"[42]—as a fallacy which has infused tragedy into history; and he insists that when the Western world accepted Christianity, Caesar conquered: "The Church gave unto God the attributes which belonged exclusively to Caesar."[43] This recurrent theme of the late Whitehead has a history at least as old as the Franciscan movement, but it received its most profound prophetic expression in William Blake, who, along with Nietzsche, became one of the two most passionate enemies of the Christian Church. Blake's prophetic attack upon Christianity fully anticipated Nietzsche and it is already present, though in an obscure form, in *The Marriage of Heaven and Hell:*

Those who restrain desire, do so because theirs is weak enough to be restrained; and the restrainer or reason usurps its place & governs the unwilling.

And being restrain'd, it by degrees becomes passive, till it is only the shadow of desire.

. . . .

It indeed appear'd to Reason as if Desire was cast out; but the Devil's account is, that the Messiah fell, & formed a heaven of what he stole from the Abyss.

This is shewn in the Gospel, where he prays to the Father to send the comforter, or Desire, that Reason may have Ideas to build on; the Jehovah of the Bible being no more than he who dwells in flaming fire.

Know that after Christ's death, he became Jehovah.

But in Milton, the Father is Destiny, the Son a Ratio of the five senses, & the Holy-ghost Vacuum!

(5-6)

Here, as elsewhere in Blake, Milton is the highest representative of the Church, and the poem, *Milton,* embodies a vision of the apocalyptic regeneration of Christianity. However, Christianity will remain enslaved to Satan so long as it remains in bondage to the Christian God. For when Jesus' body was placed in the sepulcher, Rahab (Blake's symbol of the "Mystery" of the Church), triumphed over all:

> . . . she took Jerusalem
> Captive, a Willing Captive, by delusive arts impell'd
> To worship Urizen's Dragon form, to offer her own Children
> Upon the bloody Altar.
> (F.Z. VIII, 597-600)

These lines just quoted from *The Four Zoas* are among the first expressions of that new and fuller vision that Blake had reached in the course of working upon that poem. They represent a far deeper opposition to the Christian God and the Christian Church than do the seemingly more rebellious earlier writings, and this is so because Blake had now reached the point where he could see the Christian God appearing and reappearing throughout the whole range of his vision. A decisive sign of Blake's new maturity is the fact that his symbols now flow more freely into one another. The Urizen of the early books can now take on the creative as well as the destructive forms of reason; the new symbols of the Spectre and the Selfhood, although impersonal, can fully serve as reflections of a fallen Albion; Ratio becomes more comprehensive and now clearly appears as both the ground and the consequence of the Christian God; Satan becomes manifest in his grandest form and the very triumph of his epiphany in *Milton* and in the illustrations to *Paradise Lost* reveals that Urizen, Ratio, the Spectre, the Selfhood, and "Satan" himself are no more than a series of fleeting masks of the lower reaches of Albion's sleep. All of these figures are expressions of the "Web" or "Wheel" of religion, Blake's symbol of natural religion, which had been the object of his prophetic fury throughout the whole body of his work, a fury that reaches a luminous clarity in the poem in blank verse in the address, "To the Christians," in *Jerusalem:*

> I stood among my valleys of the south
> And saw a flame of fire, even as a Wheel
> Of fire surrounding all the heavens: it went
> From west to east, against the current of
> Creation, and devour'd all things in its loud
> Fury & thundering course round heaven & earth.
> By it the Sun was roll'd into an orb,
> By it the Moon faded into a globe
> Travelling thro' the night; for, from its dire
> And restless fury, Man himself shrunk up
> Into a little root a fathom long.
> And I asked a Watcher & a Holy-One
> Its Name; he answered: "It is the Wheel of Religion."
> I wept & said: "Is this the law of Jesus,
> This terrible devouring sword turning every way?"
> He answer'd: "Jesus died because he strove
> Against the current of this Wheel; its Name
> Is Caiaphas, the dark Preacher of Death,
> Of sin, of sorrow & of punishment:
> Opposing Nature! It is Natural Religion."
> (77:45–64)

We have already seen in a passage from the *Visions of the Daughters of Albion* that the places of religion are the "self enjoyings of self denial" (7:9), so likewise the laws of religion are the "fiery joy" that Urizen perverted to the decalogue (A. 8:3), and Blake followed the mythologists of his time in identifying the most ancient and the most universal religion, an archaic religion of law and sacrifice, as Druidism. In *Milton,* Satan is Urizen drawn down into "Generation," where he dwells in a fallen space called Canaan:

And the Mills of Satan were separated into a moony Space
Among the rocks of Albion's Temples, and Satan's Druid sons
Offer the Human Victims throughout all the Earth, and Albion's

Dread Tomb, immortal on his Rock, overshadow'd the whole Earth,
Where Satan, making to himself Laws from his own identity,
Compell'd others to serve him in moral gratitude & submission,
Being call'd God, setting himself above all that is called God;
And all the Spectres of the Dead, calling themselves Sons of God,
In his Synagogues worship Satan under the Unutterable Name.
(11:6–14)

The foundation of Druidism is the sacrifice of the innocent for the
guilty, the innocent being the whole but now fallen body of humanity
and the guilty finally God or Satan who is Himself an "Eternal
Death," and who can never be redeemed but must be "new Created
continually moment by moment" (11:20), a process that occurs by
the perpetual repetition of human sacrifice. Druidism transforms
humanity into "War & Sacrifice" (J. 82:42); Albion is murdered
in "Dreams of Chastity & Moral Law" (J. 94:23), for "the Druids
rear'd their Rocky Circles to make permanent Remembrance Of Sin"
(J. 92:24).

> Every ornament of perfection and every labour of love
> In all the Garden of Eden & in all the golden mountains
> Was become an envied horror and a remembrance of jealousy,
> And every Act a Crime, and Albion the punisher & judge.

And Albion spoke from his secret seat and said:

> "All these ornaments are crimes, they are made by the labours
> Of loves, of unnatural consanguinities and friendships
> Horrid to think of when enquired deeply into; and all
> These hills & valleys are accursed witnesses of Sin.
> I therefore condense them into solid rocks, stedfast,
> A foundation and certainty and demonstrative truth,
> That Man be separate from Man . . ."
> (J. 28:1–12)

Then cold snows drift around Albion, ice covers his loins, and under-
neath him a deadly tree arises; he names it: "Moral Virtue and the
Law Of God who dwells in Chaos hidden from the human sight."

While Druidism is natural religion, it lies at the core of every historical religion, including Judaism and Christianity, and, indeed, has reached its most demonic expression in the Christian Church. However, it is difficult to avoid the suspicion that at bottom "Druidism" is intended by Blake to be nothing more and nothing less than an inverted image of the Church. The radical Christian views the established or the traditional Church not simply as the instrument of tyranny in establishing political and social repression but also as the very embodiment of repression in all its forms: the repressive authority of the Church is the source of a condemnation of all human acts, a condemnation that has shrunk human existence into a dark and turbulent sea of guilt. Nor does Blake hesitate to identify the sexual ground of the perversity of the Church. The temple of Urizen is built in the image of the human heart:

> And in the inner part of the Temple, wondrous workmanship,
> They form'd the Secret place, reversing all the order of delight,
> That whosoever enter'd into the temple might not behold
> The hidden wonders, allegoric of the Generations
> Of secret lust, when hid in chambers dark the nightly harlot
> Plays in Disguise in whisper'd hymn & mumbling prayer.
> (F.Z. VII b, 21–26)

The Jehovah who dwells in flaming fire is here seen as the repressed and secret sex of the fallen genital organs; so it is that Blake could openly speak of religion as a "Sexual Machine" (J. 44:25), and could condemn a "Vegetated Christ" and a "Virgin Eve" as the "Hermaphroditic Blasphemy" (J. 90:34), a blasphemy illuminating the sexual repression that is the source of the Church's belief. This theme is a recurrent motif of Blake's lyrics but it perhaps was given its most chilling expression in a couplet that Blake confided to his manuscript:

> Nail his neck to the Cross: nail it with a nail.
> Nail his neck to the Cross: ye all have power over his tail.
> (K. 557)

If nothing else, these lines make clear that Blake's violent attack upon the Church arose from a Christian ground. This passionate follower of Jesus reacted with apocalyptic intensity to a Rahab whose power has sealed the sepulcher of Jesus. Horrified by a Church that had aligned itself with the terror of history and become in its own law the primary agent of repression in Western history, Blake saw the Church as the "Web of Religion" built by the Spectres of all the inhabitants of earth, a web that has separated man from man, isolating each in his own Selfhood, and enslaving every man to a moral law that is the expression of the solitude of a transcendent Satan, a law directed to the destruction of energy and to a reversal of the proclamation of the forgiveness of sins. As Blake remarked with the simplicity of his master: "The Modern Church Crucifies Christ with the Head Downwards" (V.L.J. 87).

The very violence of Blake's passionate attack upon religion obscures its real ground; like Amos before him he spent so much energy in attacking priesthood and sacrifice that his deeper prophetic purpose is veiled, and there appears to be no real line of continuity between his condemnation of the Church and his affirmation of Jesus. Once again we must turn to Hegel for an elucidation of the dialectical ground of Blake's vision, and this time to his *Phenomenology,* Hegel's dialectical portrait of the gradual development of consciousness from its crude beginnings to the triumph of mind or Spirit (*Geist*). At first glance Hegel would seem to be a wholly inadequate guide to the vision of a radical Christian seer; his employment of conceptual and "speculative" thinking as a path to the Absolute, his repudiation of intuition and mystical vision, his conviction that art is inferior to philosophy in its elucidation of truth, and his belief in the forward and progressive movement of Spirit in history are all seemingly antithetical to Blake's vision, and the imagination must balk at attempting to envision the apocalyptic fury with which Blake himself might have responded to Hegel. Nevertheless, we have already seen a real coincidence in their dialectical modes of understanding and we are now confronted with a far more striking similarity in the human or existential grounds of their thinking. If the style is the man then Blake and Hegel have no common ground; their modes of expression may be taken as epitomizing the differences between the poet and the philosopher. Again it would be difficult to name two figures in history who have chosen such different ways of life: Blake the artist and craftsman, the obscure and lonely but passionate and radical seer, and Hegel the impersonal and worldly professor, who came to dominate the thought of Europe, and who ended his life as a reactionary defender of the repressive Prussian state. Yet a deeply personal crisis lies buried at the center of Hegel's thought, a religious crisis that he underwent as a young and radical theological student, a crisis that he never directly reported, but one that could be adequately described in his own language as an experience of the death of God.

Hegel's term in the *Phenomenology* for the form of consciousness that passes through a realization of the death of God is the "Unhappy Consciousness" (*unglückliches Bewusstein*); it is a necessary phase through which Spirit passes in its development in history, and it parallels St. John of the Cross's "Dark Night of the Soul" (wherein the soul loses every sense of the presence and the reality of God) in that it is an immediate prelude to the fullest epiphany of Spirit. The "Unhappy Consciousness" is the counterpart and the complement of the perfectly happy consciousness; it is the "tragic fate" that befalls certainty of self which aims at being absolute, at being self-sufficient: "It is consciousness of the loss of everything of significance in this certainty of itself, and of the loss even of this knowledge or certainty of self—the loss of substance as well as of self; it is the bitter pain which finds expression in the cruel words, 'God is dead.' "[44] Hence the "Unhappy Consciousness" is the consciousness of the "alienated soul," a consciousness of self as a divided nature, a doubled and contradictory being:

This unhappy consciousness, divided and at variance within itself, must, because this contradiction of its essential nature is felt to be a single consciousness, always have in the one consciousness the other also; and thus must be straightway driven out of each in turn, when it thinks it has therein attained to the victory and rest of unity. Its true return unto itself, or reconciliation with itself, will, however, display the notion of mind endowed with a life and existence of its own, because it implicitly involves the fact that, while being an undivided consciousness, it is a double-consciousness. It is itself the gazing of one self-consciousness into another, and itself is both, and the unity of both is also its own essence; but objectively and consciously it is not yet this essence itself—is not yet the unity of both.[45]

These difficult and even cryptic words are intended to describe a state of alienation in which consciousness is split between the here and the beyond; thereby consciousness becomes a "doubled" and contradictory being because it has left the level of self-consciousness and reverted to the condition of "mere consciousness," or the phase of conscious life in which its object is wholly external and autonomous, a simple existent or "thing."[46] Accordingly, the "Unhappy Consciousness" can only appear after Spirit has reached the level of self-consciousness and knows that self-certainty is the only ultimate portal to truth.

We cannot understand the "Unhappy Consciousness" unless we realize that it, too, like the "Dark Night of the Soul," is a transitional state between an individual and particular realization of the truth and the reality of Spirit, a realization whose very particularity demands a chasm between itself and Spirit, and a universal and total epiphany of Spirit which obliterates this chasm. The bitter pain of the alienation of the "Unhappy Consciousness" derives from its failure to realize that the Spirit which it knows in self-consciousness is identical with the Absolute Spirit that is seemingly distant and beyond. Thus the "Unhappy Consciousness" stands at that level where the particularity of consciousness and pure thought have mutually come into existence in consciousness but where they are not yet harmoniously reconciled with one another.

It rather stands midway, at the point where abstract thought comes in contact with the particularity of consciousness *qua* particularity. Itself is this act of contact; it is the union of pure thought and individuality; and this thinking individuality or pure thought also exists as object for it, and the unchangeable is essentially itself an individual existence. But that this its object, the unchangeable, which assumes essentially the form of particularity, is *its own self,* the self which is particularity of consciousness— this is not established *for it.*[47]

At this point we cannot expect to arrive at a full understanding of the "Unhappy Consciousness" if only because such an understanding demands an exposition of the movement of Spirit to total self-consciousness. Instead, let us turn to Hegel's understanding of religion in an attempt to assess the impact which the category of the "Unhappy Consciousness" had upon his conceptual understanding of the religious consciousness. Once again we are confronted with a vitally important and virtually untranslatable term, *Vorstellung;* for religion is the Absolute in the form of *Vorstellung.* The word has a large number of meanings both in German and in Hegel, the most important of which for our purpose are that *Vorstellung* is an imaginative or symbolic representation and also something that stands over against consciousness. An Hegelian scholar has this to say about its meaning:

It is not exactly the same as an image or mental picture, as one might tend to suppose, but is an image "raised to the form of universality, or thinking." What Hegel means is that Representations are thoughts which, despite their essential differences from mental pictures, none the less have some of the properties of the latter. They take whatever notions they deal with as merely given, like the things of sense, they treat them as eternal to one another like existence in Space and Time, and they merely *note* the relationships among them, instead of gaining insights into their necessity.[48]

It is also important to add that *Vorstellung* is the product of the alienation of consciousness from its object, and the degree of its alienation varies in accordance with the particular stage of the manifestation of Spirit in consciousness and in history.

The most important exposition of the meaning of religion in the *Phenomenology* for our present purpose is contained in the section devoted to the world of Spirit in "self-estrangement." First, let it be noted that Hegel, ever the dialectical thinker, maintains that Spirit only has real existence insofar as it alienates itself from itself and therefore it can only move forward by a process of self-estrangement. In a preface to this section, he says that the sphere of Spirit at this stage breaks up into two regions:

The one is the actual world, that of self-estrangement, the other is that which Spirit constructs for itself in the ether of pure consciousness, raising itself above the first. This second world, being constructed in opposition and contrast to that estrangement, is just on that account not free from it; on the contrary, it is only the other form of that very estrangement, which consists precisely in having a conscious existence in two sorts of worlds, and embraces both.[49]

Hegel, perhaps to avoid censorship, insists that he is not speaking here of religion but rather of belief or faith insofar as faith is a flight from the actual world, a flight from the present reflecting the dual state of this form of *Geist*. At this stage of Spirit, pure consciousness is alienated from its actual concrete consciousness; its essence is alienated from its existence, and consequently it exists in opposition to its own actuality. Such a self-alienated consciousness existing in estrangement from itself is only capable of living in what Hegel calls mere "belief."[50]

The immediateness which characterizes the presence of the essential reality within it is due to the fact that its object is essence, inner nature, i.e. pure thought. This immediateness, however, so far as thinking enters consciousness, or pure consciousness enters self-consciousness, acquires the significance of an objective being that lies beyond consciousness of self. It is because of the significance which immediacy and simplicity of pure thought thus acquire in consciousness that the essential reality, the object of belief, drops into being an imaginately presented idea (*Vorstellung*), instead of being the content of thought, and comes to be looked at as a supersensible world, which is essentially an "other" than self-consciousness.[51]

It lies in the very nature of belief that its object is nothing else than the real world lifted into the universality of pure consciousness, but the very alienation created by Spirit's estrangement from itself produces an object of belief that is wholly other than its present world of actuality.

In the preface to the penultimate section of the *Phenomenology* devoted to religion, Hegel remarks that the "Unhappy Consciousness" is the final shape of self-consciousness, a stage that can only know the Absolute as a "beyond," something afar off. Therefore, it becomes obvious that the understanding of the religious consciousness that Hegel reaches in his analysis of self-alienated Spirit is an understanding of the final form of that consciousness before it passes into

46

the total manifestation of Absolute Spirit. If the "Unhappy Consciousness" is the last term in an evolving series of stages of the religious consciousness, it is a stage which reveals the deepest nature of religion, and so likewise does it reveal the barriers which religion itself poses to the total epiphany of the Absolute. These barriers become fully apparent in Hegel's final discussion of *Vorstellung* in the section on revealed religion.

Since it thus, even when thinking, proceeds by way of figurative ideas, absolute Being is indeed revealed to it, but the moments of this Being, owing to this synthetic pictorial thinking, partly fall of themselves apart from one another, so that they are not related to one another through their own notion, while, partly again, this figurative thinking retreats from the pure object it deals with, and takes up a merely external relation towards it. The object is externally revealed to it from an alien source, and in this thought of Spirit it does not recognize its own self, does not recognize the nature of pure self-consciousness.[52]

But this understanding of the ground of religion is not something peculiar to Hegel himself nor is it necessarily bound to his dialectical system of understanding; it is a product of the historical stage of the modern world, of the modern form of the *Weltgeist,* and this very understanding has itself participated in the process of dissolving all previous forms of religion. Given the present historical stage of the manifestation of Spirit, traditional Christianity can find no way to appear or to be real to us; or, rather, it can retain and preserve only what is purely external or dead in belief, for the inner element in belief has now passed away.[53] Consequently, our time can only know the traditional form of the Christian faith as being directed to an empty and alien Absolute; it can only experience the established ecclesiastical form of the Church as the product of a self-alienated and estranged form of human existence; it can only encounter the Christian God by a flight from the actuality of the present moment. Need we wonder at the violence of Blake's attack upon such a Church, or at his identification of the "Christian God" as Satan, or at his realization that faith in Jesus is now possible only on the basis of the disillusion of religion?

IX. The Female

NOWHERE is Blake's symbolic power more profound, more perplexing, or more dialectical than in his portrait of the female; it might almost be said that Blake's vision of the female is a symbolic image of Hegel's absolute negativity, for the female in his vision is the primary agent of force and movement, the ruling power in nature and history, and the decisive manifestation of the dual processes of demonic destruction and divine regeneration. While the female has been deified in the form of goddesses of nature, the earth, and the dead ever since the advent of agriculture, and, indeed, received her most exalted religious expression in Indian Shaktism and Tantrism, she has nevertheless assumed perhaps her most powerful and certainly her most ambivalent epiphany in the West. One has only to think of the savior goddesses of the Greek mystery cults, the new form which the Near Eastern mystery goddesses found in the Sophia of Hellenistic Gnosticism and Eastern Christianity, the Virgin Mary of Catholicism, the Shekhinah of the Kabbalah, the strange new goddess of the uniquely Western cult of romantic love (an all too human goddess evolving from Iseult and Dante's Beatrice to the comic and tragic heroines of Shakespeare and finally coming to rest in "La belle Dame sans Merci" of modern romantic poetry and the awesome but autonomous women created by Dostoevski, Strindberg, and Proust), the realm of the Mothers in the second part of Goethe's *Faust,* the Oedipal Mother of Freud, or even the matriarchy discovered by a romantic anthropology, the Anima of Jung and D'Arcy, the White Goddess of a Robert Graves, or the existentialist understanding of woman as the Other in Simone de Beauvoir. In all these forms the female is a figure of tragic grandeur moving ambivalently between her numinous and her demonic expressions, at once the image of a lost paradise and the ruler of a present hell, the receptacle for the dreams and curses of a fallen man, whose own form has somehow become the one source of symbolic meaning in a world asleep.

If a single poet has captured in his imagery a reflection of this whole vast world of symbolic meaning, then surely that poet is Blake. We have only to remember the purity and depth of his vision of the female in his lyric poetry ("Laughing Song," "A Cradle Song," "Infant Joy," "On Another's Sorrow," "The Clod and the Pebble," "The Little Girl Lost," "The Little Girl Found," "The Sick Rose," "The Angel," "My Pretty Rose-Tree," "The Lilly," "To Tirzah," "The Mental Traveller," "The Crystal Cabinet," "The Golden Net" and "Mary"); or simply to list the major goddesses in his prophetic poetry: Ahania, Enitharmon, Vala, Jerusalem, Enion, Eno, Erin, Rahab, and Tirzah. A great deal, if not the whole, of Blake's lyric celebration of the power and the form of the female is present in the female figures of his prophetic poetry, and we must be constantly aware that Blake's goddesses are peculiarly his own; none of them is a simple transposition of a goddess from an historical mythology, nor can any of them be given a simple allegorical translation. Furthermore, the female figures of his mature poetry can flow into one another with the same deceptive, although spontaneous, movement that we have already observed in Satan; in fact, Satan himself virtually disappears as a male figure in *Jerusalem* and is present instead in a female form. Goddesses play a major role in Blake's prophetic poetry from its first symbolic expression in *America* to his final poetic work, *Jerusalem,* and while their role is minor in *Milton* they dominate *Jerusalem,* where we find a trinity of goddesses in Vala, Enitharmon, and Jerusalem, Vala being wholly demonic, Jerusalem wholly redemptive, and Enitharmon moving between these poles while at the same time symbolizing Blake's wife, Catherine. However, we should also note the significant fact that Blake's manuscript epic was first given the title, *Vala;* and it is clear that Vala was originally to have been its major protagonist, but Urizen came to usurp this role and Blake finally called the poem, *The Four Zoas.* Thus if Urizen replaced Vala's role in the earlier manuscript epic, it is clear that Vala replaced his in *Jerusalem,* and we may surmise that it was not until Blake had reached a full vision of the universal epiphany of Satan that he could create a vision of the female in all her power.

Enitharmon, the goddess first evolved in Blake's pantheon, symbolizes a fallen nature in *America*, and then in *Europe* she is identified both as the dominion of the female spreading nets to forbid all joy and as Christendom, the female dream of eighteen hundred years. This demonic role is taken up by Ahania in the books of *Urizen* and *Ahania;* in the latter book Ahania appears as the emanation of Urizen but not until Urizen has been sexually wounded by his son and his "cold loins" divide to produce the fallen sexuality of Ahania:

> Dire shriek'd his invisible Lust;
> Deep groan'd Urizen! stretching his awful hand,
> Ahania (so name his parted soul)
> He siez'd on his mountains of Jealousy.
> He groan'd anguish'd, & called her Sin,
> Kissing her and weeping over her;
> Then hid her in darkness, in silence,
> Jealous, tho' she was invisible.
> (2:30–37)

Ahania falls as a "death-shadow" into chaos, an unseen and dis-embodied mother of pestilence, and bitterly weeps on the "verge of Non-entity" at the abyss between Urizen and herself. This sequence is repeated in the third night of *Vala*, where Blake included six drawings in his manuscript of a degraded sexuality illustrating Urizen's idea of Ahania as sin. However, in this later version the role of Urizen's son is omitted and Ahania's fall becomes a direct consequence of Urizen's identification of himself as God:

> "Am I not God?" said Urizen, "Who is Equal to me?
> Do I not stretch the heavens abroad, or fold them up like a garment?"
> He spoke, mustering his heavy clouds around him, black, opake.
> Then thunders roll'd around & lightnings darted to & fro;
> His visage chang'd to darkness, & his strong right hand came forth
> To cast Ahania to the Earth; . . . .
> (F.Z. III, 106–111)

As always, Urizen in his most demonic acts takes on the form of the Creator in the Book of Job; likewise in the second night he sacrifices the Vala of eternity to establish his world. So long as Urizen dominates Blake's epic, the goddesses are thrust into the background and only appear as products of His repression and selfhood.

The full epiphany of the female in *The Four Zoas* does not take place until the eighth night when Urizen is ceasing to play an important role and is in fact already being replaced by Satan. This night was probably not written until after the apocalyptic night nine and was perhaps transcribed in its present form only after Blake had written *Milton*,[54] but here the ultimate form of the fallen female dawns in the midst of the Synagogue of Satan:

> . . . amidst them beam'd
> A False Feminine Counterpart, of Lovely Delusive Beauty
> Dividing & Uniting at will in the Cruelties of Holiness,
> Vala, drawn down into a Vegetated body, now triumphant.
> The Synagogue of Satan Clothed her with Scarlet robes & Gems,
> And on her forehead was her name written in blood, "Mystery."
> When view'd remote she is One, when view'd near she divides
> To multitude, as it is in Eden, so permitted because
> It was the best possible in the State called Satan to save
> From Death Eternal & to put off Satan Eternally.
> The Synagogue Created her from Fruit of Urizen's tree
> By devilish arts, abominable, unlawful, unutterable,
> Perpetually vegetating in detestable births
> Of female forms, beautiful thro' poisons hidden in secret
> Which give a tincture to false beauty; then was hidden within
> The bosom of Satan The false Female, as in an ark & veil
> Which Christ must rend & her reveal.
>   (F.Z. VIII, 277–293)

In eternity, Vala is the emanation of Luvah, the primordial fire of passion, but when she is sacrificed for Urizen's creation she becomes a purely female will. Yet while now existing in the state called "Satan" she is not purely satanic since that would be pure nothingness; instead she is located by her very nature at the edge of Ulro where she provides a protective boundary against Hell. Every female form is in some sense a manifestation of Vala; her own daughters are called Tirzah (the fates), she herself is called Rahab (the Mystery of the Church), and it is Vala who is the true deity of Druidism, as the passions of all humanity become victims to her priests. Meanwhile the condemned Ahania cries to Urizen:

"Will you erect a lasting habitation in the mouldering Church yard?
Or a pillar & palace of Eternity in the jaws of the hungry grave?
Will you seek pleasure from the festering wound, or marry for a Wife
The ancient Leprosy? that the King & Priest may still feast on your decay
And the grave mock & laugh at the plow'd fields, saying,
'I am the nourisher, thou the destroyer; in my bosom is milk and wine,
And a fountain from my breasts; to me come all multitudes;
To my breath they obey; they worship me. I am a goddess & queen.'
But listen to Ahania, O ye sons of the Murder'd one,
Listen to her whose memory beholds your ancient days,
Listen to her whose eyes behold the dark body of corrruptible death
Looking for Urizen in vain; in vain I seek for morning.
The Eternal Man sleeps in the Earth, nor feels the vig'rous sun
Nor silent moon, nor all the hosts of heaven move in his body."
(F.Z. VIII, 495–508)

Having delivered this dire pronouncement, Ahania in effect disappears from Blake's vision, but her words reveal the final female form of Urizen, for the "Mystery" of the female finally comes to comprehend the fallen world in its totality.

We have previously observed that in *Milton* Urizen becomes Satan but we did not note that Urizen is thereby drawn down into generation by Orc (the fallen temporal form of Luvah, the primordial passion) and the "Shadowy Female"; for the nature of a "Female Space" is this: "it shrinks the Organs of Life till they become Finite & Itself seems Infinite" (10:6). God can only appear as Satan in the fallen order of the cosmos because in that world He can only become manifest and be real in the form of a female space and time. While the female herself is created by His repressed sexuality, the solitude of His numinous transcendence, she nevertheless rules that fallen cosmos established by His very act of naming Himself the only God, and as the fall becomes all God Himself must become a female. If the female is now the Lord of the cosmos, she herself has become estranged from her lover and lives in terror of her own condition, and the "Shadowy Female" laments:

"For I will put on the Human Form & take the Image of God,
Even Pity & Humanity, but my Clothing shall be Cruelty:
And I will put on Holiness as a breastplate & as a helmet,
And all my ornaments shall be of the gold of broken hearts,
And the precious stones of anxiety & care & desperation & death
And repentance for sin & sorrow & punishment & fear,
To defend me from thy terrors, O Orc, my only beloved!"
(M. 18:19–25)

In *Jerusalem,* this terrible sovereignty of the female marks the lowest point of Albion's fall; he is bound by the cruel laws of the moral virtue of Vala's "Veil," believing that love and pity are the same— "a soft repose, Inward complacency of Soul, a Self-annihilation" (23:15)—he casts her veil into the ocean to catch the souls of the dead, and cries his last words while relapsing into his rocks and caverns:

"Blasphemous Sons of Feminine delusion! God in the dreary Void
Dwells from Eternity, wide separated from the Human Soul.
But thou, deluding Image, by whom imbu'd the Veil I rent,
Lo, here is Vala's Veil whole, for a Law, a Terror & a Curse!
And therefore God takes vengeance on me: from my clay-cold bosom
My children wander, trembling victims of his Moral Justice:
His snows fall on me and cover me, while in the Veil I fold
My dying limbs. Therefore O Manhood, if thou art aught
But a meer Phantasy, hear dying Albion's Curse!
May God, who dwells in this dark Ulro & voidness, vengeance take,
And draw thee down into this Abyss of sorrow and torture,
Like me thy Victim. O that Death & Annihilation were the same!"
(23:29–40)

The veil of Vala is a vitally important, although infrequently employed, symbolic image which Blake uses to invoke the sense of both her mystery and her universality: Vala rules the fallen world but her rule is invisible to all but the imaginative seer; she appears everywhere but she is visible only in her masks. A fallen nature is, of course, the body of this dark goddess; her womb stretches from the infinite distance of the heavens to the brute presence of a dark and lifeless matter. Hers is the face behind the mask of "Ratio"; she names the gods and cloaks religion with the costumes of her garments, the repressive laws of morality are her creation, and the most horrible outbreaks of cruelty and tyranny in history are signs of her immediate presence. However, the most agonizing rule of Vala is in a fallen sexuality where the primordial energy of life has been inverted into impotence by this whore of chastity:

> "I hear the screech of Childbirth loud pealing, & the groans
> Of Death in Albion's clouds dreadful utter'd over all the Earth.
> What may Man be? who can tell! but what may Woman be
> To have power over Man from Cradle to corruptible Grave?
> There is a Throne in every Man, it is the Throne of God;
> This, Woman has claim'd as her own, & Man is no more!
> Albion is the Tabernacle of Vala & her Temple,
> And not the Tabernacle & Temple of the Most High.
> O Albion, why wilt thou Create a Female Will?
> To hide the most evident God in a hidden covert, even
> In the shadows of a Woman & a secluded Holy Place,
> That we may pry after him as after a stolen treasure,
> Hidden among the Dead & mured up from the paths of life."
>
> (J. 34:23–35)

Once man and God have fallen into the dark caverns of Vala's womb, they can meet only in her forbidden ecstasy. An energy so turned in upon itself can move but deeper into chaos; its every movement provokes the wrath of Vala's condemnation, as every human act bears the guilt of a feminine repression. The distant and wrathful God of religion, the thou-shalt-not of the moral law, the repressive laws and institutions of society, the abstract and inhuman laws of the logical and scientific mind, and the absolute otherness of an alien nature are all inevitable consequences of Vala's triumph; but the supreme sceptre of Vala's sovereignty is the shrunken human body and that "mortal worm" that once was the "Throne of God."

Fundamentally, the dominion of Vala's "Veil" has transformed life into death; the free and joyous energy of Albion's original state has been perverted into the impotence of a shrunken sexuality; a primordial and human nature has descended into the cold and dehumanizing forces of an impersonal cosmos; an imagination originally

encompassing the totality of all things has withered into the wholly
negative activity of ratio; a primal harmony of humanity and deity
has been split asunder, with deity retreating to a vacuous slumber
and humanity falling into division and creating that chaos which is
the real ruler of history. Death is the true name of Vala:

"Once Man was occupied in intellectual pleasure & Energies,
But now my Soul is harrow'd with grief & fear & love & desire,
And now I hate & now I love, & Intellect is no more.
There is no time for any thing but the torments of love & desire.
The Feminine & Masculine Shadows, soft, mild & ever varying
In beauty, are Shadows now no more, but Rocks in Horeb."

Then all the Males conjoined into One Male, & every one
Became a ravening eating Cancer growing in the Female,
A Polypus of Roots, of Reasoning, Doubt, Despair & Death,
Going forth & returning from Albion's Rocks to Canaan,
Devouring Jerusalem from every Nation of the Earth.
(J. 68:65–69:5)

What is man? A "Polypus," an isolated selfhood who is but the
spectre of his original life, a mortal worm that once was a dragon of
desire, a cancer growing in the female who devours the source of
life: "Love may only be obtain'd in the passages of Death" (J.
81:7). Therefore Vala cries:

"The Human is but a Worm, & thou, O Male! Thou art
Thyself Female, a Male, a breeder of Seed, a Son & Husband: & Lo,
The Human Divine is Woman's Shadow, a Vapor in the summer's heat.
Go assume Papal dignity, thou Spectre, thou Male Harlot! Arthur,
Divide into the Kings of Europe in times remote, O woman-born
And Woman-nourish'd & Woman-educated & Woman-scourn'd!"
(J. 64:12–17)

As the wheels of "Satan's Mills" move onward, every living thing is
caught up and frozen into death and becomes an inverted spectre
of its original state: God becomes a female Satan, nature becomes the
empty tomb of man, and man becomes a woman's shadow. But the
satanic wheels of history and the cosmos while moving ever deeper

55

into chaos draw all things with them into the final mystery; as this mystery approaches, the circumference of a fallen totality comes into focus, and the modern prophet draws upon the New Testament Apocalypse to unveil the ultimate form of the female:

> A Double Female now appear'd within the Tabernacle,
> Religion hid in War, a Dragon red & hidden Harlot
> Each within other, but without, a Warlike Mighty-one
> Of dreadful power sitting upon Horeb, pondering dire
> And mighty preparations, mustering multitudes innumerable
> Of warlike sons among the sands of Midian & Aram.
> For multitudes of those who sleep in Alla descend,
> Lured by his warlike symphonies of tabret, pipe & harp,
> Burst the bottoms of the Graves & Funeral Arks of Beulah.
> Wandering in that unknown Night beyond the silent Grave
> They became One with the Antichrist & are absorb'd in him.
>
> (J. 89:52–62)

II

REDEMPTION

1. The Age of the Spirit

IF BLAKE were to be associated with a single theological persuasion, that could only be his prophetic and mystical identification of God and man: "God only Acts & Is, in existing beings or Men" (M.H.H. 15–17). While it is possible to trace this conviction as a constant theme in Blake's work, it must be conceded that it is a theme which takes on many colors and forms in the course of its evolution, not the least of which being the transformation effected upon it by the religious upheaval that Blake underwent while working upon *Vala* or *The Four Zoas*. No doubt Blake originally encountered this doctrine in Swedenborg, who wrote:

> In all the heavens there is no other idea of God than that He is a Man. This is because heaven as a whole and in part is in form like a man, and because it is the Divine which is with the angels that constitutes heaven and inasmuch as thought proceeds according to the form of Heaven, it is impossible for the angels to think of God in any other way. From this it is that all those in the world who are conjoined with heaven think of God in the same way when they think interiorly in themselves, that is, in their spirit.[1]

Swedenborg was also instructed in a vision that the final Age of the Spirit had begun in 1757, a date that was of great significance to Blake; it was his birthdate, and so he declared in 1790:

> As a new heaven is begun, and it is now thirty-three years since its advent, the Eternal Hell revives. And lo! Swedenborg is the Angel sitting at the tomb: his writings are the linen clothes folded up. Now is the dominion of Edom, & the return of Adam into Paradise; see Isaiah xxxiv & xxxv Chap. (M.H.H. 3)

57

His reference to Isaiah is to passages depicting the coming of the final judgment of Edom to be followed by the ultimate restoration of the faithful:

> Then the eyes of the blind shall be opened,
> And the ears of the deaf shall be unstopped.
> Then shall the lame man leap as a hart,
> And the tongue of the dumb sing:
> For in the wilderness shall waters break out,
> And streams in the desert.
>   (Isa. 35:5 f.)

However, the new age cannot be consummated until the old age has been destroyed, and, as we have seen, Blake associated religion and the Church with the old age, and reacted with wrath against the legal, the particular, and the historical claims of the Church. Few men have been so deeply offended by Christianity's claim to exclusive revelation: "The Bible or Peculiar Word of God, Exclusive of Conscience or the Word of God Universal, is that Abomination, which like the Jewish ceremonies, is for ever removed & henceforth every man may converse with God & be a King & Priest in his own house."[2]

Blake looked upon religious law as being directed both to the repression of passion or energy and to the establishment of barriers between men that would seal them in isolation from each other, thereby producing the conditions for the dominance of war and chaos in history. Such law is a product of the Fall and it serves to perpetuate and reenact the Fall, obscuring the original condition of man and binding men to the hatred generated by repression. Only the Eternal Gospel can deliver men from this bondage but the Eternal Gospel is in no sense to be equated with the gospel of the Church: "Ye are united, O ye Inhabitants of Earth, in One Religion, The Religion of Jesus, the most Ancient, the Eternal & the Everlasting Gospel" (J. 27:5 f.). This original Gospel is an eternal and everlasting Gospel; nevertheless, it has been forgotten in the sleep of fallen man, and Blake accepted and chose a prophetic vocation of resurrecting the "Religion of Jesus." Since the triumph of Rahab, Christianity has imprisoned Jesus in his tomb, but with the advent of the Age of the

Spirit the spiritual gospel of Jesus has dawned once more. There is no evidence that Blake had any actual contact with the traditions of the radical spiritual reformers in seventeenth-century England but there also can be little doubt that Blake's understanding of the spiritual gospel is intimately related to theirs. A recent study by A. L. Morton has made a solid case for Blake's relationship with the English Antinomians: many Antinomians believed that God had no other existence except in man, that the Everlasting Gospel is the spiritual revelation of the third age of the Holy Spirit, and one radical sect, the Ranters, believed only in the spiritual Jesus of the third age, practiced ritual nudism (the repetition of Adam's original state), and proclaimed that although God is present in every creature, He knows Himself only in man.[3] At all of these points and others, Blake lived in the Antinomian tradition—including the ritual nudism which is extremely important in Blake's art—and he increasingly came to deepen his conviction that he was indeed living in the spiritual age and that the end of the old world would soon be at hand. In 1800 he wrote to his friend, John Flaxman, that "the time is arriv'd when Men shall again converse in Heaven & walk with Angels"; and a year later he wrote Flaxman: "The Kingdoms of this World are now become the Kingdoms of God & His Christ, & we shall reign with him for ever & ever." This is typical Christian apocalyptic language, nor is it very rare; it seems invariably to occur in major reformers (e.g., St. Francis and Luther) and in radical sects, and in the eighteenth and nineteenth centuries it was transposed into the language of ethical and political utopianism.

The ten-year period between 1797 and 1807 was perhaps the most important in Blake's life; during this period he wrote and rewrote and finally abandoned *Vala* or *The Four Zoas,* he created many of his most important paintings and designs, and he began engraving the plates for *Milton* and *Jerusalem.* Sloss and Wallis speak of Blake's opinions undergoing a far-reaching change after 1797: "necessitarianism" gives way to a belief in a "beneficient Providence," there is a fuller use of Christian symbols, and a continuous development toward the identification of "Christianity" and "Art."[4] So likewise Damon says that in *Jerusalem* Blake for the first time identifies the Father and the Son, the Creator and the Redeemer.[5] However, it was not until G. E. Bentley Jr.'s critical study of *Vala* that the full measure of Blake's transformation became apparent. Bentley points out that by 1797 *Vala* had 2,200 lines, within ten years or so it grew to 4,000 lines and was now called *The Four Zoas,* and this growth and revision of the poem represents a progressive disintegration of its original poetic form and an increasing concentration upon mythological meaning.[6] Of the 143 symbolic names in the text, 117 appear only in added passages or in the late night eight, all of the biblical and historical names were late additions, including the name of Albion, and all of the references to Druidism are very late. In short, in the course of working upon this poem, Blake moved more and more deeply into a Christian and redemptive understanding of history and the cosmos. We have few clues to the personal ground of this transformation, the most important being a letter that Blake wrote to his patron, William Hayley, on October 23, 1804:

For now! O Glory! and O Delight! I have entirely reduced that spectrous Fiend to his station, whose annoyance has been the ruin of my labours for the last passed twenty years of my life. He is the enemy of conjugal love and is the Jupiter of the Greeks, an iron-hearted tyrant, the ruiner of ancient Greece. I speak with perfect confidence and certainty of the fact which has passed upon me. . . . Suddenly, on the day after visiting the Truchsessian Gallery of pictures, I was again enlightened with the light I enjoyed in my youth, and which has for exactly twenty years been closed from me as by a door and by window-shutters. Consequently I can, with confidence, promise you ocular demonstration of my altered state on the plates I am now engraving . . . O the distress I have undergone, and my poor wife with me: incessantly labouring and incessantly spoiling what I had done well. . . . I thank God with entire confidence that it shall be so no longer—he is become my servant who domineered over me, he is even as a brother who was my enemy. Dear Sir, excuse my enthusiasm or rather madness, for I am really drunk with intellectual vision whenever I take a pencil or graver into my hand, even as I used to be in my youth, and as I have not been for twenty dark, but very profitable years. I thank God that I courageously pursued by course through darkness.

This letter has caused a great deal of critical controversy. It seems incredible that Blake could have so condemned his earlier poetry and

art (albeit for most readers today this poetry is his only poetry); yet
some Blake scholars, such as Blackstone, have judged this letter to be
an authentic report of a genuine conversion experience, and we should
remember that Kierkegaard and Tolstoy were soon to take a similar
attitude toward their pre-conversion work. Yet theologically the most
striking thing about this letter is the fact that Blake identified the
"spectrous Fiend" who was his enemy as the tyrant God, an enemy
who has now become his servant and his friend: thus he can thank
God that he, Blake, has passed through a darkness that is presumably
God's alone.

The paradox unveiled in this letter lies at the center of Blake's
mature work and provides the key to the theological meaning of his
vision; hence we would do well to proceed with caution at this point.
Before embarking upon an examination of the Christian ground of
Blake's work, let us once more look for a Blakean parallel in Hegel. In
the preface to the *Phenomenology,* written in 1807, Hegel says that his
epoch is a birth-time and a period of transition: "The spirit of man
has broken with the old order of things hitherto prevailing, and with
the old ways of thinking, and is in the mind to let them all sink into the
depths of the past and to set about its own transformation."[7] But
the new Spirit has thus far arrived only in its immediacy, in its bare
generality. We have seen that Hegel himself first experienced this new
age of the Spirit by passing through the "Unhappy Consciousness,"
and thereby undergoing the pain of alienation and self-estrangement.
When Spirit is so estranged from itself, it is only capable of "mere
belief," and Hegel's distinction between belief and "pure insight" does
much to illuminate the new Age of the Spirit. Pure insight is con-
centrated and focused in self-consciousness; it has no content within
it because it exists for itself by negating everything in it, thereby it
negates all objectivity and all consciousness which is not self-
consciousness. Furthermore, pure insight directs itself against belief
and only appears in a genuinely active form insofar as it enters into
conflict with belief.[8]

Since belief and insight are the same pure consciousness, but in form are
opposed—the reality in the case of belief being a thought, not a Notion,
and hence something absolutely opposed to self-consciousness, while the

reality in the case of pure insight is the self—they are such that *inter se* the one is the absolute negative of the other.

As appearing the one against the other, all content falls to belief; for in its unperturbed element of thought every moment obtains definite substance. Pure insight, however, is in the first instance without any content; it is rather the sheer disappearance of content; but by its negative attitude towards what it excludes it will make itself real and give itself a content.[9]

Thus pure insight operates negatively and it can only be the negation of itself; its goal is to know the absolute negation of itself to be its own proper reality, its "self" or its "self-understanding Notion."

By analyzing the struggle between belief and insight in the period of the Enlightenment, Hegel shows how insight reveals that the object of belief is something produced by and for consciousness. One by one, belief comes to cast aside all its contents as insight works upon it, for insight makes valid in belief what is necessary to belief itself and what belief contains within it. By means of this struggle belief comes to understand itself, it comes to realize that its certainty does not carry the truth within it, and it collapses into the inarticulate state of pure feeling or intuition: "Belief is banished from its own kingdom; this kingdom is sacked and plundered, since the waking consciousness has forcibly taken to itself every distinction and expansion of it and claimed every one of its parts for earth, and returned them to the earth that owns them."[10] No doubt Blake himself went through something like this process, hence his abandonment of the contents of Christian belief and his desperate search for a new mythology, his valiant but seemingly futile effort to speak of Jesus apart from the framework of Christian belief, his realization that an allegory addressed to the corporeal understanding can only bind man yet more deeply to his fallen state, and his continual effort to create a Vision that would be a dialectical inversion and reversal of the traditional form of Christian belief. Blake, of course, was not wholly successful in this effort, and we must warn ourselves that his vision is artificial and unreal at just those points where it contains the traditional language of belief. Nor must we accept the non-dialectical principle which says that the Christian Blake is the Blake who speaks "Christian language"; such language for Blake could only be allegorical in the bad or corporeal sense; to the extent that Blake speaks this language he is either speaking ironically or failing in his purpose. When Blake attempted to transform *Vala* into a Christian epic by infusing it with the categories of traditional Christian symbolism and theology, he found that the poem simply dissolved and lost all coherent meaning. His triumph as a Christian artist and visionary came in *Milton* and *Jerusalem,* and in the illustrations to the Book of Job and to *The Divine Comedy;* and we must be prepared for the paradox that in these works Blake is most deeply Christian when his language is most anti-Christian, his vision becomes most real when it is seemingly most blasphemous or atheistic, and his images of regeneration and of Jesus become most authentic when they are furthest removed from their seeming original. All of this is in accord with the radical Christian's understanding of the Age of the Spirit, the spiritual Jesus must be antithetically related to the Church's Jesus, the Eternal Gospel must be an inversion of the temporal gospel, and God can have no existence or reality apart from that which He has in the present and immediate acts of men.

II.   Incarnation and *Kenōsis*

As EARLY as the *Songs of Innocence,* Jesus appears in Blake's poetry under the figures of the Lamb and the Shepherd and in the universal human virtues of mercy, pity, peace, and love ("The Divine Image"). But his most passionate presence is in "On Another's Sorrow," which opens with the famous lines:

> Can I see another's woe,
> And not be in sorrow too?
> Can I see another's grief,
> And not seek for kind relief?

Already we encounter a uniquely Blakean motif, for the "I" of this lyric is Jesus himself, who is identified in the penultimate stanza as

63

the maker of all those who suffer and lament; and then the poem reaches its conclusion:

> O! he gives to us his joy
> That our grief he may destroy;
> Till our grief is fled & gone
> He doth sit by us and moan.

At about the same time or shortly before he wrote this lyric, Blake had concluded the aphorisms which comprise *There Is No Natural Religion* with an affirmation of the Incarnation: "Therefore God becomes as we are, that we may be as he is." These words are doubly significant, for not only do they anticipate Blake's later work but they are also an adaption of one of the Church's earliest theological formulations of the meaning of the Incarnation, and, while this understanding of the Incarnation came to dominate the Eastern Church, it was resisted by the West, appearing there only in various apocalyptic, mystical, and heretical forms until it was reborn in the work of William Blake. Nevertheless, Christ does not appear in Blake's prophetic poetry until after his conversion or regeneration, when his prophetic activity for the first time bcame definitely Christian. Why? Surely this could only be because prior to his regeneration Blake could only know Christ as the dead body preserved in the tomb of Vala's Church; when Innocence becomes Experience the primordial energy of Luvah becomes sealed in the sepulcher:

> "The footsteps of the Lamb of God were there; but now no more,
> No more shall I behold him; he is clos'd in Luvah's Sepulcher.
>
> . . . .
>
> If God was Merciful, this could not be. O Lamb of God,
> Thou art a delusion and Jerusalem is my Sin! O my Children,
> I have educated you in the crucifying cruelties of Demonstration
> Till you have assum'd the Providence of God & slain your Father.
> Dost thou appear before me, who liest dead in Luvah's Sepulcher?
> Dost thou forgive me, thou who wast Dead & art Alive?
> Look not so merciful upon me, O thou Slain Lamb of God!
> I die! I die in thy arms, tho' Hope is banish'd from me."
>
> (J. 24:50–60)

Once the "Mystery" of Rahab has come to dominate the Church, and the Church itself has become the instrument of tyranny and the agent of repression, then the Lamb of Innocence is invisible in history and is present in Experience only in the ashes of a dead or dying passion. No way lies through the labyrinth of the Church to Jesus, no true image of Jesus is present in the dead letter of the Church's Bible, and the Church's dogma is a dark and subtle web of Vala's Veil. Therefore, when the regenerate Blake rediscovered Jesus he encountered him in a strange and radical form. Crabb Robinson reports the late Blake as eagerly asserting: "We are all coexistent with God: members of the Divine body, and partakers of the Divine nature." But these words of Blake do not bear their usual Christian meaning; he is neither referring to a transcendent and numinous God nor for that matter to any meaning of God that is present in the Christian tradition. When Robinson asked him about the imputed divinity of Jesus Christ, Blake answered: "He is the only God"—but then he added—"And so am I and so are you." This theological paradox is pervasively present in *Milton* and *Jerusalem*, where the human Imagination is called the "Divine Body of the Lord Jesus." At the end of *Jerusalem*, Jesus appears as Los, the archetypal figure symbolizing the Imagination:

> Then Jesus appeared standing by Albion as the Good Shepherd
> By the lost Sheep that he hath found, & Albion knew that it
> Was the Lord, the Universal Humanity; & Albion saw his Form
> A Man, & they conversed as Man with Man in Ages of Eternity.
> And the Divine Appearance was the likeness & similitude of Los.
> (J. 96:3-7)

In his commentary on this passage in *Jerusalem*, Joseph Wicksteed says that this vision of God as "A Man" takes us into the inmost recesses of Blake's mind and genius.[11] So it does, but the theologian might add that it is a recess that has been explored by few if any of Blake's interpreters.

A great deal has been made of Blake's equation of "Art" and "Christianity" in the Laocoon engraving of 1820, although it is not so often noticed that Blake associates Art in this passage with the

Vision of Eternity, and goes on to speak of Jesus and his apostles and disciples as artists. When Blake identifies the human Imagination with the Body of Christ, he is certainly not speaking of the imagination in a purely esthetic sense, nor is he limiting the epiphany of Christ to men who know themselves as artists. As Northrop Frye astutely analyzes this theme:

Only the creator has the divine spirit. But it would be a dreary outlook if we had to construct a new sacerdotal order out of that not especially attractive class of men whom we know as artists, and attach a superstitious reverence to their persons. The real artist is not the man creating, but the total form of his creation, his art regarded as his vision of life, and as an individual part of the archetypal vision which is the Word of God. And among artists we must distinguish a Reynolds from a Milton, and follow only the artist who is also a prophet. Through him we may learn that, just as the artist exists eternally as the total form of his art, and not as the man who created it, so the true and eternal God is not the Creator of man, but the total form of his creation, which is the larger body of man. This larger body is the human form of God, and the greatness of the great man consists in his "identity" with the unification of the divine and the human which is the body of Jesus.[12]

Moreover the divine spirit exists in every man insofar as that man is a "Minute Particular": "& every Particular is a Man, a Divine Member of the Divine Jesus" (J. 91:30). Blackstone and Wicksteed point out that Jesus is the real hero of *Jerusalem;* he is present, whether implicitly or explicitly, on virtually every page of the text as the source of regeneration; yet he seldom appears in the designs, and then never so as to show a human face. Indeed, the Jesus of Blake's vision is a truly universal Christ, in losing his particular and historical image he appears wherever there is life:

> The Divine Vision still was seen,
> Still was the Human Form Divine,
> Weeping in weak & mortal clay,
> O Jesus, still the Form was thine.
> And thine the Human Face, & thine
> The Human Hands & Feet & Breath,
> Entering thro' the Gates of Birth
> And passing thro' the Gates of Death.
> (J. 27:57–64)

Jesus is the Resurrection and the Life, and by his death he passes the limits of possibility as they appear to individual perception (J. 62:18 f.). Consequently, he is that "One Man" who is incarnate in humanity itself:

> "We live as One Man; for contracting our infinite senses
> We behold multitude, or expanding, we behold as one,
> As One Man all the Universal Family, and that One Man
> We call Jesus the Christ; and he in us, and we in him
>
> . . . .
>
> He is the Good shepherd, he is the Lord and master,
> He is the Shepherd of Albion, he is all in all, . . ."
> (J. 38:17–24)

At this point it should be apparent that Blake's prophetic and mystical identification of God and man is integrally related to his vision of Jesus, that he came to know Jesus as the eternal Word who is both the source and the substance of all life, and that the very comprehensiveness of his vision of Jesus demanded that he not only sacrifice the historical and imaginative particularity of the Church's Christ but that he was thereby likewise impelled to seek the presence of Jesus in that world of experience most estranged from the Christ of historical Christianity. The biblical source of Blake's understanding of the Incarnation is in the Greek word, *kenōsis,* meaning "emptying"; while as a noun this word is not found in the New Testament, its correlative verb occurs in Philippians 2:7, "emptied himself," in which Paul says that Christ "though he was in the form of God, did not count equality with God a thing to be grasped, but emptied himself, taking the form of a servant, being born in the likeness of men." Only in the last two centuries has a kenotic Christology appeared in the West, and it has still to be accepted in a radical form by the theologian, but a genuine kenotic mysticism is present in Meister Eckhart and his followers, as the brilliant study of Rudolf Otto has fully demonstrated.[13] Thus Eckhart declares in one of his sermons:

To deny one's self is to be the only begotten Son of God and one who does so has for himself all the properties of that Son. All God's acts

are performed and his teachings conveyed through the Son, to the point
that we should be his only begotten Son. And when this is accomplished
in God's sight, he is so fond of us and so fervent that he acts as if his
divine Being might be shattered and he himself annihilated if the whole
foundations of his Godhead were not revealed to us, together with his
nature and being. God makes haste to do this, so that it may be ours
as it is his. It is here that God finds joy and rapture in fulfilment and
the person who is thus within God's knowing and love becomes just what
God himself is.[14]

This text and the whole body of Eckhart's sermons reveal that
Christian mysticism has long known an identification of God and man
achieved in the eternal generation of the Son. In Eternity, the Father
generates the Son in his own likeness, but so likewise does the
Father generate the Son in the human soul:

The Father ceaselessly begats his Son and, what is more, he begats me
as his Son—the self-same Son! Indeed, I assert that he begats me not
only as his Son but as himself and himself as myself, begatting me in his
own nature, his own being. At that inmost Source, I spring from the
Holy Spirit and there is one life, one being, one action. All God's works
are one and therefore He begats me as he does his Son and without
distinction.[15]

Nor were these words intended to be of mere homiletic value, without
theological weight; in his own official defense Eckhart maintained
that: "the Father begats me as his Son, and the same Son, without
distinction."[16] Eckhart even coined a word to express this idea,
istigkeit, with various spellings, meaning "isness" in an immediate
sense: "God's is-ness is my isness, and neither more nor less."[17]

An implicit kenotic ground is the source of the life and vitality of
Eckhart's understanding of the eternal generation of the Son, and this
same kenotic ground is the source of the most important distinction
between Christian and non-Christian forms of mysticism, a distinction
that will gradually be explored in the course of this book. However,
Christian theology has never evolved to a genuinely kenotic form, no
doubt because it has remained too deeply bound to the dogmatic
confessions of the Church and too fully attached to the Christian
historical tradition. Therefore we must not turn to theology if we

68

wish to search out the meaning of *kenōsis,* but rather to those radical expressions of thought and vision that reflect the fruits of a spiritual reformation of Christianity. Remarkably enough, the one thinker in Christendom who self-consciously and systematically created a kenotic form of understanding was Hegel, despite the fact that this Christian foundation of his thought has only rarely been explored and has yet to be encountered by Christian theology. Historians of philosophy tell us that negation is the one specific and unique element in Hegel's dialectic, and we might add that Hegel's idea of absolute negativity cannot ultimately be dissociated from a Christian ground. The young Hegel, while discussing the meaning of sacrifice in worship, remarks that this "aimless destruction for destruction's sake . . . proves to be the only religious relation to absolute objects."[18] This conviction became the motivating center of Hegel's thought; thus, in the preface to the *Phenomenology,* immediately after having declared that everything depends upon grasping and expressing the ultimate truth not as "Substance" but as "Subject" as well, Hegel says: "The life of God and divine intelligence, then, can, if we like, be spoken of as love disporting with itself; but this idea falls into edification, and even sinks into insipidity, if it lacks the seriousness, the suffering, the patience, and the labor of the negative."[19] Negativity is the power and the process of the self-realization or the self-mediation of the Hegelian Absolute, Subject or Spirit. Accordingly, Spirit is the kenotic process of negativity, as such it is the true actuality (*Wirklichkeit*) of the world, for Spirit is the inherently negative or the negativity as found in Being *per se:* "i.e. it is absolute distinction from itself, is pure process of becoming its other."[20]

We know that Hegel had a deep love of Meister Eckhart, and we also know that the chief sources of his understanding of negation were Eckhart, Boehme, and Spinoza; furthermore, Hegel tells us that the negative process of Subject or Spirit becoming its other is mythologized in *Vorstellung* by the dogma of the eternal generation of the Son. Indeed, the most important movement of his dialectic, the negation of negation, was anticipated in a mystical form by Eckhart:

The divine One is a negation of negations and a desire of desires. What does "One" mean? Something to which nothing is to be added. The soul lays hold of the Godhead where it is pure, where there is nothing beside it, nothing else to consider. The One is a negation of negations. Every creature contains a negation: one denies that it is the other. An angel denies that it is any other creature; but God contains the denial of denials. He is that One who denies of every other that is is anything except himself.[21]

This last sentence is a concise portrait of Hegel's idea of Spirit, but it is divorced from the dialectical movement and the conceptual understanding that is the true power and greatness of Hegel's system. While Hegel's *Logic,* as we shall later see, revolves about a kenotic movement of negation, it is only in the *Phenomenology* that Hegel openly unveils the kenotic ground of his thought. The full kenotic meaning of Spirit is already given in the preface, a meaning that Hegel says is due to the modern age and its religion:

Spirit is alone Reality. It is the inner being of the world, that which essentially is, and is *per se;* it assumes objective, determinate form, and enters into relations with itself—it is externality (otherness), and exists for self; yet, in this determination, and in its otherness, it is still one with itself—it is self-contained and self-complete, in itself and for itself at once. This self-containedness, however, is first something known by us, it is implicit in its nature (*an sich*); it is Substance spiritual. It has to become self-contained for itself (*für sich*), on its own account; it must be knowledge of Spirit, and must be consciousness of itself as Spirit. This means, it must be presented to itself as an object, but at the same time straightway annul and transcend this objective form; it must be its own object in which it finds itself reflected.[22]

These words contain the heart of Hegel's system: Spirit, which exists originally and eternally in itself (*an sich*), must become historical, existing in a determinate form as object for itself (*für sich*). This transformation occurs by the process of negation, Spirit-in-itself negates itself and thus becomes Spirit-for-itself; and by the negation of negation Spirit-for-itself becomes Spirit-in-itself; but this final form of Spirit is far richer and fuller than its initial beginning.

Such an abstract and abbreviated formulation possesses, of course, very little real meaning, nor does Hegel in such formulations employ the actual word, *kenōsis*. Significantly enough we find that Hegel's deepest insights in the *Phenomenology* reach their most compelling expressions when they implicitly or explicitly employ the language of *kenōsis*. Hegel can speak of "the *kenōsis* of the eternal Being," whereby it enters the sphere of actuality, becoming sensuous and uncomprehended.[23] And he often adapts the crude language of *Vorstellung* to convey his most dialectical meaning:

The sacrifice of the divine substance, so far as it is active, belongs to the side of self-consciousness. That this concrete act may be possible, the absolute Being must have from the start *implicitly* sacrificed *itself*. This it has done in the fact that it has given itself definite existence, and made itself an individual animal and fruit on the earth. The self actively sacrificing demonstrates in actual existence, and sets before its own consciousness, this already implicitly completed self-renunciation on the part of absolute Being; and replaces that immediate reality, which absolute Being has, by the higher, viz that of the self making the sacrifice.[24]

This analysis of the cultic act of sacrifice is intended to be at once historical and ontological; the eternal movement of Spirit by the very act of *kenōsis* achieves an historical and phenomenological expression. Moreover Hegel's kenotic language is confessional, just as St. Augustine's confession of his conversion was intended to be a reflection and repetition of the universal religious process of man's fall and redemption. Hegel's analysis of the agony and despair of the "Unhappy Consciousness" is intended to be a reflection of the historical process of the birth of Spirit as self-consciousness. Spirit, here, has in it two sides:

one is this, that substance empties itself of itself, and becomes self-consciousness; the other is the converse, that self-consciousness empties itself of itself and makes itself into the form of "thing," or makes itself universal self. Both sides have in this way met each other, and, in consequence, their true union has arisen. The relinquishment or *kenōsis* on the part of the substance, its becoming self-consciousness, expresses the transition into the opposite, the unconscious transition of necessity, in other words, that it is *implicitly* self-consciousness. Conversely, the emptying of self-consciousness expresses this, that implicitly it is Universal Being, or—because the self is pure self-existence, which is at home with itself in its opposite—that the substance is self-consciousness explicitly *for the self*, and, just on that account, is Spirit.[25]

Absolute Spirit comes into existence as the unity of "Subject" and "Substance," of self-consciousness and Being-in-itself, each emptying itself of itself and becoming its own other. Self-consciousness must pass through the bitter feeling of the "Unhappy Consciousness" when it experiences the death of God because it must reach the knowledge of the pure subjectivity of Substance, the pure certainty of itself, which it lacked when it knew God as objectively existent: "This knowledge is thus spiritualization, whereby Substance becomes Subject, by which its abstraction and lifelessness have expired, and Substance therefore has become real, simple, and universal self-consciousness."[26]

We might pause momentarily at this point if only to recover from the dazzling power of Hegel's abstractions and note the decisive parallel between Hegel's philosophical and Blake's poetic themes. Both Blake and Hegel know a single movement of Spirit that comprehends all reality whatsoever, whether expressed symbolically as the fall of Albion to discord and division and his gradual reawakening as "One Man," or expressed conceptually as Spirit's original negation of itself and its consequent division into Substance and Subject, followed by the historical and the phenomenological process of these primary opposites returning into their others. A dialectical movement is the motivating power of these "systems," a movement that is kenotic in direction and form; as Spirit empties itself into its opposite, it becomes incarnate not simply *in* but rather *as* the world, and by inverting its fallen form it returns into a yet deeper unity with itself. Furthermore, Blake's most paradoxical theological affirmations take on the form of philosophical necessity in Hegel: "God only Acts & Is, in existing beings or Men" might have supplied a motto for the *Phenomenology,* where the movement of human consciousness (and unconsciousness!) unfolds itself in such a way as to reveal the essential correlation between a subjective consciousness and an objective reality, with the result that the movement from sensation to consciousness to self-consciousness comprehends the totality of *all* life and experience. Yet, most important of all for our purpose, the kenotic form of Hegel's thought can point the way to the full meaning of Blake's "Jesus." If we take Hegel's understanding of the absolute

negativity of Spirit as a conceptual formulation of the kenotic meaning of Christ, then we should be prepared to view the full scope of
Blake's vision of Jesus and to realize that the motto which Blake in
fact gave *Jerusalem*, "Jesus only," is the key to the ultimate meaning
of his vision as a whole. Remembering that Blake's Jesus is not the
historical Jesus remembered by Christendom nor the cultic Christ
worshiped by the Church, but rather the epiphany of a universal
divine Humanity, we may even be enabled to understand Hegel as
an exponent of a radically reformed and spiritual Christianity.

Indeed, Hegel freely associates the advent of Absolute Spirit with
the Incarnation. In the believing Christian community, Spirit for the
first time assumes the shape of inherent self-consciousness insofar as
the believing mind sees, feels, and hears Spirit's divinity as a definite
self-consciousness or an actual human being. Since Spirit now becomes an object for immediate experience, such belief is not fancy for
it is actual in the believer; here consciousness recognizes God in
immediate present existence, and God is known as self-consciousness
because He is beheld sensuously and immediately as an individual self.

> This incarnation of the Divine Being, its having essentially and directly
> the shape of self-consciousness, is the simple content of Absolute Religion.
> Here the Divine Being is known as Spirit; this religion is the Divine
> Being's consciousness concerning itself that it is Spirit. For Spirit is
> knowledge of self in a state of alienation of self: Spirit is the Being which
> is the process of retaining identity with itself in its otherness.[27]

Unquestionably these words record one of Hegel's clearest definitions
of Spirit, and they make it all too clear that Hegel's dialectical understanding of absolute negativity has at the very least a Christian
source. Hegel's analysis of the Incarnation also provides us with a
fuller understanding of the nature of *Vorstellung* and with the transformation of Christian belief that is effected by a spiritual reformation.
In the symbolic and mythological form of *Vorstellung*, the Incarnation must appear as an inconceivable happening, an inexplicable
paradox, and this is so because it here appears as a simple objective
fact. Belief cannot know the necessity of the reciprocal relationship
between Absolute Being and self-consciousness; therefore it can only

know that the Son of God has emptied Himself of Himself and become flesh.

This figurative idea, which in this manner is still immediate and hence not spiritual, i.e. it knows the human form assumed by the Divine as merely a particular form, not yet as a universal form—becomes spiritual for this consciousness in the process whereby God, who has assumed shape and form, surrenders again His immediate existence, and returns to His essential Being.[28]

Consequently, the full meaning of the Incarnation is that the Incarnation is a dual and dialectical process whereby God empties Himself of Himself and becomes man and man empties himself of his historical particularity and his individual selfhood and becomes God: "Therefore God becomes as we are, that we may be as he is."

It is common among contemporary scholarly interpreters of Hegel to insist that the threefold schema of thesis, antithesis, and synthesis is no part of Hegel's thought and simply represents a vulgarization of the Dialectic; yet such scholars, loyal to Hegel as they otherwise may well be, frequently deplore the arbitrariness and the artificiality of the threefold movement which again and again appears in his writings. In the *Phenomenology,* it is obvious that the Christian dogma of the Trinity is the analogue of this movement; but, as always, Hegel's dialectical understanding brings a new illumination to its source. Fundamentally, there are three moments of Spirit: (1) essential Being in which Spirit is simultaneously in and for itself; (2) explicit Self-existence, which is the express otherness of essential Being, and for which that Being is object; and (3) Self-existence or Self-knowledge *in* that other. In its third movement, essential Being beholds only itself in the objective otherness of its Self-existence:

In this emptying itself, in this *kenōsis,* it is merely within itself: the independent Self-existence which excludes itself from essential Being is the knowledge of itself on the part of essential Being. It is the "Word," the Logos, which when spoken empties the speaker of himself, outwardizes him, and leaves him behind emptied, but the "Word" is as immediately perceived, and only this act of self-perceiving himself is the actual existence of the "Word."[29]

Cryptic and dense as these words may seem, Hegel intends them to convey the meaning of the movement within itself of Absolute Being *qua* Spirit. When Spirit empties itself and enters the world, its own essential Being is left behind in an empty and lifeless form: for the Incarnation is a total and all-consuming act; as Spirit becomes the Word that empties the Speaker of Himself, the whole reality of Spirit becomes incarnate in its opposite. Spirit *is* this eternal movement of absolute self-negation; and, finally, Spirit only *is* as it is immediately experienced and perceived; only this act of "self-perceiving himself" *is* the Incarnate Word which Spirit has become. If we were to choose a modern symbolic image for the Hegelian Spirit could we do better than Blake's Shepherd of Albion who is all in all? But this choice would unveil Hegel's absolute negativity as a modern dialectical portrait of the Word of Jesus and would simultaneously veil all previous images of Jesus in a cloak of darkness.

III. Atonement and Luvah

IN 1822 Blake etched *The Ghost of Abel,* "A Revelation in the Visions of Jehovah Seen by William Blake," and the poem on this single plate was destined to be the last prophetic poetry that Blake was to write. After the death of Abel, his ghost appears, demanding vengeance, then sinks down into his grave, from which Satan arises and addresses Jehovah:

> I will have Human Blood & not the blood of Bulls or Goats,
> And no Atonement, O Jehovah! the Elohim live on Sacrifice
> Of Men: hence I am God of Men: Thou Human, O Jehovah!
> By the Rock & Oak of the Druid, creeping Mistletoe & Thorn,
> Cain's City built with Human Blood, not Blood of Bulls & Goats,
> Thou shalt Thyself be Sacrificed to Me, thy God, on Calvary.

And Jehovah thunders and replies:

> Such is My Will that Thou Thyself go to Eternal Death
> In Self Annihilation, even till Satan, Self-subdu'd, Put off Satan
> Into the Bottomless Abyss, whose torment arises for ever & ever.

Compressed as these lines are, they contain the dual theme that God must be sacrificed to Satan on Calvary, and that Satan must be self-annihilated and forever perish as Satan. This theme does not appear in Blake's work until the later revisions of *The Four Zoas*, but insofar as it identifies the sacrifice of God with the annihilation of Satan it may be taken as a clear exemplification of Blake's revolutionary transformation of Christianity. Believing that every repression of energy is a repetition of Calvary, Blake was deeply ambivalent toward the idea of atonement, but he was capable of condemning it in no uncertain terms:

"Must the Wise die for an Atonement? does Mercy endure Atonement?
No! It is Moral Severity & destroys Mercy in its Victim."
(J. 39:25 f.)

Northrop Frye's whole interpretation of Blake's vision of Christianity rests upon the position that Blake affirmed a Jesus of "action" while rejecting a Jesus of "passion." Thus, according to Frye, pure vision knows the crucified Christ as the perfected form of the sleeping Albion's dream of death: "The crucified Christ is the visible form of Man's dream state, and as whatever is completely visible is transparent, that means that the crucified Christ is a prism or lens of reality, that is, an eye, which Man is slowly trying to open."[30] Nevertheless, the fact remains that Blake's later work contains innumerable positive references to the atonement. At the end of *Jerusalem*, Jesus appears to Albion and says, "unless I die thou canst not live"; and, when Albion asks if man can exist without "Mysterious Offerings of Self for Another," Jesus replies:

"Wouldest thou love one who never died
For thee, or ever die for one who had not died for thee?
And if God dieth not for Man & giveth not himself
Eternally for Man, Man could not exist; for Man is Love
As God is Love; every kindness to another is a little Death
In the Divine Image, nor can Man exist but by Brotherhood."
(96:23–28)

We must recognize once more that Blake takes up a Christian theme only to transform it; if he was hostile to the Christian dogma of the atonement and to the traditional Christian image of the crucified Christ, it is no less true that a movement of atonement lies at the center of his work, although having lost all particularity of time and space the atonement now reaches a new totality: "Albion goes to Eternal Death. In Me all Eternity must pass thro' condemnation . . ." (J. 35:9). If we are to understand this new and universal form of the atonement, we must first examine its initial expression in *The Four Zoas*. Speaking for all of the imaginative powers, Los responds to the fallen form of Albion by saying:

"Refusing to behold the Divine Image which all behold
And live thereby, he is sunk down into a deadly sleep.
But we, immortal in our own strength, survive by stern debate
Till we have drawn the Lamb of God into a mortal form.
And that he must be born is certain, for One must be All
And comprehend within himself all things both small & great."
(F.Z. I, 290–295)

Note that it is necessary for the Lamb to become mortal, and to do so because he is the "One" who must become "All." This very necessity leads to Blake's strange identification of the Lamb with Luvah, the primordial energy or passion, whose emanation, Vala, rules over the world of generation. In the second night of *The Four Zoas*, which describes Urizen's creation—and which was probably the original night one of *Vala*—Luvah, while "reasoning" from the loins of "Ulro's night," cries out:

". . . . O Lamb
Of God clothed in Luvah's garments! little knowest thou
Of death Eternal, that we all go to Eternal Death,
To our Primeval Chaos in fortuitous concourse of incoherent
Discordant principles of Love & Hate. I suffer affliction
Because I love, for I was love, but hatred awakes in me,
And Urizen, who was Faith & certainty, is chang'd to Doubt;
The hand of Urizen is upon me because I blotted out
That Human delusion to deliver all the sons of God
From bondage of the Human form. O first born Son of Light,
O Urizen my enemy, I weep for thy stern ambition,
But weep in vain. O when will you return, Vala the Wanderer?"
(II, 99–110)

With these words, Blake is struggling to create a new vision of the Crucifixion, a vision that will unveil Calvary as a sacrifice of God to God, the sacrifice of a broken and even castrated divine Humanity to a transcendent and sovereign God who is the Spectre of the "Great Humanity Divine." When atonement is understood in this sense, it becomes identical with the Incarnation, for the Lamb who is offered to the Father is the final manifestation of the alienated and emptied God, as Blake seems to be saying in this late addition to the second night:

> For the Divine Lamb, Even Jesus who is the Divine Vision,
> Permitted all, lest Man should fall into Eternal Death;
> For when Luvah sunk down, himself put on the robes of blood
> Lest the state call'd Luvah should cease; & the Divine Vision
> Walked in robes of blood till he who slept should awake.
> (II, 261–265)

There is no figure in the whole range of Blake's mythology that has created more confusion and more controversy than Luvah, and there is good reason for this: Luvah is not a consistent figure, nor does Luvah ever appear in full clarity; rather Luvah is the figure through whom Blake primarily expressed his own imaginative breakthroughs, and he embodies all the ambivalence of an initial stroke of vision. Percival, who believes that Luvah is the very substance of Blake's myth, has given us the best definition of this paradoxical figure:

He is the point of man's departure from Eden, and the goal of his return. At the summit he is Christ; at the nadir he is Satan.[31]

But Percival, as usual, insists upon fitting Blake into a classical mystical pattern, and hence he does not acknowledge that Eternity itself has fallen through Luvah—"Eternity appear'd above them as One Man infolded in Luvah's robes of blood & bearing all his afflictions" (F.Z. I, 363 f.). Nor does Percival, or any other critic for that matter, realize that Luvah is a figure symbolizing the universal process of Crucifixion. For example, on the 25th plate of *Jerusalem* we find a design depicting Albion on his knees and wreathing back in agony. Lording it over him are three spectrous female figures who have complete dominion over fallen man: Vala,

who spreads her veils over his fallen form, and her daughters, Tirzah
and Rahab, the one drawing Albion's umbilical cord from his navel
and the other gazing into his agonizing eyes with the look of hypnotic
temptation. Among the lines etched in the upper quarter of the plate
are these:

"As the Sons of Albion have done to Luvah, so they have in him
Done to the Divine Lord & Saviour, who suffers with those that suffer;
For not one sparrow can suffer & the whole Universe not suffer also
In all its Regions, & its Father & Saviour not pity and weep."

Such lines should warn us against following Frye, who interprets
Luvah merely as the fallen body of Albion; fallen yes, but Luvah's
is a redemptive fallenness, and a fallenness that extends through all
history. The Lamb of God descends to redeem when clothed in Luvah's
robes of blood; thus the daughters of humanity greet the Lamb:

"We now behold . . . .
Where death Eternal is put off Eternally.
Assume the dark Satanic body in the Virgin's womb,
O Lamb Divine! it cannot thee annoy. O pitying one,
Thy pity is from the foundation of the World, & thy Redemption
Begun Already in Eternity. Come then, O Lamb of God,
Come, Lord Jesus, come quickly."
                              (F.Z. VIII, 239–245)

The apocalyptic prayer which brings this passage to a close has an
exact parallel in the earliest liturgy of the Church, and it shows that
the Lamb cannot be fully incarnate until he assumes the dark "Satanic
body," where eternal death is put off eternally.

Consequently, Luvah is a deeply ambivalent figure: (1) he symbolizes the sacrificial movement of energy or passion from its initial fall
to its ultimate self-sacrifice in Christ, and thence to the repetition of
this sacrifice in the suffering of humanity; and (2) he also embodies
the dark or evil forces of passion and must himself become Satan if
he is to accomplish his work.

"Satan is the State of Death & not a Human existence;
But Luvah is named Satan because he has enter'd that State:
A World where Man is by Nature the Enemy of Man,

Because the Evil is Created into a State, that Men
May be deliver'd time after time, evermore. Amen."
(J. 49:67–71)

If only because of Blake's dialectical realization that redemption cannot be total apart from an incarnation of the "Eternal Great Humanity
Divine" in the fearful symmetry of its opposite, Satan, he was forced
to cast aside the non-dialectical redemptive symbols of the Christian
tradition, at crucial moments abandoning even the name of Christ,
while searching for a language that could record his vision of a
coincidentia oppositorum. One result of this rebellion against the
ecclesiastical tradition is that Blake frequently seems to employ
ancient Gnostic ideas and imagery in the elucidation of his more
paradoxical prophetic themes. In a line in *Milton* that is apparently
unrelated to the other contents on the page, he says: "Christ took
on Sin in the Virgin's Womb & put it off on the Cross" (5:3). We
must turn to Blake's notebook poem, *The Everlasting Gospel,* to seek
a direct development of this motif:

> The God of this World raged in vain:
> He bound Old Satan in his Chain,
> And bursting forth, his furious ire
> Became a Chariot of fire.
>
> . . . .
>
> And in his Body tight does bind
> Satan & all his Hellish Crew;
> And thus with wrath he did subdue
> The Serpent Bulk of Nature's dross,
> Till He had nail'd it to the Cross.
> He took on Sin in the Virgin's Womb,
> And put it off on the Cross & Tomb
> To be Worship'd by the Church of Rome.
> (b. 31–57)

Cryptic and private as the full meaning of these lines must remain, we
can see that a Gnostic language is here being directed to a non-Gnostic
and dialectical goal. An "evil" God of this world employs Satan, the
very personification of a dead natural world, as His means of annihilat-

ing evil and effecting redemption. But the "Sin" that Christ takes on in the virgin's womb is annulled or negated in the Crucifixion, the Body of Christ has become the "Serpent Bulk of Nature's dross" as a means of binding Satan and his powers: Satan is one with that Body, and Satan perishes on the cross. While Blake's language borders upon Gnosticism, it may more properly be regarded as an inversion of Gnosticism: Christ assumes the dark satanic body of the natural world to put off death eternally, that world dies in his death, and, most paradoxically of all, the God whose wrath nails Christ's Body to the cross is the God who Himself must perish in Christ's death.

At this juncture of Blakean scholarship it is not possible to arrive at either a clear or a full meaning of Blake's understanding of the atonement. It both accepts and rejects the Christian tradition, for atonement does occur through the Crucifixion and its repetition, but atonement is by no means to be understood as a sacrifice or restitution offered to the wrath or justice of a Father God, nor, as we shall see, is Jesus' humility an atoning example for man. And at the heart of Blake's vision of atonement lies a conception of the redemptive work of Satan:

> The Synagogue of Satan therefore, uniting against Mystery,
> Satan divided against Satan, resolv'd in open Sanhedrim
> To burn Mystery with fire & form another from her ashes,
> For God put it into their heart to fulfill all his will.
> (F.Z. VIII, 614–617)

Keeping in mind the fact that Blake's symbolical figures dialectically flow into one another, that Satan is a figure simultaneously symbolizing the dark abyss of evil and nothingness as well as the redemptive work of passion or energy, and that Satan is openly identified as Luvah and therefore implicitly as Christ, we must be prepared for the possibility that Satan is Blake's name for the atoning power of Christ. The very horror of the sacrifice which Satan demands in all his forms is finally a redemptive horror, a darkness that must become light, and this is so because the movement of the energy of passion is kenotic or sacrificial, both in origin and in goal, and therefore an energy becoming incarnate in the flesh must be self-subdued in self-annihilation. In his commentary on *Jerusalem,* Wicksteed notes—but unfortunately he fails to develop or explicate this insight—that Blake's Christ is the redeemer of the Creator.[32] He is the redeemer because he is the very epiphany of kenotic energy, but the Creator is the redeemed because He is the source of the repressed energy that is transmuted in self-sacrifice; He is the spectrous "shadow" of a fallen and inverted energy, and His shadow disappears in the passion of self-sacrifice and self-annihilation. "I am not a God afar off," declares the Saviour in *Jerusalem* (4:18), but in the Lamb's presence the distant God is self-annihilated and forever perishes as Satan: "Thou shalt Thyself be Sacrificed to Me, thy God, on Calvary."

Finally, the slain Lamb of God or the divine Body that is crucified is the "Human Imagination" (J. 24:23), and, as such, the Crucifixion is a universal process operating wherever the dark satanic mills evolve history and the cosmos; its movement cannot be fully traced until we have moved through all the stages of Blake's vision. However, at this point we can recognize the ground of Blake's hostility to a Church that is bound to the mere remembrance of the dead body of Jesus or the "Vegetated Christ," believing that the literal body on the cross and in the sepulcher is the foundation of Christianity. As Frye so justly says: "On this level the essence of Christianity is the compulsory acceptance of a vanished event, and if we pull the words 'compulsory' and 'vanished' out of that clause we may see that tyranny and mystery, the two marks of the Beast, are still involved in such an acceptance of Christianity."[33] If we take Blake and Hegel as primary representatives of a radically reformed or spiritual Christianity, then it cannot be without significance that it was not until their time that the modern historical consciousness was born, a consciousness that for the first time grasped the particularity and the uniqueness of human events, knowing every past event as autonomous and unique, enclosed within its own time and situation. Unquestionably, Hegel is the philosophical father of historical understanding; he was the first thinker to arrive at a systematic conception of the essential correlation between history and consciousness, just as he was the first philosopher to understand the history of philosophy as the necessary and inevitable process of the evolution of consciousness. Hegel, moreover, employed this new historical consciousness to reach the conclusion that the Christ of faith must become a "mere" historical figure if faith itself is to become fully self-conscious. Speaking of the Incarnation in the *Phenomenology,* he says:

This individual human being, then, which Absolute Being is revealed to be, goes through in its own case as an individual the process found in sense existence. He is the *immediately* present God; in consequence His being passes over into His *having* been. Consciousness, for which God is thus sensuously present, ceases to see Him, to hear Him: it *has* seen Him, it *has* heard Him. And it is because it only *has* seen and heard Him, that it first becomes itself spiritual consciousness; or, in other words, He has now arisen in Spirit, as He formerly rose before consciousness as an object existing in the sphere of sense.[34]

By this circuitous means, Hegel is saying that the Crucifixion is the inevitable culmination of the Incarnation: Christ himself must die and perish as an individual and historical being so that he may be resurrected in the universal form of Spirit. Yet the existence of the historical Jesus is essential to the epiphany of Absolute Spirit; the Crucifixion, or the disappearance of the immediate existence of what is known to be Absolute Being, is the "negative moment" of that epiphany: only through the negation of the individual form of Spirit's self-consciousness can consciousness itself be brought to the level of self-consciousness.

While Blake struggled with great difficulty and confusion to create a dialectical vision of the atonement as a universal process, Hegel's philosophical method leads to a conception of the ground of such a vision, and for that very reason the philosopher's ideas can once again illuminate the dark if deeper vision of the poet. Hegel is all too Blakean in understanding the Crucifixion as the sacrifice of the abstract and alien God. For the Crucifixion can only fully appear in consciousness when God is known as being alienated from Himself, existing in a dichotomous form as Father and Son or sovereign Creator and eternal Word: to maintain His existence as the transcendent Creator He must continually cancel or negate the world, but to move toward His universal epiphany as the Word He must negate His sovereign Divinity. Consequently, God is here known as existing in opposition to Himself, but the dissolution of this opposition only takes place when each form of the Godhead (by virtue of its inherent independence) dissolves itself in itself: "Therefore that element which has for its essence, not independent self-existence but simple being, is what empties and abandons itself, gives itself unto death, and so reconciles Absolute Being with its own self."[35] Absolute Being now becomes manifest as Spirit; yet it comes to its own fulfillment in the sphere of the immediate and sensuous present, as the dissolution of the alienated forms of the Godhead reconciles that Godhead with the actuality of immediate existence. Through the events that faith knows as the Incarnation and the Crucifixion, God has emptied Himself of His sovereignty and transcendence, and not only does this kenotic sacrifice effect the dissolution of the opposition between Father and Son in the new epiphany of God as Spirit, but so likewise vanishes the opposition between God and the world. As the full meaning of this sacrifice dawns in consciousness, the factuality and historicity of Jesus' "particular self-existence" is negated as that existence now becomes "universal self-consciousness": "The death of the mediator is death not merely of his *natural* aspect, of his particular self-existence: what dies is not merely the outer casement, which, being stripped of essential Being, is *eo ipso* dead, but also the abstraction of the Divine Being."[36]

Therefore, spiritual Christianity, as Hegel conceives it, understands the atoning death of Christ as the manifestation of the transition of Spirit from its alienated form in "Substance" or objective Being to its absolute form in "Subject" or total self-consciousness. This transition is effected by the death of the abstract and alien God in the kenotic process of Incarnation and Crucifixion, but faith in the form of *Vorstellung* can only grasp this process as a series of events that are autonomous and external to consciousness itself:

We see self-consciousness at its last turning-point become inward to itself and attain to knowledge of its inner being, of its self-centeredness. We see it relinquish its natural existence, and reach pure negativity. But the positive significance—viz. that this negativity, or pure inwardness of knowledge is just as much the self-identical essential Being: put otherwise, that Substance has here attained to being absolute self-consciousness—that is, for the devotional consciousness, an external other. . . . In other words, it is not really aware as a fact that this depth of pure self is the power by which the abstract essential Being is drawn from its abstractness and raised to the level of self by the force of this pure devotion. The action of the self hence retains towards it this negative significance, because the relinquishment of itself on the part of substance is for the self something *per se;* the self does not at once grasp and comprehend it, or does not find it in its *own* action as such.[37]

Only when the death of God appears in all its bitterness in the "Unhappy Consciousness," and consciousness thence comes to know the dissolution of the Wholly Other, can a spiritual form of conceptual or dialectical understanding arise that will know the death of God as the epiphany of Spirit. So long as consciousness remains bound to *Vorstellung,* it must exist in an alienated form, closed to the inner reality of itself by its very belief in an alien Other. Faith in this traditional form is the product of a divided consciousness: it can only know redemption as a reconciliation with an Other that lies beyond itself, and must experience the actuality of the present as a world that merely awaits its transfiguration.

The world is no doubt implicitly reconciled with the essential Being; and that Being no doubt knows that it no longer regards the object as alienated from itself, but as one with itself in its Love. But for self-consciousness this immediate presence has not yet the form and shape of spiritual reality. Thus the spirit of the communion is, in its immediate consciousness, separated from its religious consciousness, which declares indeed that these two modes of consciousness inherently are *not* separated; but this is an implicitness which is not realized, or has not yet become an equally absolute explicit self-existence.[38]

Question as one may the scholastic and now dated form of Hegel's language, need we search further than Hegel's dialectical system for a schema that brings conceptual meaning to the universal kenotic process of Eternity passing through condemnation in Albion's "Eternal Death"?

iv. Creation

MORE critics have been led astray by Blake's vision of Creation than by any other phase of his vision. Critic after critic has seen fit to interpret this vision in Gnostic terms, whether implicitly or explicitly, basing their judgment primarily upon the early and pre-Christian prophetic poetry, a number of pictorial designs, and a few random comments of the late Blake. Without pausing to comment upon the validity of this procedure, let us first note the key sentences that Blake wrote in his notebook sometime about 1810:

> Thinking as I do that the Creator of this World is a very Cruel Being, & being a Worshipper of Christ, I cannot help saying: "the Son, O how unlike the Father!" First God Almighty comes with a Thump on the Head. Then Jesus Christ comes with a balm to heal it.
>
> . . . .
>
> Error is Created. Truth is Eternal. Error, or Creation, will be Burned up, & then, & not till Then, Truth or Eternity will appear. It is Burnt up the Moment Men cease to behold it. I assert for My Self that I do not behold the outward Creation & that to me it is hindrance & not Action; it is as the Dirt upon my feet, No part of Me. "What," it will be Question'd, "When the Sun rises, do you not see a round disk of fire somewhat like a Guinea?" O no, no, I see an Innumerable company of the Heavenly host crying, "Holy, Holy, Holy is the Lord God Almighty." I question not my Corporeal or Vegetative Eye any more than I would Question a Window concerning a Sight. I look thro' it & not with it.
>
> (V.L.J. 92–95)

Toward the end of 1825, when Blake had just completed the engravings for the Job illustrations and was working upon the designs for the Dante illustrations, he is reported by Crabb Robinson to have said:

> The eloquent descriptions of Nature in Wordsworth's poems were conclusive proofs of atheism, for whoever believes in Nature, said Blake, disbelieves in God. For Nature is the work of the Devil. On my obtaining

86

from him the declaration that the Bible was the Word of God, I referred
to the commencement of Genesis—In the beginning God created the
Heavens and the Earth. But I gained nothing by this, for I was triumphantly told that this God was not Jehovah, but the Elohim; and the doctrine
of the Gnostics repeated with sufficient consistency to silence one so un-
learned as myself.

We have examined in some detail the comprehensiveness of Blake's
vision of the Fall, and we have learned that, when Vision is radically
grounded in the Fall, all things whatsoever will appear in a fallen
form. But the very universality of fallenness stands witness to an
inherent possibility of the apocalyptic and total transfiguration of a
fallen cosmos: and the universality both of fallenness and of
apocalyptic transfiguration are antithetically related to the dualistic
and world-negating spirit of Gnosticism. No one with any historical
knowledge of ancient Gnosticism could imagine for a moment that
Blake's vision is Gnostic; we need only remember the deep hostility
to art that is characteristic of true Gnosticism (and when a few
Gnostic books were finally unearthed they proved to be not "books"
at all, but either non-narrative collections of oral teachings or strange
narrations of myth of such crude expression and dark obscurity as to
be virtually unreadable).

No, we cannot take a few private statements of an artist and
prophet and believe that they are sufficient in themselves to lead us
into the meaning of a major theme of his work—obviously it is his
work itself that must supply the data for our analysis. Nevertheless,
the fact remains that Blake's early prophetic poetry is pervaded with
Gnostic ideas, particularly the *Book of Urizen,* and that during this
period Blake fully and perhaps totally identified the Creation with the
Fall. No one who has ever seen even a black and white reproduction
of the frontispiece to *Europe,* generally known as "The Ancient of
Days Striking the First Circle of the Earth," depicting Urizen
separating light from darkness with the compasses held in his left or
"sinister" hand, could forget this image of a fallen or falling Creator;
nor could Blake himself, for he is reported to have drawn a version of
it while on his deathbed, and ironically enough this was his last completed work of art. Even Blake's magnificent illustrations to the *Book*

of Urizen—which some critics believe so overshadow the poetry of the book that the poetry itself could only have been intended to be illustrative of the engraved designs—depict the terrible Creator with compassion, if not with pity, and Urizen himself remains a heroic figure in Blake's vision until the last revisions of *The Four Zoas*. Therefore, it would be misleading to consider this early prophetic work to be of a genuinely Gnostic character. No authentic Gnostic myth could admit the dramatic quality of the following lines, which Margoliouth has reconstructed as the probable original opening of *Vala:*

> . . . Man calld Urizen & said. Behold these sickning Spheres
> Take thou possession! take this Scepter! go forth in my might
> For I am weary, & must sleep in the dark sleep of Death
>
> Urizen rose from the bright Feast like a star thro' the evening sky
> Exulting at the voice that calld him from the Feast of envy
> First he beheld the body of Man pale, cold, the horrors of death
> Beneath his feet shot thro' him as he stood in the Human Brain
> And all its golden porches grew pale with his sickening light
> Pale he beheld futurity; pale he beheld the Abyss
> Where Enion blind & age bent wept in direful hunger craving
> All rav'ning like the hungry worm, & like the silent grave
> Mighty was the draught of Voidness to draw Existence in[39]

This fragment from the manuscript epic is illustrative of a central theme in the early Blake since it reveals that while Creation is a consequence of the Fall, and of the fall of the Eternal Man, Urizen, the Creator, is neither an eternal cosmic power of evil nor an alien and inhuman force of darkness, for He arises from the human brain and His epiphany as the Creator is captured with the exuberant imagery of Blake's lyric genius. As one of the four Zoas, or the divided quarters of the fallen body of the Eternal Man, Urizen is shrunk into the opposite of his original and integrated nature, becoming doubt and fear, and his very lust for power and sovereignty stands witness to His alienation from the Zoas: Luvah, Tharmas, and Urthona. Yet, after Blake had undergone what Bentley calls his personal "Last Judgement,"[40] he was forced to radically revise this epic in an attempt to fit it into a Christian scheme, finally introducing a providential "Council of God" to replace the directing agency of the Zoas (which is one reason why Urizen is the only Zoa who appears with clarity in the manuscript). We can easily see the results of this far-reaching change by noting the opening lines of the final version of night eight:

> Then All in Great Eternity Met in the Council of God
> As one Man, Even Jesus, upon Gilead & Hermon,
> Upon the Limit of Contraction to create the fallen Man.

The Creator has now become the personification of Eternity (the "one Man," Jesus), the temporal order of Creation and Fall has been reversed, and the creation itself is grounded in a redemptive purpose. However, this formulation represents the extreme point of Blake's movement in the direction of traditional Christianity. It is abandoned in *Milton* and *Jerusalem;* nevertheless, Blake was ever thereafter unable to dissociate the creation from a redemptive ground, and, while there is little traditional Christian imagery in the mature Blake, he is now able to go far beyond such imagery in unveiling the redemptive direction and goal of a fallen and still falling cosmos. Urizen disappears with the full unfolding of Blake's vision of Creation, and with Him disappears anything resembling a genuine creation myth. Gradually the Creator becomes a universal but unseen redemptive power, operative throughout the vast stretches of a fallen time and space, but visible only in the fullness of Experience, where He becomes manifest as the "one Man," Jesus.

As early as 1788, in his annotations to Lavater's aphorisms, Blake could say: "It is the God in *all* that is our companion & friend . . . creation is God descending according to the weakness of man, for our Lord is the word of God & every thing on earth is the word of God & in its essence is God." Evidence of this order should serve to remind us that despite everything, Blake's vision underwent a consistent and organic development, and was never wholly divorced from a Christian foundation. Despite the fact that many if not most of Blake's most important commentators maintain that he invariably views Creation either as the inevitable consequence of the Fall or as a beneficent but lower order mercifully provided for the weakness of man, the fact remains that quite a different meaning of Creation is present in *Jerusalem*, where Blake provides his fullest poetic portrait of the creation. All of the Blakean meanings of the Creation are present in *Jerusalem*; once more we learn:

> (But whatever is visible to the Generated Man
> Is a Creation of mercy & love from the Satanic Void).
> (13:44 f.)

And, to cite again Blake's reference to the Kabbalah in his address, "To the Jews":

> You have a tradition, that Man anciently contain'd in his mighty limbs all things in Heaven & Earth: this you received from the Druids.
> "But now the Starry Heavens are fled from the mighty limbs of Albion."
> Albion was the Parent of the Druids, & in his Chaotic State of Sleep, Satan & Adam & the whole World was Created by the Elohim.
> (27:13–17)

Indeed, virtually every page of Blake's supreme epic is devoted to a ritual-like repetition and even celebration of the Creation as the Fall: Albion's fallen body is revealed in innumerable colors and forms, as every act of the epic is yet a further repetition and renewal of the Fall, and every ray of light is refracted by Blake's vision into an image of darkness. But the very universality of this fallenness, as well as its dynamic life and movement—"everything that lives is holy"—gives hope of its ultimate transformation. For example, we find these words engraved on a plate containing a beautiful illustration of the Ark of Salvation:

> . . . but Albion dark,
> Repugnant, roll'd his Wheels backward into Non-Entity.
> Loud roll the Starry Wheels of Albion into the World of Death,
> And all the Gate of Los, clouded with clouds redounding from
> Albion's dread Wheels, stretching out spaces immense between,
> That every little particle of light & air became Opake,
> Black & immense, a Rock of difficulty & a Cliff
> Of black despair . . .
> (44:5–12)

CREATION

Blake tries—and I believe fails—to give even these words an external redemptive form by following them with the reassuring assertion that: "The Family Divine hover around the darken'd Albion." It is rather the dramatic vitality of Blake's vision of Albion's dread Wheels which more truly contains the seeds of regeneration.

Only on the 49th plate of *Jerusalem* does Blake's redemptive vision of Creation appear in its clearest form, and, while this vision pervades the whole body of his mature work, we cannot understand its full meaning until we have passed through all the phases of Blake's vision, and have fully grasped its component moments and the dialectical form of its movement and ground. At this point we can only hope to assess something of the theological significance of a redemptive meaning of Creation that is inseparable from the brute actuality of the fallen form of the cosmos. After having bitterly lamented the shrunken state of the fallen Albion—"become One Great Satan Inslav'd to the Most powerful Selfhood"—and having condemned the murder of the Divine Humanity, Blake suddenly cries:

"Rush on! Rush on! Rush on, ye vegetating Sons of Albion!
The Sun shall go before you in Day, the Moon shall go
Before you in Night. Come on! Come on! Come on! The Lord
Jehovah is before, behind, above, beneath, around.
He has builded the arches of Albion's Tomb, binding the Stars
In merciful Order, bending the Laws of Cruelty to Peace."
(49:50–55)

When we remember that the natural bodies move into external space in response to Albion's fall—"The Sea, the Stars, the Sun, the Moon, driv'n forth by my disease" (J. 21:10)—it is startling to discover that the sun and moon guide the sons of Albion in the direction of mercy; and that Jehovah, who is everywhere present, has built the tomb of fallen man even while binding the stars in a merciful order, and bending the terrible tyranny of history in the direction of peace. This vision of a cosmos that is terror and mercy at once is only meaningful when we understand the Creation as a kenotic process, and realize that Eternity itself has become incarnate in the creation:

Wonder siez'd all in Eternity, to behold the Divine Vision open
The Center into an Expanse, & the Center rolled out into an Expanse.
(J. 57:17 f.)

The 73rd plate contains a design showing Los, the personification of
the prophetic powers and of the creative movement of time, striking
the sun on his anvil; Wicksteed says of this design: "Los, with his
feet and knees held down by mother Earth, is *driving down* the Sun
in the West that it may be forced to follow the dread passage through
the underworld that leads eventually to Dawn in the East."[41] And
the prophetic words on the plate inform us that:

Where Luvah's World of ·Opakeness grew to a period, It
Became a Limit, a Rocky hardness without form & void,
Accumulating without end; here Los, who is of the Elohim,
Opens the Furnaces of affliction in the Emanation,
Fixing the Sexual into an ever-prolific Generation,
Naming the Limit of Opakeness, Satan, & the Limit of Contraction,
Adam, ...
(73:22–28)

Once again we confront Blake's doctrine of Satan and Adam as the
"Limits" of opacity and contraction, but now we see more clearly
that these limits of the creation are an inevitable effect of the redemptive process of Creation.

If we return from these difficult pages of *Jerusalem* to the more
luminous poetry of *Milton*, we learn that it is the Divine Saviour who
named the Opake, Satan, and the Solid, Adam (29:39). Moreover,
in this poem Blake was able to evoke the merciful nature of the
temporal movement of creation with something approaching a joyous
acceptance of its dark forms:

Some Sons of Los surround the Passions with porches of iron & silver,
Creating form & beauty around the dark regions of sorrow,
Giving to airy nothing a name and a habitation
Delightful, with bounds to the Infinite putting off the Indefinite
Into most holy forms of Thought; such is the power of inspiration.
They labour incessant with many tears & afflictions,
Creating the beautiful House for the piteous sufferer.
(28:1–7)

On their surface, these lines seem to say that the artist transmutes evil into joy, but Blake's vision of the Imagination transcends all that language knows as "art": the holy forms of "Thought" that put off the "Indefinite" by binding the Infinite are themselves expressions of the process of Creation. The fullness of Blake's vision effects a coalescence of time and the imagination; the temporal process itself becomes the expression of an artistic and prophetic activity, as Blake created the vision of a creative process that was soon to become the province of a Hegel or a Whitehead. One of his proverbs of Hell states quite simply that: "Eternity is in love with the productions of time" (M.H.H. 7); and in 1800 he wrote William Hayley a letter of condolence in which we find these words:

I know that our deceased friends are more really with us than when they were apparent to our mortal part. Thirteen years ago I lost a brother & with his spirit I converse daily & hourly in the Spirit & See him in my remembrance in the regions of my Imagination. I hear his advice & even now write from his Dictate. Forgive me for Expressing to you my Enthusiasm which I wish all to partake of Since it is to me a Source of Immortal Joy: even in this world by it I am the companion of Angels. May you continue to be so more & more & to be more & more perswaded that every Mortal loss is an Immortal Gain. The Ruins of Time builds Mansions in Eternity.

Fantastic and even outrageous as this expression of "spiritualism" must appear to the rational mind, at bottom it is no more scandalous than Blake's prophetic poetry, for Blake's work is finally meaningless apart from its ability to evoke the presence of a human and imaginative Eternity in the concrete moments of real time.

When Blake says that the ruins of time build mansions in Eternity, he can only be speaking from the perspective of a kenotic understanding of the Creation: not only is Eternity present in the ruins of time, but Eternity is also enhanced and expanded by the seemingly destructive process of temporal duration. Eternity empties itself and becomes time so that time itself might lead Eternity to its goal. Refusing to imagine time as an aged man, Blake always insisted upon personifying it as an eternal youth, a youth who is the "Spirit of

Prophecy" and the deliverer of the deadening inertia of a one-dimensional matter:

> Time is the mercy of Eternity; without Time's swiftness,
> Which is the swiftest of all things, all were eternal torment.
> (M. 24:72 f.)

As Blake's vision unfolded he gradually moved beyond his initial insight that the world of time and space is a realm of mercy created as a beneficent haven for those who cannot endure the inward, the immediate, and the infinite. Believing, as we shall see, in a lower paradise called Beulah, a romantic paradise of Innocence, he was continually tempted to imagine the mercy of time as the presence of Beulah:

> But others of the Sons of Los build Moments & Minutes & Hours
> And Days & Months & Years & Ages & Periods, wondrous buildings;
> And every Moment has a Couch of gold for soft repose,
> (A Moment equals a pulsation of the artery),
> And between every two Moments stands a Daughter of Beulah
> To feed the Sleepers on their Couches with maternal care.
> (M. 28:44–49)

Thus far this passage has not moved beyond the level of a romantic celebration of Innocence, but a few lines later a cosmic orientation is introduced, and with it a paradoxical relation between time and Eternity:

> Each has its Guard, each Moment, Minute, Hour, Day, Month & Year.
> All are the work of Fairy hands of the Four Elements:
> The Guard are Angels of Providence on duty evermore.
> Every Time less than a pulsation of the artery
> Is equal in its period & value to Six Thousand Years,
> For in this Period the Poet's Work is Done, and all the Great
> Events of Time start forth & are conciev'd in such a Period,
> Within a Moment, a Pulsation of the Artery.
> (28:59–29:3)

Six thousand years is Blake's symbolic limit of history, but so likewise is it the limit of time, since time for Blake is simultaneously a human and a natural process. Accordingly, every fragment of imaginative time becomes paradoxically identical with Eternity; as Blake said in the opening stanza of "Auguries of Innocence":

> To see a World in a Grain of Sand
> And a Heaven in a Wild Flower,
> Hold Infinity in the palm of your hand
> And Eternity in an hour.

But such a celebration of Eternity must be merely romantic if it is not grounded in a vision of Creation, a vision that actually sees the presence of Eternity in time, and therefore can know time as the *emptied* form of Eternity. Blake struggled valiantly toward and finally achieved a vision of an Eternity that can only appear, can only exist, in the imaginative meaning of the spatial and temporal process of the cosmos:

> For every Space larger than a red Globule of Man's blood
> Is visionary, and is created by the Hammer of Los:
> And every Space smaller than a Globule of Man's blood opens
> Into Eternity of which this vegetable Earth is but a shadow.
> (M. 29:19–22)

Finally, Blake would see that the earth is the shadow of Eternity only in the sense that the creation is the ruins of a once glorious Eternity that has emptied itself and become time so that time itself might become Eternity:

> But Jesus, breaking thro' the Central Zones of Death & Hell,
> Opens Eternity in Time & Space, triumphant in Mercy.
> (J. 75:21 f.)

v. The Female

WE HAVE previously observed that one of the most striking differences between the religions of East and West lies in the role of the female. In the Far East, goddesses have never played more than a minor and peripheral role, despite the fact that the female has enjoyed a profound if elusive symbolic significance in Chinese mysticism. The valley and the female, like the infant and water, are Lao Tzu's favorite symbols for Tao, and this is so because they stand for vacuity, vastness, openness, all-inclusiveness, and humility:

> The Spirit of the valley never dies.
>   It is called the subtle and profound female.
> The gate of the subtle and profound female
>   Is the root of Heaven and Earth.
> It is continuous, and seems to be always existing.
> Use it and you will never wear it out.[42]

No doubt a redemptive meaning of the female is present in this classic passage from the *Tao Tê Ching,* but Chinese mysticism has never personified the mysterious female, perhaps because of the passive ground of its own quest for the Tao. A comparable if more complex phenomenon is found in India where goddesses almost certainly played a major role in pre-historic times, only to be thrust into the background by the orthodox religion of the Vedas, and then to be reborn in Shivism and Tantrism. But the emanations or Shakti of Shiva are invariably demonic and destructive goddesses, and, most particularly so is his most popular emanation, Mother Kali, who is celebrated by her devotees as the supreme ogress of bloody sacrifice and chaos. If we wish to discover a redemptive goddess in the full sense of the word we must turn to the Near East and the West, where remarkably enough, by Oriental standards, goddesses have probably played a more predominant redemptive role over the millennia than have their counterparts, the savior gods. Moreover, it is only in this part of the world that an ancient and pervasive quest for individual union with a mother or savior goddess may be found, a quest that surely lies behind the Western cult of romantic love and the contemporary cult of the Oedipus Complex. Yet Blake's ecstatic celebration of Jerusalem, the universal emanation of Jesus, is surely the most profound and the most comprehensive vision of the savior goddess that has thus far been evolved in the West.

Blake is probably the only major prophet and mystic in the world whose vision has been integrally related to and in large measure even a product of an intimate experience with a woman. Most of his

biographers and critics are agreed that the revolutionary transformation that he underwent while working upon *Vala* and then beginning
Milton and *Jerusalem* was probably initiated by a new and deeper
conjugal relationship which he reached with his wife, Catherine. The
Enitharmon of *Jerusalem,* not withstanding the wide variety of her
roles, is almost certainly in part a portrait of Catherine:

> Enitharmon is a vegetated mortal Wife of Los
> His Emanation, yet his Wife till the sleep of Death is past.
> (14:13 f.)

While the early Blake saw the female as the primary agent of that
repression which is the source of all that we know as history, the
mature Blake, although deepening this vision of her demonic role
in his renewed symbolic portrait of Vala, came also to see the female
as the willing repository of male negation and the sacrificial victim
of a universal kenotic process. Blake took up, and then orchestrated
on a cosmic scale, the ancient Christian teaching that, if man fell by
woman, it is by woman that he is redeemed. Indeed, the sheer horror
of the female's role as the high priestess of sacrifice is open dialectically to her opposite and complementary role as the chief instrument
of salvation. In night eight of *The Four Zoas,* after the female has
spread herself through the Web of Religion, and her web has fallen,
altering the vortexes and misplacing every center, lust begins and
tangles Urizen in his own net of repentance:

> Enitharmon wove in tears, singing songs of Lamentations
> And pitying comfort as she sigh'd forth on the wind the spectres
> And wove them bodies, calling them her belov'd sons & daughters,
> Employing the daughters in her looms, & Los employ'd the sons
> In Golgonooza's Furnaces among the Anvils of time & space,
> Thus forming a vast family, wondrous in beauty & love,
> And they appear'd a Universal female form created
> From those who were dead in Ulro, from the spectres of the dead.
> And Enitharmon named the Female, Jerusalem the holy.
> Wond'ring, she saw the Lamb of God within Jerusalem's Veil;
> The Divine Vision seen within the inmost deep recess
> Of fair Jerusalem's bosom in a gently beaming fire.
> (F.Z. VIII, 182–193)

After Enitharmon names the universal female form Jerusalem, the sons of Eden behold redemption and sing glory to the Lamb of God: "Who now beginneth to put off the dark Satanic body."

From this passage, we gather that Jerusalem only fully appears when Jesus casts off his mortal body and assumes a universal form. Nor is Jerusalem visible to the eye of generation. She, too, wears a veil, a veil disguising the presence of the Lamb within her, and, like Vala's, her veil encompasses her secret parts where the fire of Jesus' redemption lies hidden. This fire remains entombed in the fallen body of Albion until the Incarnation, for Jerusalem is the first victim of the Fall. A fascinating design on the 23rd plate of *Jerusalem* represents Jerusalem's gentle surrender to her vicarious fate as Albion utters his falling curse. Wicksteed says of this design:

> Blake has taken pains to represent her as following in the steps of her Saviour Himself as she takes on the sins and woes of the world. At her feet we see the little Star of Bethlehem and at her head the lily of Calvary. Stamped upon the feathers of her outstretched wings is a series of small Golgotha crosses. Above her head the long coil of the intestines rolls like a cloud; for to go through this World she must endure hunger and thirst and enter into "a devouring Stomach."[43]

Jerusalem, in fact, is the incarnate body of Jesus: she is present wherever there is pain and suffering, for she is the "I" of every sufferer, the passive self or *anima* of all pain. Moreover, Jerusalem's sacrificial role is established by the Creation. Most of the 35th plate of *Jerusalem* is occupied by an illustration of the creation of Eve from Adam's rib, but Blake followed Milton in believing that the Son was the Creator of Eve, and in this design the Saviour hovers over the newly-born woman with the stigmata on his hands and feet. Woman is born, then, under the destiny of the stigmata, her passion is finally the Passion of the Cross, and that passion is the most immediate manifestation in Experience of Jesus' "fire." As Wicksteed interprets Blake's portrait of Jerusalem on the 32nd plate of her epic, when she greets Vala's proffered veil not with hatred and horror but with sacrificial love: "It was a bold inspiration of Blake's to anticipate the grand climax of the whole drama (the closing plates of Chapter 4) by representing the tender naked loveliness of Woman yielding itself to the dark way through the Underworld to save mankind by her vicarious sacrifice, and thus preparing a way through Hell by which to receive her Lord in the hour of his final descent, upbearing him in her eager embrace."[44]

Finally, Vala, Enitharmon, and Jerusalem are all faces of one love, multiple forms of a single passion, and that passion itself bears the masculine names of Luvah, Satan, and Christ. Creation, Incarnation, and Redemption are but seemingly distinctive acts of one kenotic process, a process that woman literally enacts in time, even when she is twisted into her most perverse and destructive form. The female has no real identity apart from her destructive and creative roles:

> "There is a limit of Opakeness and a limit of Contraction
> In every Individual Man, and the limit of Opakeness
> Is named Satan, and the limit of Contraction is named Adam.
> But when Man sleeps in Beulah, the Saviour in Mercy takes
> Contraction's Limit, and of the Limit he forms Woman, That
> Himself may in process of time be born Man to redeem."
> (J. 42:29–34)

Woman is born of Adam, the limit of Albion's contraction, so that the Saviour may become incarnate in that limit. It is the female's destiny to maintain and perpetuate that limit until the consummation of the kenotic process, and this she does by her dual destructive and creative roles: Jerusalem's sacrifice goes hand in hand with Vala's repression, compassionate suffering is the opposite pole of cruel restraint, love and death are united in the priestess who is simultaneously the offerer and the victim of sacrifice. In one of the more enigmatic passages in *Jerusalem*, Vala, while pleading for mercy from Jesus, cries out:

> "My Father gave to me command to murder Albion
> In unreviving Death; my Love, my Luvah, order'd me in night
> To murder Albion, the King of Men; he fought in battles fierce,
> He conquer'd Luvah, my beloved, he took me and my Father,
> He slew them. I revived them to life in my warm bosom.
>   .   .   .   .

But I, Vala, Luvah's daughter, keep his Albion's body, embalmed
  in moral laws
With spices of sweet odours of lovely jealous stupefaction,
Within my bosom, lest he arise to life & slay my Luvah.
Pity me then, O Lamb of God! O Jesus pity me!
Come into Luvah's Tents and seek not to revive the Dead!"
                    (80:16–31)

Of the many twisted threads in this labyrinth, we might note that
Albion has once conquered Luvah, and is now embalmed in the repressive veil of Vala lest he rise and murder Luvah, while Vala, who
is both the daughter and the beloved of Luvah, has been ordered by
Luvah to murder Albion in "unreviving Death." We may assume that
Albion conquered Luvah in his own initial fall, that Albion's energy
is now bound in repressive laws lest he wholly destroy the primordial
passion, and that Vala is Albion's guardian. But what is Vala's
relationship to Luvah?

Remembering the deeply ambivalent and yet universal role of
Luvah, a role that extends from Satan to Christ, and that Vala, as
every daughter of Eve, has a special and derivative relationship with
the energy of passion, we must be prepared to see in Vala an incarnation of Luvah. Earlier in *Jerusalem*, Albion, who has first experienced
Vala's presence as an eclipse of the "Divine Vision" and as the fading
of all life and joy, asks of Vala her identity, and she replies:

"I was a City & a Temple built by Albion's Children.
I was a Garden planted with beauty. I allured on hill & valley
The River of Life to flow against my walls & among my trees.
Vala was Albion's Bride & Wife in great Eternity,
The loveliest of the daughters of Eternity when in day-break
I emanated from Luvah over the Towers of Jerusalem,
And in her Courts among her little Children offering up
The Sacrifice of fanatic love! why loved I Jerusalem?
Why was I one with her, embracing in the Vision of Jesus?
Wherefore did I, loving, create love, which never yet
Immingled God & Man, when thou & I hid the Divine Vision
In cloud of secret gloom which, behold, involves me round about?
Know me now Albion: look upon me. I alone am Beauty. . . ."
                    (33:36–48)

Now Albion is Vala's eternal husband, and Vala is an emanation of
Luvah who was once identical with Jerusalem, but who has since
created a love that hides the Divine Vision by separating God and
man. Vala is the "Female Will" that hides the most evident God
in her sexual parts (J. 34:32), but her will, as the emanation of
Luvah, is the fallen primordial passion. Again, let us remember that
in *Milton* it is the "Shadowy Female" that draws down Urizen as
Satan into generation.

> The nature of a Female Space is this: it shrinks the Organs
> Of Life till they become Finite & Itself seems Infinite.
> (10:6 f.)

On the following plate of *Milton,* Satan calls himself God and enslaves humanity to laws deriving from his fallen identity: whereupon
a "Great Solemn Assembly" says:

> "If the Guilty should be condemn'd he must be an Eternal Death,
> And one must die for another throughout all Eternity.
> Satan is fall'n from his station & never can be redeem'd,
> But must be new Created continually moment by moment. . . ."

Then, without warning, a strange female figure named Leutha—whom
Frye identifies as Satan's harlot mistress, the original "female will"
of the Fall[45]—appears and identifies herself with Satan's "Sin":

> But when Leutha (a Daughter of Beulah) beheld Satan's condemnation,
> She down descended into the midst of the Great Solemn Assembly,
> Offering herself a Ransom for Satan, taking on her his Sin.
>
> . . . .
>
> She spake: "I am the Author of this Sin! by my suggestion
> My Parent power Satan has committed this transgression. . . ."

This whole sequence occurs in the midst of the story of Satan and
Palamabron, one of Blake's least successful and most confusing
prophetic myths, but, as we shall see, the female's vicarious identification with the guilt of Satan initiates the whole history of salvation

from Lucifer to the Lamb. After Leutha has freely taken upon herself
the sin of Satan, she speaks these final words:

> "All is my fault! We are the Spectre of Luvah, the murderer
> Of Albion. O Vala! O Luvah! O Albion! O lovely Jerusalem!
> The Sin was begun in Eternity and will not rest to Eternity
> Till two Eternitys meet together. Ah! lost, lost, lost for ever!"
>   (M. 13:8–11)

Insofar as these events take place in Eternity, they must be understood as underlying the forms and processes of time and history;
thus the very destiny of the female is created by her sacrificial offering
of herself as a ransom for Satan. Not only does the female take on
the guilt of Satan's "Selfhood," but by this very act she herself also
becomes incarnate as the fallen form of Luvah's passion; then her will
and body become enclosed in the dark passivity that is an archetypal
image of the victim on the Cross. In truth, Jerusalem has become
Vala, just as finally Vala will become Jerusalem: but the kenotic
process by which passion sacrifices itself and freely accepts a repressed
and broken form is the source of that energy by which Albion moves
between his fallen and his apocalyptic forms. Consequently, the
eternal female is at once the incarnate body of Satan and the redemptive passion of Luvah. The fallen forms of her body and will
are simultaneously both the primary agents of repression and the
most immediate instruments of redemption. If woman has created
her destiny by freely choosing to actualize in a fallen form the paradoxical identification of Satan and Christ, then the female form is
the paradigmatic exemplification of the creative and destructive
energies of a fallen cosmos, and must itself disappear when Albion
is awakened from his sleep of death: "Sexes must vanish & cease
to be when Albion arises from his dread repose" (J. 92:13).

VI. Generation and Regeneration

ONE of the most difficult theological problems posed by Blake's work
derives from the question of its Christian ground. Is Blake's vision

authentically and uniquely Christian? Or must his Christian symbols be judged to have only a local and a personal significance, deriving from the simple historical accident that Blake was born and lived in Christendom, and having no intrinsic relationship to his vision of redemption? When we recall that the deeper thrust of Blake's vision continually transmutes the particularity and the historical uniqueness of Christian symbols and dogmas into a universal and all-encompassing form, is this not sufficient evidence that Blake was a Christian only in an accidental sense, and that he truly belongs to a universal mystical tradition that by its very essence transcends all particular historical expressions? Such is the judgment of many of Blake's most astute critics, but this judgment has three grave limitations: first, it must derogate the particularity and uniqueness of Blake's poetic and artistic genius; second, it must isolate the essential meaning of Blake's vision from his own particular and historical situation, thereby discounting the significance of Blake's relation to the political, social, artistic, intellectual, and religious currents of the modern West; and, finally, it rests upon an inadequate and uncritical theological ground. The first limitation speaks for itself, the second depends upon the value that one gives to history and to Blake as a prophetic precursor of the contemporary world, but the third obviously requires further elucidation. Indeed, in turning from the confident dogmatic persuasion of either the particularist Christian or the universalist mystic to the actual historical phenomenon of religion, we find that neither the imperialistic Christian claims of uniqueness nor the esoteric mystical claims of universality can stand up to critical examination. On the one hand, there is not a single Christian dogma or symbol that does not have a clear parallel or parallels in non-Christian religions of varying types and forms; but, on the other hand, there is not a single "universal" doctrine or symbol that is not integrally related to a particular religious tradition. If it is true that the history of religions has discovered the whole spectrum of Christian doctrine throughout the vast world of religion, it is no less true that it has demonstrated the impossibility of dissociating even such exalted mystical ways as the Vedanta and Zen from their respective Indian and Chinese roots, and no way has yet been found of correlating the symbols of the

Vedanta and Zen, to say nothing of the problem of arriving at a genuine historical synthesis of all the mystical forms of religion in the world. Therefore we cannot make the judgment that Blake was not a "particular" Christian but was a "universal" mystic without doing violence to the historical categories of particularity and universality.

A more critical way of approaching this problem would be that of identifying certain religious motifs which are peculiarly characteristic of Christianity and are uniquely Christian insofar as they cannot elsewhere be found in this particular form. To follow this procedure, for example, would be to discard the mere listing of certain dogmas, such as the Creation, the Fall, and the Incarnation, with the hope that these dogmas in themselves contain the key to the uniqueness of Christianity. No, the more reliable path is to search for the particular trust or direction of the Christian "way," and then to see if this direction affects the foundations of Christianity in such a manner as to clearly show its distinction from the non-Christian religions. Surely one such motif that illustrates this thrust is the profound emphasis that Christianity places upon the Fall. This emphasis itself is uniquely Christian and so likewise is the fact that Christianity tends to find the Fall embedded throughout the whole range of human experience. Moreover, this vision of fallenness does not have simply a negative function in Christianity, for it provides both the arena for redemption and the source of salvation, insofar as Christianity knows an Incarnation that has actually happened in the fallen world, and has no meaning or reality apart from its fallen form. By employing this approach, we see yet another dimension of Christianity's uniqueness, and that is its special emphasis upon the future realization of the Kingdom of God as a state transcendent to the original Innocence that precedes the Fall. The Fall, accordingly, assumes a primary importance in Christianity as it does in no other religion, and for that very reason it takes on a unique form: (1) it is a real and in some ultimate sense a historical event; (2) it pervades the whole of experience, even including the experience that the believer knows as grace and redemption; (3) it is the necessary ground for salvation apart from which there could be no movement either from Innocence to Experience or from Paradise to Apocalypse; and (4) it alone makes possible the sacrificial movement of *kenōsis* and the redemptive process of Incarnation and Atonement. Seen in this perspective, it is the vision of the Fall that provides the foundation for the overwhelming emphasis that Christianity places upon the concrete actuality of history and experience, an emphasis that must inevitably lead to a total Vision of the Incarnation as a universal kenotic process, arising from within the heart of the Godhead, and operative throughout the totality of history and the cosmos. Christianity assumes its most unique and particular form when it is seen as placing such a radical emphasis upon the Fall. Moreover, when the Fall is comprehended as a universal movement it can be known as the source of Creation and Incarnation, and, finally, Fall, Creation, and Incarnation will appear as particular moments of a single kenotic process. True, no form of Christian doctrine has yet arrived at such an understanding of the Fall. But the way to this understanding has been established by radical Christian mystics such as Eckhart and Boehme, and in Blake's work we may discover a comprehensive vision of the Fall that leads through all the movements of redemption.

Simply by taking up the problem of Blake's relationship to Christianity we have also arrived at an essential ground of his opposition to the traditional form of the Christian faith. A doctrine that knows the Trinity in the forms of a sovereign and almighty Creator, an obedient and sacrificial Son, and a universal but disincarnate Spirit can grasp neither the uniqueness of Christianity nor the particular and special meaning which it brings to *kenōsis*, a meaning that faith celebrates when it knows Jesus as the Incarnate Lord who is the sole agent of redemption. The traditional Christian doctrine of God and the Trinity not only contains numerous parallels with non-Christian conceptions, but for that very reason it also obscures and distorts a kenotic process that comprehends all reality whatsoever, and can only provide an authoritarian and repressive basis for the acceptance of Jesus as the eternal Word who is everywhere incarnate as the source of a universal process of salvation. Blake's "atheism," just as Hegel's, is in part a radical and prophetic reaction to a non-redemptive God of power and judgment who stands apart from the kenotic movement of the Incarnation, and whose absolute sovereignty must finally sanction the fallen order of history and the cosmos. By coming to know the *total* presence of God in the Incarnation, Blake and every radical Christian is liberated from the God who is Wholly Other than man, and likewise liberated from the authority of a heteronomous Law and an autonomous Creator. Again, in rebelling against an institutional Church and its ideological expression in Christendom, Blake came to realize the repressive and anti-Christian reality of a salvation-history whose authority derives from the codified memory of a series of events that are irrevocably past and intrinsically irreversible. To know the particular and historical Jesus of Nazareth as the eternal Word of salvation is to bind oneself to his dead body in the sepulcher and to refuse his resurrected presence in the redemptive energy of the cosmos. Blake's prophetic pilgrimage led him to a vision of the omnipresence of the passion of Jesus, and, once having seen that presence in every pain and sorrow, he could celebrate the naked horror of experience as an epiphany of the crucified Lamb of God.

"Experience," as Percival says, "is with Blake the essence of regeneration."[46] But experience is found only in the fallen world of generation, a world that Blake symbolically associated with the loins, for the very purpose of generation is its gift of life. Having long believed that everything that lives is holy, Blake finally came to see the world of generation as the incarnate body of Christ:

"O holy Generation, Image of regeneration!
O point of mutual forgiveness between Enemies!
Birthplace of the Lamb of God incomprehensible!
The Dead despise & scorn thee & cast thee out as accursed,
Seeing the Lamb of God in thy gardens & thy palaces
Where they desire to place the Abomination of Desolation."
(J. 7:65–70)

Generation, or the fullness of passion that is present in sexual energy, is not simply the source of life, but in its own form and direction is the temporal image of the process of redemption. Consequently, generation will not have fulfilled its function until it makes Christ manifest in the fullness of experience. Experience itself therefore is only

truly consummated in the passion of generation where the spontaneous expression of bodily energy duplicates and even makes incarnate
in each individual body the universal process of *kenōsis*. The Lamb
of God sports in the gardens of sexual delight because these gardens
are palaces of self-annihilation and mutual forgiveness; the ecstasy
of liberation that is the gift of sex reverses the repressed energy of a
fallen body, and resurrects the dead who are enslaved to an alien
Law and an inhuman Creator. Yet Satan has sealed the process of
generation in Vala's Veil; the sheer immediacy of delight has passed
under condemnation and become the very essence of the forbidden,
as the "Abomination of Desolation" has been erected in the temple
of Christ. Not until the body of Satan is transformed into Jerusalem
will the Incarnation be complete, and then the passion of Jesus will
appear in its full form as a regenerate Experience.

Paradoxically, sexual generation simultaneously appears in Vision
both as the repressed product of Satan's "mills" and as the most
immediate arena of the process of regeneration. Jesus, who is the
incarnation of the primordial passion of Luvah, is at once the dark
body of Satan and the redemptive body of holiness:

> "A Vegetated Christ & a Virgin Eve are the Hermaphroditic
> Blasphemy; by his Maternal Birth he is that Evil-One
> And his Maternal Humanity must be put off Eternally,
> Lest the Sexual Generation swallow up Regeneration.
> Come Lord Jesus, take on thee the Satanic Body of Holiness!"
> (J. 90:34–38)

Despite those who cite this fragment of Blake's vision as evidence
of a Gnostic hatred of the body, we have only to recall his continual
and ecstatic celebration of sexuality and the body to recognize these
lines as containing a vision of the regeneration and reversal of a
fallen sexuality. The hermaphroditic blasphemy is a generated or
vegetated Christ *and* a virgin Eve; the Church castrated Jesus when
it locked the memory of his generation in the image of a virgin birth,
just as it dehumanized and falsely spiritualized his body in its belief
in the Ascension. Jesus continually reverses his "Maternal Humanity"

by becoming incarnate in a satanic body of holiness; his very existence in a generated body challenges Vala's repression and initiates
the process of reversing the fallen energy of the body. This movement
of reversing the world of experience is the process of regeneration,
and it occurs only in the full actuality of the body, for the living
energy of the body is the image of regeneration and therefore is itself
the most immediate manifestation of the incarnate body of Jesus.
What the Church knows as the descent of Christ into Hell is not,
according to Blake's vision, a descent apart from the body, but rather
a descent into the very depths of bodily repression, a descent that is
only consummated in the identification of Jesus' "Satanic Body of
Holiness" with the totality of the cosmos, and its consequent presence
as the redemptive fire of passion throughout the whole body of humanity.

Finally, if we are to be prepared to explore Blake's vision of Experience, we must note the significance of the reversal pattern in the
Jerusalem designs. One of the most fascinating results of Wicksteed's
analysis of the *Jerusalem* illustrations is his demonstration of the
way in which Blake reversed the traditional designation of right and
left as symbols of good and evil or the spirit and the body. For example, Plate 7 contains a simple marginal illustration of Los discovering the formula or the "pass" to salvation, with his left arm
pointed up and his right down:

Los no longer appears here as a figure crouching under the oppression of
the illusions of Time, but as the poet and prophet of Futurity, liberated by
his vision to act the part of the Human Councillor and Saviour which we
shall discover to be his Divine role in the culmination of the drama on
page 97. But the end is not yet, and while foreseeing it he helps to speed
it on. Thus the very significant attitude of his right and left arms symbolizes together with the rising spirit above, and the falling one below, a
constant theme directing us prophetically to the Way of Salvation that
each must labour to pursue himself. This Way is indicated for mortals
as demanding that the Left (or bodily) side must ascend to sublimation,
while the Right (or spiritual) side must endure the pangs of mortal
existence and, if need be, must sound the "well of sanguine woe." This
in another form is identical with the claim that Innocence must be beatified
and Experience must be tried in the furnaces of affliction. [47]

However, we must not surmise that Los's way is simply a way for mortals; the fact that Los symbolizes the "Human Imagination" is equivalent in Blake's vision to his symbolizing the "Divine Body of Jesus," for it is the kenotic movement of the Incarnation that reverses the significance of right and left. Just before the drama of *Jerusalem* reaches its conclusion, there appears one of Blake's most important portraits of Los on plate 97, showing him lifting up the sun from the depths of fallen time to Eternity:

Los's symbolical attitude reverses that of the Frontispiece. There, as he passed over the threshold from Eternity into Time, he raised his Left hand to open the dread portal, bearing the lamp of Eternity in his dropped Right. Here still stepping forward with Right foot and springing from the stony Earth with his Left, he raises his Right hand to shield his eyes from the fierce light of Eternity, while thrusting down his Left into the nether Abyss to lift his Eternal "globe of fire."[48]

Wicksteed misses the full theological significance of this theme by his failure to grasp the import of Blake's revolutionary transformation of Christianity: Jesus or the "Human Imagination" raises his *right* hand to shield his eyes from the destructive rays of an Eternity that dawns for the first time with this cosmic reversal; the Apocalypse reverses the total order of the Fall, including the order of morality and religion; therefore, the right hand is powerless to participate in this ultimate process of redemption, whereas it is the *left* hand that is thrust into the depths of Hell to redeem the eternal sun of passion.

III

HISTORY

1. History and Vision

TO SILENCE all those who would question the Christian ground of Blake's work, we need only point to the pervasive role that history plays in his vision: for history is at once the incarnation of Eternity and the arena of Albion's fall and redemption. Like his precursor, Milton, Blake became a biblical poet by choosing the prophetic vocation of recreating the form of the biblical epic—an epic that is invisible in an age of unbelief—out of the materials of the history and consciousness of his own time and space. This vocation itself must remain meaningless both to those who reject the Bible as fable and fantasy and to those who believe that the literal words of the Bible are revealed truth. For Blake must offend both the rationalist who scorns the reality of Vision and the Christian who believes that memory and tradition can record the presence of Eternity. Both are fundamentally opposed to everything that Blake called "Vision," and are closed to the possibility of a total experience occurring here and now in the present moment. Indeed, the whole body of Blake's mature work proclaims an Eternal Gospel that is present *only* in immediate Vision. Remembering that Blake defined Vision or Imagination as a representation of what eternally exists, and regarded fable or allegory as formed by the "daughters of Memory," let us note the older Blake's repudiation of the Greek muses in the name of the "Inspiration" of the Bible:

Reality was Forgot, & the Vanities of Time & Space only Remember'd & call'd Reality. Such is the Mighty difference between Allegoric Fable & Spiritual Mystery. Let it here be Noted that the Greek Fables originated in Spiritual Mystery & Real Visions, which are lost & clouded in Fable &

Allegory, while the Hebrew Bible & the Greek Gospel are Genuine, Preserv'd by the Saviour's Mercy. The Nature of my Work is Visionary or Imaginative; it is an Endeavour to Restore what the Ancients call'd the Golden Age.

(V.L.J. pp. 71–72)

But to *restore* the "Golden Age" is to make the primordial paradise incarnate in the immediate moment and to treat the concrete actuality of history as the sole arena of paradise. There is no possibility in this vision of either a Gnostic flight to another world or of the religious security which the ecclesiastical Christian finds in the saving acts of a past and sacred history. Once it is granted that Eternity fully dawns in the present moment of concrete actuality, there can be neither a return to a moment of the past nor a total negation of time itself.

Not only do we find a Christian ground in the role of history in Blake's vision but we should also further note that no other Christian artist or mystic has given history the comprehensive role that it plays in Blake's work. Blake is the only Christian seer to whom these words of Percival could apply:

Blake's system has a twofold source. It is at once a reading of history and an interpretation of his mystical experiences. He found the two in accord. The macrocosm, Albion, and the microcosm, Blake, descend and return by the same path.[1]

Northrop Frye, who believes that the merging of imagination and time is the axis upon which all Blake's thought turns,[2] finds Blake's vision of history to be the real clue to the meaning of his work:

In Deism the nation has reached the point at which "common sense," or the fallen vision of the world, becomes its dogmatic confession of faith. But this faith assumes the finality of the two primary categories of common sense, time and space. Hence the third course open to the poet in an age of Deism is, first, to visualize the reversibility of time and space, to see the linear sequence of history as a single form; and, second, to see the tradition behind him as a single imaginative unity. These are, more or less, the themes of *Jerusalem* and *Milton* respectively.[3]

111

Moreover, Frye maintains that it is only an actual *reversal* of concrete time and space that can create a vision of history as Eternity:

A larger human brain will be developed by Man when the whole of human life is seen and understood as a single mental form. This single mental form is a drama of creation, struggle, redemption and restoration in the fallen life of a divine Man. This drama is the archetype of all prophecy and art, the universal form which art reveals in pieces, and it is also the Word of God, the end of the journey of our intellectual powers. And here the antithesis between imagination and memory, the intellectual powers and the corporeal understanding, the vision of life and the vision of death, reaches its crisis. Everything that has ever happened since the beginning of time is part, Blake says, of the literal Word of God. The ordinary historical conception of human existence as a dissolving flux in linear time is therefore the literal approach to life, the corporeal understanding based on memory. History as the total form of all genuine efforts of human culture and civilization is the canon or Scripture of human life. History as linear time is the great apocrypha or mystery which has to be rejected from it.[4]

Having thus been warned that Blake's vision of history negates all that which the profane consciousness knows as literal or lineal history, we should nevertheless be prepared to see that Blake's goal was the creation of a Christian epic that would celebrate the whole of history as the human body of the eternal Jesus.

In his *Descriptive Catalogue,* while speaking of the Everlasting Gospel, or the religion of Jesus, Blake attacks the "reasoning historian," repudiates the historiography of the classical historians from Herodotus to Gibbon, and insists that: "Acts themselves alone are history." Quite obviously he is saying that the "Why" of the reasoning historian destroys the "What" of historical acts, and this is so because only the dead shell of the original living act can be preserved in the memory, the records, and the tradition that the historian chooses as his data. Both as an artist and prophet, and as a "spiritual" Christian, Blake was violently opposed to any understanding of history that would subordinate its human reality to the lifeless matter of a fallen nature. The inevitable consequence of this radical choice, as Blackstone observes, was that Blake became the expounder of an idealism more thoroughgoing than Plato's or Berkeley's, and this he did because he totally identified history and humanity: "History thus becomes an exteriorization of psychology: what is perpetually going on in the mind of Man manifests itself in the pattern of events."[5] Perhaps at no other point is Blake's vision so startling to the mind of modern man; but in Blake alone may we see the full meaning of an historical as opposed to a natural understanding of man, for a consistent historical vision must finally identify history and the cosmos. This point is astutely made by Peter F. Fisher:

> Blake combines the individual human observer with the field of his observation, and places both within the dream of a Giant Man who is the universal expression of experience as Blake sees it. In other words, he sees the world as history and not as nature, as a process of perception in living minds and not as a reality apart from human experience.[6]

When the cosmos itself is understood as a human experience, there can be no question of subordinating mind to matter or of looking upon consciousness as the product of an external temporal process; rather, as Fisher says, "the productions of time are the effects of conscious activity which remains prior to them and contains them."[7] Therefore history is the underlying human reality of time; it is neither the product of an external time and nature nor an internal realm dualistically isolated from nature: history or humanity is the totality of experience.

The great danger of formulating Blake's understanding of history in abstract terms is that it will appear to be identical with archaic and Oriental modes of understanding. We can avoid this danger by examining a passage in *Milton* (and the crucial words in this passage are repeated on the 75th plate of *Jerusalem*):

> I am that Shadowy Prophet who Six Thousand Years ago
> Fell from my station in the Eternal bosom. Six Thousand Years
> Are finish'd. I return! both Time & Space obey my will.
> I in Six Thousand Years walk up and down; for not one Moment
> Of Time is lost, nor one Event of Space unpermanent,
> But all remain: every fabric of Six Thousand Years
> Remains permanent, tho' on the Earth where Satan

Fell and was cut off, all things vanish & are seen no more,
They vanish not from me & mine, we guard them first & last.
The generations of men run on in the tide of Time,
But leave their destin'd lineaments permanent for ever & ever."
(22:15–25)

These words of Los speak for every Christian prophet or visionary and are representative of the redemptive movement of time. But the redemption to which they point is not effected by annihilating or dissolving concrete moments of actual time. When all events of time and space remain permanent, and the "destin'd lineaments" of humanity will exist forever, we are far from the horizon of either a cyclic vision of time or of a movement of redemption that annuls the concrete contingency of spatial and temporal events. It is precisely this acceptance and affirmation of the eternal reality of the contingency of the cosmic process that constitutes a genuine historical understanding. Once again we see how integral Blake's vision of the Fall is to his understanding of redemption and how his kenotic understanding of Creation leads inevitably to a total fusion of time and Eternity. Not only is a fallen or falling humanity the only reality, but that very reality is also inseparable from the actual occasions of its movement in time and space, and the order of a fallen spatial-temporal process becomes paradoxically identified with the history of salvation.

That which is at once profoundly Christian and deeply modern in Blake's vision of history is its acceptance of the actual processes of time and its will to meet this time as the immediate presence of Jesus, the incarnation of a divine Humanity. We find no Gnostic longing for an escape from time in Blake, but rather a Christian will to reverse an actual and present temporal process, a reversal that accepts the contingent processes of time and space as the sole arena of redemption. It is not without theological significance that a seminal contemporary study of Blake, David Erdman's *Blake: Prophet Against Empire,* could find the great body of Blake's poetry to be directed to a political or social reality of Blake's day; and his poetry met that reality with a revolutionary will to invert its tyranny and repression and thus to transform its deepest horror.

Nowhere else in history, not even in the Old Testament, can we find a prophet or mystic who so chose to direct the fullness of his vision to the actual historical events about him: for Blake is absolutely unique among all visionaries in that he chose to confront the awesome reality of history as the total epiphany of the sacred. Blake alone among Christian seers can meet the challenge of an archaic and Oriental vision of redemption, a challenge that has so effectively been presented in our own day by Mircea Eliade. Eliade has demonstrated conclusively that religious patterns the world over are intended to effect an annihilation or dissolution of concrete historical events. Only the Near Eastern prophetic tradition and its later developments in Judaism, Christianity, and Islam stand in any decisive way apart from this opposition to history; but this tradition has been swallowed up in the contemporary West by a radically profane historicism that in granting an ultimate value and reality to historical events has abolished any meaning lying beyond them.

Again, Eliade, speaking with the prophetic voice of all those who resist the tyrannical power of history, makes the telling point that it is only those peoples who have gained historical dominance—and we might add that such peoples include not only Western Christians but also monarchic Jews, medieval Muslims, and Confucian mandarins— who have dared to affirm the redemptive reality of history; the overwhelming mass of humanity has been doomed to know history as a realm of alienation and terror. As Eliade says:

Modern man's boasted freedom to make history is illusory for nearly the whole of the human race. At most, man is left free to choose between two positions: (1) to oppose the history that is being made by the very small minority (and, in this case, he is free to choose between suicide and deportation); (2) to take refuge in a subhuman existence or in flight.[8]

Yet, according to Eliade—and almost the whole body of European spokesmen for faith—even the special freedom of this elite minority must disappear with the collapse of Christendom and the advent of a new nihilism and a consequent rebirth of various forms of totalitarianism. Never before has the West been so pervasively tempted by the call of a Gnostic retreat from history and a subsequent return to an archaic and Oriental refusal of the finality of destiny. Only the radical Christian can meet this temptation with the faith that a totally fallen history is finally the redemptive epiphany of Christ. When Eliade says that Christianity is the religion of modern and historical man because only the Christian faith can promise an absolute emancipation from the ontological constitution of the universe, he is speaking to those who know the terror of history as a chaos pervading the whole of experience, and is joining the primitive and the sectarian Christian in demanding a final and definitive end of the world. The fact that this plea has been made in so many forms in our time and with such compelling power is evidence itself of the eclipse of the traditional form of faith with its belief in the redemptive movement of history. Now the time has come for faith to engage in its deepest confrontation with history. Can faith meet this challenge with a final Yes-saying to history, or must it utter a final No to a history that has lost all its moorings in Christendom? No doubt a traditional faith must say this No, but Blake's vision points the way to a total acceptance, if ultimate reversal, of the full reality of a fallen history.

II. Paradise and History

THE overwhelming importance which Blake's vision gives to history can be seen in his understanding of Innocence and Experience as the two contrary states of the soul, and in his full employment, yet radical transformation, of ancient myths of paradise. Corresponding to the dual states of Innocence and Experience, his vision knows two forms of paradise, called Beulah and Eden, the one a dreamy and passive realm of repose intermediate between spiritual and physical existence, and the other a total union between God and man obliterating all distinction between the creature and the Creator. Eden is both the pre-kenotic form of the Godhead—and in this form it is now lost to Vision—and the final apocalyptic epiphany of Albion as the cosmic body of Jesus. But Beulah is present wherever there are visions of Innocence:

There is from Great Eternity a mild & pleasant rest
Nam'd Beulah, a soft Moony Universe, feminine, lovely,
Pure, mild & Gentle, given in Mercy to those who sleep,
Eternally created by the Lamb of God around,
On all sides, within & without the Universal Man.
The daughters of Beulah follow sleepers in all their Dreams,
Creating spaces, lest they fall into Eternal Death.

(F.Z. I, 94–100)

Nor does Beulah simply play a static role in Blake's "system." *The Four Zoas* introduces a "Circle of Destiny" that conceives Experience as a remedial and circular path descending from Beulah into Ulro and then ascending from Ulro by way of Generation into Beulah again, where it finally opens into Eden. Percival has written a clear analysis of this circle, although he has abstracted it from the deeper and more radical thrust of Blake's vision:

The two levels of existence in Eternity become four when the soul fails to maintain even the lower paradisical level. This occurs when man, doubtful of energy and proud of repose, tries to perpetuate his repose. With this negation of energy, spiritual sleep deepens into spiritual death. The infinite universe shrinks into the finite. The ethereal body, hardening into flesh, becomes a tomb for the imprisoned spirit. This is the world of Ulro. But man is not permitted to perish utterly. A way of salvation is provided. A shaft of light pierces the tomb. Energy reappears and struggles for release from the temporal and the finite. This is the world of Generation, Eden and Beulah, the two unfallen levels, together with Ulro and Generation, the two fallen levels, constitute Blake's four worlds. They represent four states of the soul, corresponding to four degrees of spiritual vision.[9]

Blake's "system" can only be portrayed in this Gnostic form by wholly isolating it from Blake the poet and artist, but it remains an accurate analysis of the "Circle of Destiny," providing we correct it by realizing that all four of Blake's worlds are fallen!

Since Blake scholarship has not yet given us a study of Blake's twofold vision of paradise and Fall, it will be necessary for us to take up this theme at this point, both to indicate its integral role in his total vision and to establish yet another ground of Blake's uniqueness as a Christian and a universal seer. A late addition to the first night of *The Four Zoas* contains a passage recording a vision of the creation of history out of paradise:

> Then Eno, a daughter of Beulah, took a Moment of Time
> And drew it out to seven thousand years with much care & affliction
> And many tears, & in every year made windows into Eden.
> She also took an atom of space & opened its centre
> Into Infinitude & ornamented it with wondrous art.
>
> (222–226)

Toward the end of the fourth night of *The Four Zoas,* after Urizen or the "Eternal Mind" has been bound to the creation, and the endless chain of sorrows making up the links of fate has been forged, the Council of God weeps over the "Body of Man" clothed in Luvah's robes of blood, and the daughters of Beulah see the Divine Vision:

> "Lord Saviour, if thou hadst been here our brother had not died,
> And now we know that whatsoever thou wilt ask of God
> He will give it thee; for we are weak women & dare not lift
> Our eyes to the Divine pavilions; therefore in mercy thou
> Appearest cloth'd in Luvah's garments that we may behold thee
> And live. Behold Eternal Death is in Beulah. . . ."
>
> (253–258)

The muses of Innocence, who have initiated the fall from paradise into history, now lament over Albion's corpse. But they are saved from Experience by a vision of the atoning Lamb of God, who appears to them at the very moment that "All Eden was darken'd" (264). Thus we see that the fall from paradise into history or experience results in the obliteration of Eden and the consequent transformation of the Divine Humanity into its broken or kenotic form. Not only is Eden darkened, but "all Beulah fell in dark confusion" as well (VII a, 258); and in the apocalyptic night nine we are informed by one of the Eternals of the present fallen form of Beulah:

> "Man is a Worm; wearied with joy, he seeks the caves of sleep
> Among the Flowers of Beulah, in his selfish cold repose
> Forsaking Brotherhood & Universal love, in selfish clay
> Folding the pure wings of his mind, seeking the places dark
> Abstracted from the roots of Science. . . ."
>
> (627–631)

However, it is only in the perspective of the apocalyptic epiphany of the "Eternal Man" that the dark nature of a fallen Beulah is revealed: Beulah must finally perish—although there are passages in *Milton* which speak of its eternal necessity for those who are hardened in Selfhood—that the new Eden may reign triumphant over all.

Theologically considered, it is essential that the primordial Eden not only be darkened but also that it fully pass away, if a new and apocalyptic Eden is to be resurrected out of Albion's fallen body. Blake, it is true, never went so far in his portrait of Eden, but we must remember that Blake, the man, had an inevitable tendency to linger in a "fourfold vision," just as Blake, the apocalyptic seer, could already speak of the new Eden that he believed was already dawning. Let us turn to a somewhat cryptic passage in *Jerusalem* where Blake employs Ezekiel's famous throne-chariot vision (an archetypal vision of paradise for all mystics in the Judeo-Christian tradition) to portray the fourfold movement in Golgonooza or the gradually developing City of God:

Fourfold the Sons of Los in their divisions, and fourfold
The great City of Golgonooza: fourfold toward the north,
And toward the south fourfold, & fourfold toward the east & west,
Each within other toward the four points: that toward
Eden, and that toward the World of Generation,
And that toward Beulah, and that toward Ulro.
Ulro is the space of the terrible starry wheels of Albion's sons,
But that toward Eden is walled up till time of renovation,
Yet it is perfect in its building, ornaments & perfection.
(12:45–53)

Golgonooza, as we shall later see, is the reversed movement of a fallen humanity, a movement in all directions of "the four Faces towards the Four Worlds of Humanity in every Man" (12:57), and therefore it is a cosmic movement of redemption. Yet in this cosmic movement the space toward Eden is "walled up" until the final time of apocalyptic transfiguration. A passage of decisive theological significance in *Jerusalem* associates the apocalyptic Eden with the universal body of Jesus:

"Mutual in one another's love and wrath all renewing
We live as One Man; for contracting our infinite senses
We behold multitude, or expanding, we behold as one,
As One Man all the Universal Family, and that One Man
We call Jesus the Christ; and he in us, and we in him
Live in perfect harmony in Eden, the land of life,
Giving, recieving, and forgiving each other's trespasses.
He is the Good shepherd, he is the Lord and master,
He is the Shepherd of Albion, he is all in all,
In Eden, in the garden of God, and in heavenly Jerusalem."

(38:16–25)

The very fact that this Eden is an apocalyptic garden of paradise means that this vision is not to be interpreted as being analogous with Indian visions of the eternal evolution and involution of the Godhead. Consequently, just as the expansion of our infinite senses will only be consummated in the Apocalypse, their contraction occurs only in the Fall; and, while the Fall is a continuous event, it is a perpetual if kenotic movement into darkness, and it is ultimately the primordial Eden which is kenotically emptied and darkened by the Fall.

We must not search for clarity and consistency in Blake; rather, the true task of the theologian who chooses to interpret Blake is the ascertainment of the theological implications of the deeper thrusts of his vision at precisely those points where it is most obscure. Nevertheless, we must not lose sight of Blake's text, and significantly enough it is Beulah and not Eden to which the larger body of his vision of paradise is directed. Two passages in *Jerusalem* are particularly significant in revealing the ambivalence with which Blake treated Beulah, the first of which is:

There is a Grain of Sand in Lambeth that Satan cannot find,
Nor can his Watch Fiends find it; 'tis translucent & has many Angles,
But he who finds it will find Oothoon's palace; for within
Opening into Beulah, every angle is a lovely heaven.
But should the Watch Fiends find it, they would call it Sin
And lay its Heavens & their inhabitants in blood of punishment.
Here Jerusalem & Vala were hid in soft slumberous repose,
Hid from the terrible East, shut up in the South & West.

(41:15–22)

At the very least, the "Grain of Sand" in this passage is the sexual delight that religion will call sin, while the terrible East refers to the realm of Generation, and the South and West to Eden and Beulah. Only an Innocence that is isolated from Experience can be a lovely heaven, but this is a primordial and pre-historic state of sleep. Jerusalem and Vala have not yet become incarnate in Experience, but when they do, the gates of this lovely heaven become closed, as we see in our second passage:

> Beneath the bottoms of the Graves, which is Earth's central joint,
> There is a place where Contrarieties are equally true:
>
>   .   .   .   .
>
> From this sweet Place Maternal Love awoke Jerusalem;
> With pangs she forsook Beulah's pleasant lovely shadowy Universe
> Where no dispute can come, created for those who Sleep.
>
> Weeping was in all Beulah, and all the Daughters of Beulah
> Wept for their Sister, the Daughter of Albion, Jerusalem,
> When out of Beulah the Emanation of the Sleeper descended
> With solemn mourning, out of Beulah's moony shades and hills
> Within the Human Heart, whose Gates closed with solemn sound.
>   (48:13–25)

This terrible separation of Jerusalem from Beulah marks the full advent of Experience; now Innocence must be confined to childhood, dreams, and sleep, for to

> The Sons of Eden the moony habitations of Beulah
> Are from Great Eternity a mild & pleasant Rest.
>   (M. 30:13 f.)

Underlying Blake's vision of the twofold paradise of Beulah and Eden is not only his knowledge of Innocence and Experience as the two contrary states of the soul but also his realization that Innocence *must* become Experience. This motif became a dominant theme of his work from the time he engraved *The Book of Thel* (1789), and it illustrates a uniquely Christian ground of his vision: a Fall that culminates in Apocalypse must be a fall of paradise, a paradise lost that is regained in a transfigured form. If a primordial Eden is to become an apocalyptic Eden, then not only must that original Eden be lost forever, but with it must also perish every paradise that might otherwise be present in Experience. Indeed, Blake's very category of Experience is created by the irrevocable loss of Innocence. Blake was the first visionary to discover the final loss of the original paradise and its corresponding heaven, and, while we may take this fact as indicative of the full arrival of the Age of the Spirit, we should also note that it brings new light to the uniqueness of Christianity, for Christianity is the only religion that has abandoned a primordial paradise. This truth must have remained largely hidden until the advent of a radical Christianity, inasmuch as a revolutionary form of faith must rebel against its own tradition, and identify even a Christian nostalgia for paradise as a selfish flight to the sleep of Beulah. As Frye says: "To the individual visionary the upper limit of Beulah is the limit of orthodox vision, and as far as a church of any kind will take him."[10] Moreover, an understanding of Beulah as a lower and now fallen form of paradise can deliver the Christian from the pagan temptation of seeking paradise in a past moment of time and prepare him for a final darkness in which all traces of Innocence will have passed away and history will have become totally identical with Experience. Terrible as this reality will be—for it will have lost all images and memories of paradise—it is the *only* path to an Apocalypse in which Jesus will be all in all. Only when the primordial paradise has fully been drawn into Experience will history have been prepared for its final apocalyptic role.

III. Cosmos and History

DESPITE the fact that Blake lived in an age that had witnessed the dawn of the European historical consciousness and in a period that was soon to culminate in a great outburst of historical creativity— we must remember that fortunately Blake did not receive a single day of formal education—he himself lived beyond his time and anticipated the dissolution of the Western historical and ontological consciousness that was later to be proclaimed in Nietzsche's vision of Eternal Recurrence. If the historical consciousness isolated man from nature and the transcendent, and gave itself to a quest for the reproduction and reliving of the unique experiences created by the variety and particularity of man's historical situations, then Blake passed through this consciousness of historicity by drinking deeply of the well of Albion's corpse and recognizing that an absolutely autonomous humanity must finally be enclosed within the darkness and the solitude of its own Selfhood. Just as Hegel and Marx were soon to discover the alienation of man from nature, and Nietzsche and Freud were shortly thereafter to discover repression as the origin of history, so the revolutionary Blake came to know history as an all-encompassing Experience obliterating all hope and joy, and finally annihilating the meaning and order of the cosmos. To know historicity as a uniquely human experience is not only to isolate man from the cosmos, but also to accept a self-created meaning as the source of its own reality. When meaning is confined to a series of acts that are both radically contingent and wholly autonomous, then not only does the knower face the relativism of historicism, but also the dissolution of the knowing process itself. A romantic and existentialist retreat to an interior realm of pure subjectivity is an inevitable consequence of the triumph of historicity, for a fully consistent historical thinking must dissolve all meaning that lies beyond the unique and individual knower, and ultimately reduce the whole of reality to the instantaneous and fleeting moments of a solitary consciousness.

That the older Hegel communicated with the *Weltgeist* by reading his daily newspaper may possibly be indicative of a belief in the omnipresence of an objective Absolute, but so likewise may it be interpreted as an all too modern realization that there is no meaning of human events which transcends their immediate occurrence. Hegel's posthumously published lectures are perhaps the noblest expression of the bourgeois belief in the progress and pattern of history—although we may well wonder if Hegel himself would have approved their publication—but they have only a limited basis in his own

Phenomenology and *Logic,* and were never to be followed by serious studies by others reflecting a comparable belief in the order of history. Rebel that he was, the early Blake was inspired by the French and American revolutions to attempt the project of writing a series of epics recording the rise and fall of civilizations leading from the original rebellion of Orc to the final victory of freedom. But even these minor epics are infused with a cyclical understanding of history, and his mature epics altogether abandoned a belief in a universal pattern or order in history. Or, rather, *Milton* and *Jerusalem* are grounded in a radical faith in a redemptive movement of history arising from the progressive disintegration of its meaning and form. This is one reason why these poems are so exceedingly difficult, and, if it were not for its poetic power, *Jerusalem* could be ranked for its obscurity with the writings of Boehme and the Kaballah, and could challenge in its dark density the most abstruse sutras of Mahayana Buddhism. Indeed, Buddhism can prepare us for a reading of *Jerusalem,* for the Buddhist's initiatory passage through an experience of the loss of self-consciousness and a collapse of all cognitive meaning has a clear analogy in the pages of Blake's epic. Blake probably intended, in his later work, to shatter all of the primal categories of Western thought and experience; this was essential to his project of arriving at a vision of the death and resurrection of Albion, just as it had gradually revealed itself to be an essential presupposition of his lifelong quest for a vision of the universal presence of Jesus. To reach the Jesus who is the resurrected Albion, Blake was forced to seek for a cosmic reversal of history.

While avoiding the question of Blake's success in creating a symbolic portrait of this reversal, we must openly acknowledge that his images and symbols of this process are ambivalent and confusing, perhaps inevitably so since he was forced to create a whole new language of vision. His most important symbol of the cosmic reversal of history is the "Mundane Shell," and we might begin our investigation of its meaning by following Sloss and Wallis' analysis of the multiple levels of its symbolic significance: (1) it is the sky and the movement of the heavenly bodies; (2) it is the illusory universe of single vision, whether conceived as the world created by the agents of Urizen, or the shadow of the ideal world, or as the individual's conception of the universe which, in turn, regulates his own perceptions; (3) it is the religious history of humanity; and (4) it is the mortal environment of the spirit's reawakening, built through mercy or Los.[11] Obviously, the Mundane Shell is simultaneously a demonic and a redemptive symbol and it portrays both a kenotic and an historical movement of the cosmos. On the one hand, it is a shadow of the earth:

> The Mundane Shell is a vast Concave Earth, an immense
> Harden'd shadow of all things upon our Vegetated Earth,
> Enlarg'd into dimension & deform'd into indefinite space,
> In Twenty-seven Heavens and all their Hells, with Chaos
> And Ancient Night & Purgatory. It is a cavernous Earth
> Of labyrinthine intricacy, twenty-seven-folds of opakeness,
> And finishes where the lark mounts; here Milton journeyed
> In that Region call'd Midian among the Rocks of Horeb.
> For travellers from Eternity pass outward to Satan's seat,
> But travellers to Eternity pass inward to Golgonooza.
> (M. 17:21–30)

On the other hand, it meets the Eternity beyond the stars:

> The Vegetative Universe opens like a flower from the Earth's center
> In which is Eternity. It expands in Stars to the Mundane Shell
> And there it meets Eternity again, both within and without,
> And the abstract Voids between the Stars are the Satanic Wheels.
> (J. 13:34–37)

However, the "blue" Shell is not solely a cosmic or celestial region. For Los built the Mundane Shell in the four regions of Humanity as the "Net & Veil of Vala among the Souls of the Dead" (J. 42:81). Paradoxically enough, a celestial transcendence undergoes an epiphany in the dark regions of the dead, as the ancient holiness of the sky is seen in Vision to be incarnate in the dark tyranny of Vala's Veil.

Thus we see that the Mundane Shell is at once a cosmic symbol reflecting a fallen historical process and an historical symbol reflecting a cosmic fall. Moreover, the Shell is simultaneously a labyrinthic chaos and the actual place of redemption:

> For the Veil of Vala, which Albion cast into the Atlantic Deep
> To catch the Souls of the Dead, began to Vegetate & Petrify
> Around the Earth of Albion among the Roots of his Tree.
> This Los formed into the Gates & mighty Wall between the Oak
> Of Weeping & the Palm of Suffering beneath Albion's Tomb.
> Thus in process of time it became the beautiful Mundane Shell,
> The Habitation of the Spectres of the Dead, & the Place
> Of Redemption & of awaking again into Eternity.
>
> (J. 59:2–9)

If the Mundane Shell is a hardened shadow of all things upon earth, enlarged and deformed into indefinite space, it is also a beautiful place of redemption. This paradox can only be unveiled by the realization that the destructive "Veil of Vala" is the temporal pole of the Mundane Shell, and both are expressions of the kenotic movement of the Fall. The Shell and the earth are polar forms of one cosmic and historical movement; a dialectical relation exists between these forms, each reversing the form and movement of the other: "Whatever is visible in the Vegetable Earth, the same is visible in the Mundane Shell revers'd, in mountain & vale" (J. 72:46 f.); and "Whatever is seen upon the Mundane Shell, the same be seen upon the Fluctuating Earth woven by the Sisters (J. 83:38 f.). It is the female who mediates the movements of the Mundane Shell to a fallen earth:

> "And sometimes the Earth shall roll in the Abyss & sometimes
> Stand in the Center & sometimes stretch flat in the Expanse,
> According to the will of the lovely Daughters of Albion;
> Sometimes it shall assimilate with mighty Golgonooza,
> Touching its summits, & sometimes divided roll apart.
> As a beautiful Veil, so these Females shall fold & unfold,
> According to their will, the outside surface of the Earth,
> An outside shadowy Surface superadded to the real Surface
> Which is unchangeable for ever & ever. Amen: so be it!"
>
> (J. 83:40–48)

A rolling earth, moving to and from the abyss, the center and the expanse, and moving according to the will of the female, can only be an image of history. Finally, history and the cosmos are dialectical images of one reality, a totality divided by the Fall. In their fallen form, cosmos and history, the outer and the inner realms, invert one another; but no matter how far they may pass from one another, they remain bound together by a dialectical relationship, as each records in a reverse form the form and movement of the other.

Did Blake believe that there is a "real Surface" of the earth beneath history that is forever unchangeable? Perhaps so; as far as we know Blake never reached a fully consistent belief, and it is readily apparent that he was often tempted to fall back upon a Gnostic dualism. Yet it is unquestionable that such a belief is incompatible with the deeper thrust of his vision and it violates his own portrayal of the historical movement of the Mundane Shell. To understand this movement, we must examine the 37th plate of *Milton* and the 75th plate of *Jerusalem.* The first plate records the culminating sequence of *Milton;* here Milton's shadow appears to Blake as the "Covering Cherub," and within it stand Satan and Rahab ("in an outside which is fallacious, within, beyond the outline of Identity, in the Selfhood deadly"). Blake sees Milton

> Descending down into my Garden, a Human Wonder of God
> Reaching from heaven to earth, a Cloud & Human Form,
> I beheld Milton with astonishment & in him beheld
> The Monstrous Churches of Beulah, the Gods of Ulro dark,
> Twelve monstrous dishumaniz'd terrors, Synagogues of Satan,
> A Double Twelve & Thrice Nine: such their divisions.
> (13–18)

All of these Beulah churches and Gods of Ulro are within the Mundane Shell, and Blake sees the history of religion from Baal to Isis and Osiris to Saturn and Jove as the movement of the twelve gods who are the twelve spectre sons of the Druid Albion. Then he has an apocalyptic vision of the twenty-seven heavens and their churches, beginning with Adam and reaching

Abraham, Moses, Solomon, Paul, Constantine, Charlemaine,
Luther, these seven are the Male-Females, the Dragon Forms,
Religion hid in War, a Dragon red & hidden Harlot.
(41–43)

All of these are seen in Milton's shadow, or the spectre of Albion,
in which the spectre of Luvah inhabits the "Newtonian Voids" between the substances of creation. These voids of chaos are outside the
stars and invisible to earth, and stretched out, they compose the
Mundane Shell, a mighty incrustation

Of Forty-eight deformed Human Wonders of the Almighty,
With Caverns whose remotest bottoms meet again beyond
The Mundane Shell in Golgonooza; but the Fires of Los rage
In the remotest bottoms of the Caves, that none can pass
Into Eternity that way, but all descend to Los. . . .
(54–58)

Only in the perspective of the dawning Apocalypse—Milton thereafter almost immediately comes to "Self Annihilation"—does the
Mundane Shell appear as an absolute chaos through which there
is no way to Eternity; and, only in this apocalyptic moment, does
Blake have a vision of the twenty-seven heavens and their churches
within the Shell as "a Dragon red & hidden Harlot."

This plate of *Milton* can only be understood by relating it to its
analogue, the 75th plate of *Jerusalem*. The latter plate is set in the
context of an apocalyptic judgment; it begins with the line, "And
Rahab, Babylon the Great, hath destroyed Jerusalem," and concludes
with Blake's favorite image of the Fall: "But now the Starry Heavens
are fled from the mighty limbs of Albion." There is a design in the
middle of the text of the seraphim of Eden who are united by inter-
secting rings of endless love, and beneath the text there is an illustration of Jerusalem locked in the serpentine coils of the apocalyptic dragon (this interpretation is not Wicksteed's but my own). These
designs illustrate the paradoxical nature of the text, which portrays
the final encounter of Heaven and Hell. Rahab is depicted with her
twenty-seven "Poisons":

And all her Twenty-seven Heavens, now hid & now reveal'd,
Appear in strong delusive light of Time & Space, drawn out
In shadowy pomp, by the Eternal Prophet created evermore.
For Los in Six Thousand Years walks up & down continually
That not one Moment of Time be lost, & every revolution
Of Space he makes permanent in Bowlahoola & Cathedron.

(4–9)

Bowlahoola and Cathedron are obscure images of fallen man, and we
see that Los directs history—including that of the twenty-seven
churches—with the intention that not one fragment of its time or
space will be lost. Blake then repeats almost word for word the
passage in *Milton* naming the twenty-seven heavens and their
churches, but he transforms its meaning by adding these words:

But Jesus, breaking thro' the Central Zones of Death & Hell,
Opens Eternity in Time & Space, triumphant in Mercy.

(21 f.)

Here, the "Mystery" of the apocalyptic dragon is revealed at the very
moment when Jesus mercifully opens Eternity in time and space.
Notice that Eternity opens *in* time and space, and only now does
the redemptive form of the Mundane Shell fully appear.

Thus are the Heavens form'd by Los within the Mundane Shell.
And where Luther ends Adam begins again in Eternal Circle
To awake the Prisoners of Death, to bring Albion again
With Luvah into light eternal in his eternal day.

But now the Starry Heavens are fled from the mighty limbs of Albion.

(23–27)

We must postpone an examination of the meaning of the "Eternal
Circle" and the apocalyptic dragon until the final part of our study,
but it is clear that the Mundane Shell brings Albion *and* Luvah into
eternal light. Already we have seen that Luvah occupies the darkest
chaos of the Mundane Shell, and this chaos awakens *with* Albion on
the eternal Day.

129

Blake's vision of universal redemption is unique if only because it is both mystical and apocalyptic: it comprehends history and the cosmos as a single if divided process, finally celebrating the absolute chaos of a totally fallen cosmos as the spatial and temporal point of resurrection. The Mundane Shell is the historical movement of the cosmos in response to the death and resurrection of Albion, and the chaos of its "Newtonian Voids" is the sepulcher of a fallen history awaiting its reversal. This reversal occurs at the very point where the Mundane Shell appears in all its horror; then the epiphany of the Mundane Shell as the "Dragon red & hidden Harlot" reveals the redemptive goal of a fallen history, and initiates the apocalyptic transformation of the cosmos. One of Blake's most vibrant water colors, entitled "The Great Red Dragon and the Woman Clothed with the Sun," depicts a winged and serpentine dragon in human form descending upon a luminous daughter of light who could only be Jerusalem, and their two bodies form one organic whole. Again, the fifteenth of the Job illustrations, "Behold now Behomoth which I made with thee," contains a design of the primordial monsters, Behomoth and Leviathan, created as pillars in the deepest Hell who are erected to reach the heavenly arches above. Wicksteed says in response to this design: "And no phase of life can be regarded as permanently blessed until we have experienced its obverse or breakdown and found that blessed too."[12] So it is that the vast stretches of an infinite and impersonal cosmos are not simply the illusions of a fallen "Ratio," but, more truly considered, are the bodily reflections of a fallen humanity which will themselves be transfigured with the resurrection of the body. The dead matter of Ulro is the fallen body of Luvah, the primordial energy; so likewise is it the indefinite space of the Mundane Shell that appears on earth as Vala's Veil, and will finally burst into life on the eternal Day. No dualism is possible in this vision, as every fragment of space and time remains permanent in its fallen form that Jesus may open Eternity in its midst; for apart from the actuality of the fallen cosmos, there could be no history of salvation, and thus no final Apocalypse.

IV. God and History

AN increasingly major motif of Christian theology from St. Augustine's *City of God* to the most recent schools of Catholic and Protestant theology has been the identification of Christianity as an historical faith or religion, a thesis that postulates a peculiarly historical realm as the arena of salvation, frequently maintaining that the uniqueness of Christianity lies in its mediation of redemption to the actual processes of history. Few historians of religions would accept this latter claim, for in many respects Confucianism and Islam have gone beyond Christianity in their immersion in history—and Islamic theologies of history anticipated Vico and Hegel in their understanding of a universal historical process—to say nothing of monarchic expressions of religion the world over that have given themselves to the pursuit of the redemption of history. Whether Jewish, Christian, or Islamic, or even Hindu and Buddhist, the monarchic quest for power and dominance in history has invariably expressed itself in some form of a messianic hope, and radical believers in many faiths have long rejected this hope as a priestly and all too human expression of the will to power. William Blake was such a believer, and he was at one with a universal prophetic fraternity in rebelling against a salvation that is associated with the worldly power and the sacred authority of a king, despite the fact that such a salvation is inscribed in the texts of scripture. If it is possible to distingush an Old Testament and a New Testament form of the biblical epic and to say that the latter differs from the former because it reverses its pattern of salvation—for an eschatological faith in the *end* of the world must invert a messianic hope in the *fulfillment* of history— then Blake's epic poetry is not only a modern repetition of the biblical epic but it also brings a new and deeper prophetic light to the Bible at just those points where the Bible itself is most obscured and distorted by a priestly and literal theology.[13] Just as the Old Testament legal and historical writings understand the history of salvation

131

in terms of Torah, cult, and king, the New Testament follows the Old Testament prophetic tradition in proclaiming a Kingdom of God that is a New Covenant, an apocalyptic dawning of a final salvation that reverses the forms and structures of history, abolishing the authority of priest and Torah, and offering a new and total union between man and God. When an ecclesiastical Christianity arose to dissolve this eschatological foundation of the New Testament, it once again exalted the authority of law and cult, transformed Jesus himself into a monarchic Lord and cosmic Logos, and finally reached a tyrannical form in the Church's claim to be the absolute religion. Blake and every radical Christian point to a return to primitive Christianity by way of shattering this claim.

The very conception of Christianity as the absolute religion, with its correlative beliefs in the Bible as the unique and final revelation of God, the Church and its cultus as the sole path to salvation, and Jesus Christ as the one Redeemer, derives from the belief in one absolutely sovereign Triune God who demands a total and universal submission to His manifestation in the words and events of a particular historical tradition. The Christian God is a God of overwhelming power whose presence induces a numinous response of adoration and abject humility, and who is incarnate not in the poor and humble prophet of Nazareth (orthodox Christologies have never succeeded in evolving to a kenotic form) but only in the historical epiphany of an eternal Logos. Likewise, the Christian Messiah or Christ is worshipped in the form of a universal Monarch, is known to be the Suffering Servant on the Cross only to the extent that He appears as the voluntary and atoning Victim for a sinful humanity, and is dogmatically defined as the Second Person of a Trinity having but a single divine nature, which is conceived as an absolutely sovereign transcendence. The success of Christianity in evolving to an absolute form can be seen in the degree to which Christian doctrine negates the original message of Jesus: an original proclamation calling upon brokenness and forgiveness as the way to the Kingdom of God has been followed by an exaltation of its proclaimer to the status of cosmic Lord and transcendent Redeemer. The Christ of orthodox Christianity is not the breaker but the upholder of an absolute Law;

He sanctions the "justice" of rulers and the institutions of society, and He redeems only to the extent that His believers submit to His sovereign and transcendent power. Consequently, the spiritual or the radical Christian, who is loyal only to Jesus, must rebel against the Christian Messiah. Having chosen lowliness as the path to the Kingdom, rejected all worldly power and authority as the province of Satan, and accepted the apocalyptic and mystical goal of the total union of God and man, the radical Christian must finally recognize that the Christ of traditional faith is merely a disguise of the almighty and wholly other Creator, and therefore he must defy the orthodox Christ as the ultimate author of repression and the Lord of a fallen and guilty humanity.

Blake was the first Christian atheist, and his atheism was born out of a hatred of repression and a joyous response to a new and universal epiphany of Jesus. But he was no atheist in the ordinary sense; he knew that the Christian God is every bit as real as the reality of repression, that the sovereignty and transcendence of God is created by the Fall, and that this wholly other God has died to make possible the advent of the Apocalypse. We have already seen how Blake unveils the Christian God as Satan, and how he interprets the atonement as effecting the death of Satan, but we have not yet directly approached his understanding of the death of God. Orthodox Christianity has never been able to accept the full reality of the Crucifixion because it is bound to a conception of Christ as the eternal Logos and can only conceive the Crucifixion as an atonement for the sin of humanity. So long as guilt is limited to humanity, and divinity is known as an eternal reality, there can be no real acceptance of the Crucifixion: for the Crucifixion can finally be no more than a Gnostic mirage if it is not understood as culminating in the death of God. If a real event underlies the Crucifixion, that event must be the death of God, for the suffering of Christ can have no ultimate meaning unless it is the Passion of God, and faith itself knows that passion as a passage into death. Radical Christianity knows that the God who dies on the Cross is the God who is manifest to fallen man, the transcendent Creator and the sovereign Lord, and it celebrates the Resurrection as the advent of the "Eternal Great

Humanity Divine" of an apocalyptic Eden. When the Resurrection is understood as the triumph of the Lordship of Christ over the mortal humanity of Jesus, the Crucifixion must be conceived as a repetition of a non-kenotic Creation, the separation of light from darkness, and the exaltation of a sovereign Lord over a fallen and guilty creation. To the spiritual Christian, the Resurrection of Christ is the resurrection of the divine Body of a fallen humanity, the apocalyptic rebirth in a glorious and transfigured form of the primordial "Humanity Divine" that fell into death and repression when Urizen or Satan named himself as the only God.

Once again we see how Christianity has only reached its full and radical form with the coming of the Age of the Spirit, and only in this form does Christianity appear in its genuine uniqueness. Death has been a dominant theological motif throughout the Christian tradition; whether in meditation upon the Passion of Christ, or in the ecstatic celebration of poets and seers, all true forms of Christianity have known death as the path to resurrection and to authentic human existence. Buddhism presents a significant contrast to Christianity at this point, for, while Buddhist meditation centers upon the image of death, it does so to dissolve the illusion of selfhood and the consequent pain of *samsara,* whereas Christianity experiences death as an event leading to resurrection, and not simply as the fallen condition of a guilty humanity. The Buddhist meditates upon death to dissociate himself from a temporal and painful condition; Christian meditation upon death, however, is an interior repetition of the Crucifixion, a real co-experiencing of Christ's dying and rising again. Through dying with Christ to the fallen form of the human condition, the Christian identifies himself with the resurrected Body of the Divine Humanity. True, Buddhist meditation upon death effects an annihilation of the fallen human condition. But in Buddhism death cannot be a once-and-for-all decisive event effecting a final transfiguration because Buddhism is closed to the ultimate reality of spatial and temporal events: Christianity, alone among the world religions, celebrates the concrete factuality of death as the path to regeneration. Yet this regeneration must remain a mere illusion or an unrealizable ideal if it involves no more than the free acceptance of a particular

and individual death. Only when death is concretely experienced as
the real and final death of the God who alone is God can it be consummated in the resurrection of the fallen body of humanity. Psychoanalysis tells us that we are forever destined to reenact the murder of
the repressive Father, but a radical form of faith knows that the death
of the Father brings a new freedom from guilt and repression; and,
unlike psychoanalysis, that faith can experience the death of the
Father as a once-and-for-all decisive event, an event that is final
and irrevocable, and once it has freely and fully been accepted it
can never recur in a "repetition compulsion." If Christianity is the
only religion that knows the totality of fallenness, so likewise it alone
has given birth to a form of faith that knows a solitary Divinity and a
transcendent holiness as consequences of the Fall; and only radical
Christianity can live the death of God and His holiness as the path
to an apocalyptic reversal and transfiguration of history and the
cosmos.

Although the identification of God as Urizen or Satan is a consistent and dominant motif of Blake's work, his later writings record
a dark if powerful vision of a contrary motif, a vision of a kenotic
movement in the Godhead leading to the redemption of a cosmic
humanity. This vision arises in the context of a new and apocalyptic
understanding of the "Mystery" of the Godhead. When Blake sees
Satan within the dark Selfhood of Milton's shadow, he therein sees
a "Human Wonder of God" reaching from heaven to earth, a "Human
Form" revealing the monstrous Churches of Beulah and the dark
Gods of Ulro (M. 37:14–16). There follows an apocalyptic epiphany
of these Gods in the twenty-seven heavens and their churches of the
Antichrist. But in *Jerusalem,* as we have seen, this epiphany is
consummated in Jesus' triumphantly breaking through the central
zones of death and Hell and opening Eternity in time and space
(J. 75:21). God only appears in His Ulro form with the dawn of the
Apocalypse; then He is fully incarnate as Hell or Ulro, and Jesus
must break through that Hell to usher in Eternity. This vision stands
within the Christian theosophical tradition of Erigena, Boehme,
and Schelling, with its witness to the dialectical and historical movements of the Godhead; but Blake's vision is more consistently

kenotic for it fully identifies God with the dark abyss or evil potency
of the Godhead even while unveiling the goal of this potency as being
wholly redemptive. If the early Blake said that God became man
that man might become God, the late Blake might well have said that
god become God that man might become Man. Such a simplification
obviously distorts Blake's vision—and Blake himself was rarely able
to formulate his later vision in clear and simple terms—but it should
prepare us for an understanding of Blake's paradoxical identification of Satan as a redemptive form of God. He left us few texts
upon which we might base a reconstruction of this meaning. However,
the early Blake delighted in greeting Satan as a redemptive figure,
and, while Blake was to be overwhelmed and almost crushed by his
realization of the deeper consequences of the divine identity of
Satan, he never wholly lost sight of the regenerative potencies of
evil, and, as we have seen, a kenotic meaning of the Fall is an intrinsic
ground of his vision as a whole.

Blake created only a single symbolic image of the kenotic movement of God, and this image of the "Seven Eyes of God"—an image
derived from the Book of Revelation—always appears in an obscure
and fragmentary form, for the few passages in which this image may
be found are strangely isolated from the body of their respective
texts. At the conclusion of the first night of *The Four Zoas*, the
"Family Divine" elected seven, "called the Seven Eyes of God &
the Seven Lamps of the Almighty."

> The Seven are one within the other; the Seventh is named Jesus,
> The Lamb of God, blessed for ever, & he follow'd the Man
> Who wander'd in mount Ephraim seeking a Sepulcher,
> His inward eyes closing from the Divine vision, & all
> His children wandering outside, from his bosom fleeing away.

We must assume that the seven Eyes of God are related to the historical symbol of the seven ages of man (M. 3:1–28), and that the eyes
or lamps are windows through which a fallen man looks beyond himself when his own eyes are closed to the Divine vision. In the eighth
night of *The Four Zoas*, after Satan has been condemned by a
"Great Solemn assembly," Satan and his companions roll down into
a dark and deadly world.

"Jerusalem, pitying them, wove them mantles of life & death,
Times after times. And those in Eden sent Lucifer for their Guard.
Lucifer refus'd to die for Satan & in pride he forsook his charge.
Then they sent Molech. Molech was impatient. They sent
Molech impatient. They sent Elohim, who created Adam
To die for Satan. Adam refus'd, but was compell'd to die
By Satan's arts. Then the Eternals sent Shaddai.
Shaddai was angry. Pachad descended. Pachad was terrified.
And then they sent Jehovah, who leprous stretch'd his hand to Eternity.
Then Jesus came & Died willing beneath Tirzah & Rahab."

(397–406)

Here we see that the seven Eyes of God are progressive historical manifestations of God who are "sent" by the Eternals to redeem a fallen Satan until the last Eye, Jesus, "came" and freely died. Not only is Jesus an Eye of God, but he is also the one Eye who freely accepts and enacts his chosen destiny. This text is repeated in a somewhat modified form in *Milton,* where after the leprous Jehovah stretched his hand to Eternity: "the Body of Death was perfected in hypocritic holiness, Around the Lamb, a Female Tabernacle woven in Cathedron's Looms" (13:25 f.). This reference to Jehovah's creating the dead body of Jesus in the tomb reveals the deep antithesis between the first six Eyes of God and their opposing counterpart in Jesus. We also learn in *Milton* that the seven Eyes of God may not sleep because they are to walk through all the twenty-seven heavens "even to Satan's Seat" (M. 35:64).

One significant reference to the seven Eyes of God appears in *Jerusalem;* this occurs on the 55th plate when the eternals gather into a solemn assembly after seeing a vision of Jesus as the "Eternal Man." Some of the eternals refuse to follow Jesus into the land of the dead:

But others said: "Let us to him, who only Is & who
Walketh among us, give decision: bring forth all your fires!"

So saying, an eternal deed was done: in fiery flames
The Universal Concave raged such thunderous sounds as never
Were sounded from a mortal cloud. . . .

. . . .

137

Then far the greatest number were about to make a Separation;
And they Elected Seven, call'd the Seven Eyes of God,
Lucifer, Molech, Elohim, Shaddai, Pahad, Jehovah, Jesus.
(17–32)

Thus we see that the seven Eyes of God are elected when a body of the
eternals wills to make the kenotic movement of Incarnation. Wicksteed interprets the seven Eyes as seven forms of God seen variously
by mankind in general as: (1) a proud and masterful authority
(Lucifer); (2) a punitive tyrant demanding the sacrifice of the
noblest in man (Molech); (3) the Creator, Designer, Law-giver and
Law-enforcer (the triple Elohim); (4) the impatient, magisterial, and
final authority who crushes any appeal or complaint from the human
sufferers in his charge (Shaddai, the Almighty in the Book of Job);
(5) the fear that is both more terrible and more sustaining for being
a divine voice within the human soul (Pahad); (6) the War God of
Hosts who both led his people in battle and inspired their prophets
(Jehovah); and (7) the Divine Humanity in its supreme earthly
manifestation (Jesus).[14] Perhaps little more can be said about the
meaning that Blake intended to lie behind these seven Hebrew
names of God except to correct Wicksteed by insisting that Blake
could only have intended all six of the First Eyes to represent demonic
or satanic forms of God. Each of these Eyes stands for a form of
sovereign transcendence that Blake had long regarded as a manifestation of Satan; each of them represses and destroys all that which
is truly human, and yet the Eyes themselves were elected in response
to the initial movement of the kenotic process of redemption. However, in terms of Blake's own vision, the strangest fact about this
symbol is that Jesus could appear as the culmination of an historical
series of *divine* forms.

That Blake could name Jesus as an Eye of God is startling, not only
because of the passion and joy with which he had always celebrated
the humanity of Jesus, or simply because the name of God had almost
invariably inspired rebellion and defiance within him, but also more
deeply because the Jesus whom he knew was the bringer of a Humanity that is born out of the tomb of God: "Thou art a Man, God is
no more" (E.G. c, 41). Since the Eyes of God are an historical series
of the forms of God, and are intended in their sixfold form to embody

138

the demonic movement of the Mundane Shell, they must culminate
in the "Dragon red & hidden Harlot" of the Antichrist. Thus the
Eyes must walk through all the twenty-seven heavens even to "Satan's
Seat," and this is so because the Eyes were "sent" in response to
the fall of Satan. Now when we remember that Blake discovered
Satan's fall to be the birth of the solitary and sovereign God, and
that this vision of God as Satan underlies his mature work as a whole,
it must seem absurdly paradoxical to entertain the supposition that
the Eyes of God were sent in response to the fall of God, particularly
so since six of these Eyes are demonic or satanic forms of Deity.
Yet each of these Eyes fails to fulfill its appointed destiny: Lucifer
refused to die, Molech was impatient, Elohim wearied, Shaddai was
angry, Pahad was terrified, and Jehovah stretched his hand to Eternity
to perfect the "Body of Death" around the Lamb. Not only do each
of them fail, but each of the Eyes also embodies a particular pattern
or movement of the fallen or falling Satan: six of the Eyes reflect
the falling Satan in their own form. Their movement through the
twenty-seven heavens is the moving shadow of Satan on the Mundane
Shell, a shadow that reaches its final apocalyptic epiphany in the
revelation of the "Mystery" of the Gods of Hell. Blake, of course,
adopted his apocalyptic imagery from the Book of Revelation, and
there we read: "And I beheld, and, lo, in the midst of the throne
and of the four beasts, and in the midst of the elders, stood a Lamb
as it had been slain, having seven horns and seven eyes, which are
the seven Spirits of God sent forth into all the earth" (5:6). Here,
the Eyes of God are the eyes of the slain Lamb, but Blake reverses the
New Testament text by seeing the Eyes as being sent *before* the Lamb.
This reversal makes possible Blake's vision of the death of the Eyes
in the death of the Lamb of God: Jesus, as the seventh and the
final Eye, comes and dies *willingly* beneath the "Dragon Red & hidden
Harlot." Jesus alone among the seven Eyes accepts his destiny of
death. But his death is the culmination and fulfillment of the movement of the seven Eyes; through his death the Eyes of God fulfill
their kenotic role, and that death becomes the once-and-for-all decisive event effecting the transfiguration of a fallen cosmos. Jesus dies
the death that is God's destiny, in that death the fallen forms of

Satan are annihilated, and the concrete factuality of the death of God becomes in Jesus the path to regeneration.

v. Jesus

BLAKE was an apostle to the Gentiles and his message brings forth the same offense in his readers that is always induced by an authentic proclamation of the Gospel. That offense is most deeply present in Blake's devotion to "Jesus only" (the motto of *Jerusalem*), in his call to all mankind to accept the goal of becoming identical with Jesus, and in his conviction that Jesus is the "Universal Humanity" (J. 96:5). If only because of his faith in Jesus we must acknowledge that Blake was a Christian seer, but he is by far the most Christocentric of Christian visionaries, despite the fact that his revolutionary vision of Jesus arose out of a rebellion against the Christian Christ. Why should the rebellious Blake have given such reverence to the name of Jesus? Why believe that Jesus' passion is present throughout history, that Jesus is the lamb who is slain in all his children, and that only Jesus can save us from our destructive Selfhood (J. 45:16)? How could a prophet who was so overwhelmingly committed to the universal redemption of humanity make such absolute claims for a particular historical figure? What is present in Jesus that is not present in a Siddhartha Gautama, a Krishna, a Lao Tzu, or even a Socrates or a Gandhi? Was Blake's devotion to Jesus simply the expression of a bhakti faith that can have no validity beyond its particular historical context? The force of these questions must multiply beyond all bounds when it is realized that Blake thoroughly and consistently repudiated all Christian claims to the effect that Jesus is the Son of God, or the Word of God, or the Incarnate Lord (although Blake brought a new and radical meaning of his own to each one of these titles). It was the simple humanity of Jesus that attracted Blake's devotion; he saw that humanity wherever there is pain or joy; and, while condemning all notions of an abstract or general humanity, he profoundly believed that Jesus is the body of humanity, and is present in every human face and hand:

JESUS

The Divine Vision still was seen,
Still was the Human Form Divine,
Weeping in weak & mortal clay,
O Jesus, still the Form was thine.
(J. 27:57–60)

The bard who could sing of his own land as having once shown forth with the countenance of Jesus knows that Jesus is always present no matter how deep the darkness:

Jesus replied, "I am the Resurrection & the Life.

. . . .

Come now with me into the villages, walk thro' all the cities;
Tho' thou art taken to prison & judgment, starved in the streets,
I will command the cloud to give thee food & the hard rock
To flow with milk & wine; tho' thou seest me not a season,
Even a long season, & a hard journey & a howling wilderness,
Tho' Vala's cloud hide thee & Luvah's fires follow thee,
Only believe & trust in me. Lo, I am always with thee!"
(J. 62:18–29)

The full use that is made of the Gospels in such passages should not deceive us into thinking that Blake was yet another Christian poet in the conventional sense. He commonly employs a biblical passage only to invert and deepen its usual and literal meaning—his success as a dialectical interpreter of the New Testament can most easily be seen in his manuscript poem, *The Everlasting Gospel*[15]—and we might best approach our problem by first examining Blake's inversion of the Church's image of Christ. Sloss and Wallis remark that Blake's vision of Christ differs in almost all respects from the Christ of religious orthodoxy,[16] and the truth of this judgment can be seen simply by recalling Blake's understanding of the Atonement. There is a puzzling passage at the beginning of the ninth night of *The Four Zoas* when Los and Enitharmon are building Jerusalem and weeping

Over the Sepulcher & over the Crucified body
Which, to their Phantom Eyes, appear'd still in the Sepulcher
But Jesus stood beside them in the spirit, separating
Their spirit from their body.

Once again, we must reject any interpretation that would ascribe such passages to a Gnostic hostility to the body. The resurrected Jesus is separated from the crucified body, although that broken body is imprisoned by the Church in "Luvah's Sepulcher" (J. 24:51). When Jesus died he passed the limits of possibility as they appear to individual perception (J. 62:19), and it is precisely this passage through death that makes possible his epiphany in a universal form. Jesus alone among the Eyes of God assumed a mortal form, and his mortal destiny is the path by which he reaches the "Universal Humanity."

> "And that he must be born is certain, for One must be All
> And comprehend within himself all things both small & great."
> (F.Z. I, 294 f.)

At the conclusion of *Jerusalem*, when Jesus appears to Albion as a "Man,"

> Albion said: "O Lord, what can I do? my Selfhood cruel
> Marches against thee, deceitful, from Sinai & from Edom
> Into the Wilderness of Judah, to meet thee in his pride.
> I behold the Visions of my deadly Sleep of Six Thousand Years
> Dazling around thy skirts like a Serpent of precious stones & gold
> I know it is my Self, O my Divine Creator & Redeemer."

> Jesus replied: "Fear not Albion: unless I die thou canst not live;
> But if I die I shall arise again & thou with me.
> This is Friendship & Brotherhood: without it Man is Not."
> (J. 96:8–16)

During this final moment before the apocalyptic transfiguration of the cosmos, Albion's Selfhood appears as the God of Sinai; this is the Selfhood which underlies the deadly sleep of a fallen history and which will die in Jesus' death so that Albion can live. Indeed, humanity can only exist through this death of God in Jesus:

> Jesus said: "Wouldest thou love one who never died
> For thee, or ever die for one who had not died for thee?
> And if God dieth not for Man & giveth not himself

JESUS

Eternally for Man, Man could not exist; for Man is Love
As God is Love; every kindness to another is a little Death
In the Divine Image, nor can Man exist but by Brotherhood."
(J. 96:23–28)

Thus God dies for man and gives himself eternally for man, and this death is repeated in every man when he exists in brotherhood; for Jesus is present wherever an autonomous and solitary Selfhood freely wills its own annihilation.

If it is the "Divine Mercy" that redeems man in the body of Jesus (J. 36:54), it does so only by freely dying in Jesus, and that death is both a once-and-for-all event that annihilates God as the Wholly Other, and a death that is repeated in God's eternal death for "Man." A death that is consummated in such an eternal repetition is obviously not confined to the particular body of Jesus, nor can an eternal repetition of the divine death be enclosed within the faith and liturgy of the Church: to the extent that the death of God in Jesus is limited to a particular time and space, the full reality and comprehensiveness of that death is negated, and God dies only to be resurrected in His original and fallen form. Blake's hatred of religion was primarily directed against its destructive movement of repetition; a repetition that re-presents a spatial and temporal moment of the past must bind its celebrant to an eternal repression, for a submission to a past moment of concrete time isolates the believer from the reality of both the present and the future, and enslaves him to an alien moment that is alien just because it is past. When the death of Jesus is known only as an occurrence of the past, it cannot be repeated as a universal and eternal event because it remains enclosed within its own particularity. Such a "religious" understanding of the Crucifixion is closed moreover to the finality of Jesus' death; it must resurrect him in the form of an exalted Lord, and thereby annul both the reality of his death and its redemptive consequences. The radical Christian seer knows that God has truly died in Jesus and that His death has liberated humanity from every reality that appears beyond the human hand and face. Consequently, a true humanity is born only through the death of Jesus; that death obliterates the repressive authority of the Wholly Other, and therefore dissolves every form of humanity that is the victim of repression, with the result that the triumphant Body of the crucified Jesus is the freedom and universality of the "Human Imagination" (M. 3:3).

Northrop Frye interprets Blake's vision as unveiling the final revelation of Christianity to be not that Jesus is God, but that "God is Jesus."[17] This crucial phase is to be found in the Laocoon engraving of 1820 where Blake identifies the Eternal Body of Man, the Imagination, the Divine Body of God himself, and Jesus. Every man is a member of this Eternal Body of Jesus for this Body is the God who is all in all. Thus the first chapter of *Jerusalem* opens with Blake's most poignant and ever-recurring song:

> This theme calls me in sleep night after night, & ev'ry morn
> Awakes me at sun-rise; then I see the Saviour over me
> Spreading his beams of love & dictating the words of this mild song.

> "Awake! awake O sleeper of the land of shadows, wake! expand!
> I am in you and you in me, mutual in love divine:
> Fibres of love from man to man thro' Albion's pleasant land."
> (4:3–8)

Although the "Divine Vision" is now darkened, and lovely Jerusalem is hidden from sight, Jesus calls his sleeping brothers to a realization of their identity with himself:

> "I am not a God afar off, I am a brother and friend;
> Within your bosoms I reside, and you reside in me:
> Lo! we are One, forgiving all Evil, Not seeking recompense.
> Ye are my members, O ye sleepers of Beulah, land of shades!"
> (4:18–21)

We sleep in the shades of Beulah when we imagine Jesus as a distant Lord or are bound to a belief in a God who is other than Jesus. To know a God, or a Spectre, or a Selfhood who is other than Jesus is to exist in a repressed or fallen form, and to be a stone upon the grave of Jesus, a stone that will not move because it is hardened by its own solidity and enclosed within its own isolated point in space. Contracting our infinite senses we behold an isolated multitude, but expanding we behold as one: "and that One Man we call Jesus the Christ" (J. 38:20).

JESUS

Is the Jesus who Blake named as the "Universal Humanity" and the "Human Imagination" simply a symbol of humanity itself? Has Blake merely given a poetic and symbolic expression to an Enlightenment humanism in his vision of Jesus? Does the Jesus who dwells "in" us represent an essential core of human nature which transcends the frailties of weakness and vice? These questions can be answered in the affirmative only by denying the great body of Blake's vision: they altogether ignore the violence of Blake's opposition to the "Deism" of his day, just as they set aside his continual pleas for a radical transformation of the natural man, and ignore his total repudiation of all forms of moralism: "If Morality was Christianity, Socrates was the Saviour."[18] It is not Socrates or the Buddha or the artist or the common man who is the Saviour, but *only* Jesus; and only Jesus *is* God. Humanity is deified *in* Jesus, not Jesus in humanity. The real problem posed by Blake's vision of Jesus is the identity of the Saviour; for he is not simply the particular man, Jesus of Nazareth; nor is he the Jesus who is present in the cultus and the images of the Church; nor, for that matter, can Jesus the Saviour be equated with the Lamb of Innocence. No, the Jesus who "is" God can only be the Jesus of Experience, the Jesus who is actually and fully incarnate in every human hand and face. This is the Jesus who is most foreign to either the believer or the natural man; for this is the Jesus who resists every title, every name, and every notion by which the mind of man might weaken and ensnare him. We must remember Blake's rejection of the generalizing activities of the mind:

To Generalize is to be an Idiot. To particularize is the Alone Distinction of Merit. General Knowledges are those Knowledges that Idiots possess.[19]

The idiot of whom Blake speaks is the man who is asleep, the man who is the victim of an alien nature, whose acts are but conditioned reflections of an external law or history, and who has no individual identity because he is bound to a cosmic and historical fate.

Even if we grant that Blake was in quest of a "Universal Humanity" that is incarnate in Experience, why did he seize upon the name of Jesus? How can the particular name of Jesus symbolize the fullness of Humanity? Why employ the literal name of Jesus in a vision that promises to go beyond Christianity and point to the awakening of a cosmic Albion? The name of Albion can help us at this point: for Albion is an English name, its sound and letters embody a particular and actual historical tradition, and it is intended to awaken a latent and buried experience in its readers. The actual name of Jesus was just as sacred to Blake as it is to those Eastern practitioners of Hesychism who pronounce the name of Jesus as the path to salvation. And this is so because Jesus' name has an historical actuality for us that is matched by no other. True, such names as Krishna and Kali, and Amithabha and Avalokitesvara, have a comparable redemptive power to the bhakti Hindu and Buddhist; but bhakti religion, whether in its Christian or non-Christian form, has an inevitable tendency to dissociate the sacred name from the actualities of concrete experience. Blake passionately resisted this transformation of Experience into Innocence, and, while he could not always withstand the temptations of a traditional Christian imagery and iconography, he did so in his greatest visions (e.g., the human face of Jesus is not present in the designs of *Jerusalem*). No doubt the name of Jesus will disappear in the Apocalypse, and the spiritual Christian need have no reason to believe that it must be employed by the non-Christian; yet the reality underlying that name is the innermost reality of faith; it symbolizes the total union of God and man, and gives witness to a concrete reversal of history, and a dawning apocalyptic transformation of the cosmos. The very name of Jesus embodies the promise of these final things while simultaneously calling for a total identification with our neighbor. Truly, to pronounce his name is to give oneself to Jesus as he is manifest in the weak and broken ones about us, and as he is present in the darkness, the anonymity, and the chaos of a fallen history; for the repetition of the name of Jesus is a repetition of God's eternal death for man, a reliving of an ultimate cosmic reversal, a participation even now in the End which he has promised.

To the radical Christian the name of Jesus makes present once again the actuality of the death of God; through that name he participates in the concrete factuality of God's death, and knows that the bars of alienation and repression have finally been broken.

With the death of God every alien law and authority has been stripped of its foundation, the spaces separating man from man have been bridged, and the irreversibility of past moments of time has been annulled: for the God who eternally dies for man is the God who is kenotically incarnate in every Other; His dying dissolves that Other; and His free acceptance of His death in Jesus initiates the Apocalypse. Once God has died in Jesus, He is present only in Jesus' resurrected Body, and that Body is the eternal Body of a transfigured Humanity. No way to that Body is present in the memories and traditions of the Church; for the Church can only know the past and particular body of Jesus, the crucified body in the tomb, since the Lord of the Ascension has negated the human and living body of Jesus. The Body that is created by Jesus' passage into death—by the voluntary death of God *in* Jesus—is the Body of the incarnate God who has totally identified Himself with Experience. Jesus is the name of the totality of Experience, an experience that is born with the abolition of repression, and that is potentially present wherever there is life. To pronounce the name of Jesus is to pierce the darkness of a fallen condition and to give witness to the ultimately human reality of Experience. The Blake who declares that Jesus *is* God is the Blake who simultaneously envisioned the total fallenness of experience and the totally human and imaginative reality of Experience: and Jesus is the name of the God who has become totally incarnate in experience—even unto death—and His death has been consummated in the birth of a "Universal Humanity" and a "Human Imagination." Through Blake and every radical Christian seer, we may realize that, to know the full horror of experience, we must relive God's death in Jesus; but the God who is all in all in Jesus is present wherever there is death and darkness; and His death has transformed that darkness into light.

vi. States and the Individual

THE Blake who was so fully persuaded both as artist and seer that Vision appears in its "Minute Particulars" was hostile to every general law or moral principle that would claim to encompass, direct, and define the human individual, for: "General Forms have their vitality in Particulars, & every Particular is a Man, a Divine Member of the Divine Jesus" (J. 91:30 f.). Today we are confronted with the terrible irony of a Western civilization which can justly claim to have discovered the depths of the human person and to have honored at the cost of a great moral and political struggle the rights and liberties of the individual, but which has since produced the most demonic totalitarian regimes in history and has witnessed the human individual in its midst progressively dissolve in the direction of solitude, anonymity, and mass impersonal existence. As Blake wrote to a devoted friend four months before his death:

I know too well that a great majority of Englishmen are fond of The Indefinite which they Measure by Newton's Doctrine of the Fluxions of an Atom, A Thing that does not Exist. These are Politicians & think that Republican Art is Inimical to their Atom. For a Line or Lineament is not formed by Chance: a Line is a Line in its Minutest Subdivisions: Strait or Crooked It is Itself & Not Intermeasurable with or by any Thing Else. Such is Job, but since the French Revolution Englishmen are all Intermeasurable One by Another, Certainly a happy state of Agreement to which I for One do not Agree. God keep me from the Divinity of Yes & No too, The Yea Nay Creeping Jesus, from supposing Up & Down to be the same Thing as all Experimentalist must suppose.

Blake's poetry was transformed by his bitter disappointment that the French Revolution failed to usher in an age of universal liberty; no longer could he celebrate Los as the chief agent of political brotherhood, nor could he look upon history as a progressive if cyclical movement to justice and freedom. Blake like Newman, Kierkegaard, Dostoevski, and Nietzsche prophetically foresaw the darkness that was to fall upon the European quest for freedom and autonomy; and, like his prophetic compeers, he knew that the Western choice of an autonomous Selfhood could only be followed by the destruction of the individual. Yet, despite the fact that Blake abandoned his political prophecy—and it might be remarked that no prophet has succeeded in playing a pragmatic political role—his regeneration as an artist and seer led him to a vision of the "Minute Particular" that gives promise of saving the concrete individual from the self-destructive consequences of our history.

We might pause at this point and consider briefly the uniqueness of the Christian and Western vision of the human person. First, we might note that it is doubtful if a representative of a traditional Eastern culture could have written: "A Line is a Line in its Minutest Subdivisions." While it is true that Buddhist philosophy produced what is probably the most radically nominalistic logic in the world, the "point-instant" (*ksana*)—which that logic knows as the ultimately real event—is a transcendent pure existence or pure efficiency that is both non-empirical and unutterable.[20] The Eastern man of vision, moreover, refuses to speak of an interior life that is unique and individual, regarding a personal consciousness as the product of ignorance and illusion, and his very call for a life of compassion assumes the ultimate identity of all sentient creatures. Thus, the great Buddhist philosopher, Asanga, could describe the compassion of the Bodhisattva in these terms:

The world is not able to bear its own misery. How much less, then, can it endure the misery of the mass of others. The Bodhisattva is the opposite of this; he is able to bear the misery of the whole mass of living creatures, of all who are in the world. His tenderness towards creatures is the highest miracle in the universe; or rather no miracle at all, since he is identical with others, and creatures are like himself to him.[21]

Or, as Hubert Benoit, in the best Western book on Zen Buddhism, could remark while describing the attainment of *satori:* "In short, I am unconscious of that in which I am real, and that of which I am conscious in myself is illusory."[22] If all which we consciously know as the self is illusory, there obviously is no possibility in this Eastern orientation of affirming the ultimate reality of the individual person. Western Christendom alone among the great cultures of the world has evolved to an understanding of the human person as a unique and ultimately real entity; only in the modern West do we find a culture which has placed an absolute value upon the individual, and only in the Judeo-Christian-Islamic tradition do we find a total quest for the salvation of the "Minute Particular." Yet in choosing to make an absolute affirmation of the freedom and the autonomy of the individual, the West has wholly isolated the individual from both God and the cosmos, an isolation which has produced the most secular culture in history, resulted in an unparalleled form of society in which individuals are hopelessly alienated from one another, and created a unique interior experience revolving about a solitary subjectivity. All the power of the Western valuation of the individual would seem to rest upon the discovery of the autonomous person, but a wholly autonomous person must necessarily be isolated both from other persons and from nature and the sacred, and doomed to exist within a solitude that is its own creation.

We find no celebration of the conscious self or the autonomous person in Blake's vision, or at least no typically Western affirmation of the individual; in many respects, his fourfold vision of Albion is closer to Eastern than to Western psychology, and his free and almost spontaneous usage of mythical symbols testifies to the immense distance separating his visionary world from the dominant modes of Western thought and experience. Nevertheless, the whole body of Blake's work is saturated with an ecstatic joy in the life and experience of the individual. What Eastern poet or thinker could have known an Experience which is both contrary to Innocence and yet so rich and overwhelming in its concrete actuality? What other major poet in East or West has been so immersed in the political and social problems of his day, or so rebelliously dedicated to a quest for individual and actual freedom? And where else in Christendom can we find a prophet or seer who envisioned the resurrected Jesus as being wholly incarnate in the concrete individual? This revolutionary vision of the "Minute Particular," while still being a deeply Christian affirmation, is the product of an inversion of the Christian tradition; and it does much to illuminate a Christian vision of the individual that has been lost in the priestly and positivistic forms of modern Christian theology. At the end of *Milton*, there is a cryptic passage to the effect that: "the Starry Eight became One Man, Jesus the Saviour, wonderful!" (42:10). Not until the 55th plate of *Jerusalem* does the symbol of the "Starry Eight" appear again and there it is associated with the redemptive movement of God:

And they Elected Seven, call'd the Seven Eyes of God,
Lucifer, Molech, Elohim, Shaddai, Pahad, Jehovah, Jesus.
They nam'd the Eighth: he came not, he hid in Albion's Forests.
(31–33)

Frye believes that the Starry Eight is the eighth Eye of Jesus' second coming: "The latter is pure vision, as the former is the hearing of the Word, the lesser revelation to the ear (cf. Job xlii, 5) which also ceases at the upper limit of Beulah."[23] If so, the eighth Eye is the totally incarnate form of God in which God has become both fully present and wholly enclosed in the concrete individual; for as Wicksteed has interpreted the Shadowy Eighth: "He is beyond doubt the single individual, the Minute Particular, the YOU and ME and all other Definite and Determinate Identities of which reality is composed, and without which not Jesus himself, nor all the powers of Heaven, can effect a final Redemption."[24] However, we might more accurately say that Jesus (the seventh Eye) and all the powers of Heaven (the first six Eyes) are now present in the Shadowy Eighth and present *nowhere* else: the Incarnation is consummated in the total and final identification of God with the determinate identity of each human individual.

If the eighth Eye of God is now hidden in Albion's forests—buried in the "Minute Particulars"—there can be no question of the ultimate reality of an autonomous person who is wholly and simply human, just as there can be no possibility of a human communion with a distant and heavenly God. Furthermore, since the resurrected Jesus is the underlying and hidden reality of every person, the states in which that person appears—both to himself and to others—cannot be identified with the individual himself. In his manuscript notes, Blake says that the states a man passes through remain forever because everything is eternal; and then he goes on to say:

In Eternity one Thing never Changes into another Thing. Each Identity is Eternal. . . . Lot's Wife being Changed into a Pillar of Salt alludes

151

to the Mortal Body being render'd a Permanent Statue, but not Changed or Transformed into Another Identity while it retains its own Individuality. A Man can never become Ass nor Horse; some are born with shapes of Men, who may be both, but Eternal Identity is one thing & Corporeal Vegetation is another thing.

(V.L.J. p. 79)

When every minute particular is an "Eternal Identity," possessing an individuality that cannot be changed or transformed into another, then the particular state of the individual must be either a destructive and illusory mask or a concrete means of redemption. On the 35th plate of *Jerusalem,* as we have seen, there is a floating figure of Jesus, seen only from behind, showing the stigmata on his hands and feet. It illustrates the depths of Albion's tragic fall recorded in the text: "Albion hath enter'd the State Satan!"—necessitating the entrance of the Lamb of God into that state in order to redeem it; his mission being to make the state permanent so that individuals may thereby be enabled to pass through it.[25]

> "Albion goes to Eternal Death. In Me all Eternity
> Must Pass thro' condemnation and awake beyond the Grave.
>
> .   .   .   .
>
> Albion hath enter'd the State Satan! Be permanent, O State!
> And be thou for ever accursed! that Albion may arise again.
> And be thou created into a State! I go forth to Create
> States, to deliver Individuals evermore! Amen."
>
> (J. 35:9–16)

The eternal death which Albion reaches by falling to the state of Satan—the limit of opacity, a limit that like Adam (the limit of contraction) exists in every man—is a state of guilt and vengeance in which man is the enemy of man.

"But Vengeance is the destroyer of Grace & Repentance in the bosom
Of the Injurer, in which the Divine Lamb is cruelly slain.
Descend, O Lamb of God, & take away the imputation of Sin
By the Creation of States & the deliverance of Individuals Evermore.
     Amen."

(J. 25:10–13)

152

States are the fallen form of Albion, the products of guilt and repression, through which the individual passes on his way to Eternity: "But many doubted & despair'd & imputed Sin & Righteousness To Individuals & not to States, and these Slept in Ulro" (J. 25:15 f.).

The satanic and adamic limits of opacity and contraction are not the work of a cruel God; they are rather expressions of an inevitable movement from Innocence to Experience, a kenotic movement through the totality of fallenness to the final transfiguration of the Apocalypse. All of the moral and historical states through which humanity is destined to pass are therefore essential to this movement of redemption: "Because the Evil is Created into a State, that Men May be deliver'd time after time, evermore" (J. 49:70 f.). Once again we see how a radical vision of the Fall knows the depths of fallenness as an Experience terminating in redemption. If Innocence must become Experience, and if Innocence must pass away that a true and total Experience may be born, then that Experience must be the brute actuality of a history which has lost all its roots in the sacred, a history that is a wholly isolated and wholly autonomous mode of existence. On one of the most important plates of *Milton,* we read:

"Distinguish therefore States from Individuals in those States.
States Change, but Individual Identities never change nor cease.
You cannot go to Eternal Death in that which can never Die.
Satan & Adam are States Created into Twenty-seven Churches.
And thou, O Milton, art a State about to be Created,
Called Eternal Annihilation, that none but the Living shall
Dare to enter, & they shall enter triumphant over Death
And Hell & the Grave: States that are not, but ah! Seem to be."
(32:22–29)

While states remain permanent forever (J. 73:45), they are only temporary paths for the human traveler who is an "Individual Identity." That traveler is bound for an apocalyptic destiny, but such a destiny can be reached only through an "Eternal Death," a death that is not possible so long as the individual remains bound to a particular state or historical identity.

"Judge then of thy Own Self: thy Eternal Lineaments explore,
What is Eternal & what Changeable, & what Annihilable.

153

The Imagination is not a State: it is the Human Existence itself.
Affection or Love becomes a State when divided from Imagination.
The Memory is a State always, & the Reason is a State
Created to be Annihilated & a new Ratio Created.
Whatever can be Created can be Annihilated: Forms cannot:
The Oak is cut down by the Ax, the Lamb falls by the Knife,
But their Forms Eternal Exist For-ever. Amen. Hallelujah!"
(M. 32:30–38)

Finally, the states of the individual are created so that they may be annihilated. This process of "Eternal Annihilation" is the redemptive process of history; it becomes possible only through the creation of human states that are both real and "divided from Imagination"; and the annihilation of these states is the innermost goal of Experience.

This vision cannot be meaningful if the "Individual Identity" is understood to be eternal in a static sense. Such an identity cannot be an *Atman* underlying the conscious self: "You cannot go to Eternal Death in that which can never die." No, the "Starry Eight" or the eighth Eye of God—which is now solely manifest in the definite identity of each minute particular—is the totally fallen body of Albion. That body can only realize itself by annihilating all which it creates: but this process of self-annihilation creates the "Identity" that will be consummated in the Apocalypse. When history or Experience is known to be an ultimate process of self-annihilation, it assumes a redemptive reality that is present upon no other plane of faith, and the movement of redemption becomes inseparable from the movement of the Fall. Albion must die so that he may be resurrected in the minute particulars of Experience:

> For God himself enters Death's Door always with those that enter
> And lays down in the Grave with them, in Visions of Eternity,
> Till they awake & see Jesus . . .
> (M. 32:40–42)

The Jesus who is seen only after death is not the particular and historical Jesus of Nazareth, nor is he the lamb of Innocence or the cultic Christ of traditional faith: he is the God who only "Acts

& Is in existing beings or Men." Furthermore, this final Eye of God only appears and only exists in the self-annihilation of Experience. The individual who is created by this "Eternal Death" has passed through all the states of Experience, his "Individual Identity" is the product of the historical and fallen process of self-annihilation, and it is precisely the fact that he has passed through the historical states of Experience that gives his identity a unique and individual form. Consequently, the eighth Eye of God must be hidden in Albion's forests if it is to pass through the self-annihilation of Experience and be resurrected in the definite identities of the minute particulars of the universal body of Jesus.

IV

APOCALYPSE

1. America

ODD as it may seem to the mid-twentieth century American there was a time not long distant when many Europeans looked upon the new nation of America as the initial historical epiphany of a new heaven upon earth. William Blake was such a believer—or so he was at a crucial point in his work. *America* (1793) was his first fully symbolic prophetic poem; it is the first expression of a total vision that was to culminate in *Milton* and *Jerusalem* and the late illustrations, and it records his first full vision of the Christian God as Urizen. Blake had just written the *Visions of the Daughters of Albion*, a vision of the transition of Oothoon from Innocence to Experience, and Oothoon is identified as "the soft soul of America" (1:3). Moreover, in the second "Memorable Fancy" of *The Marriage of Heaven and Hell*, Ezekiel answers Blake's question as to why he ate dung and lay so long on his right and left sides by replying: "the desire of raising other men into a perception of the infinite: this the North American tribes practise...." In the "Preludium" to *America*, history itself is redefined by the American Revolution,[1] for Blake had come to believe that the American Revolution was the first sign of a dawning Last Judgment. Now the Golden Age of the primordial Beginning is returning in a new and final form. As Frye analyzes this theme:

In the Golden Age before the Fall, humanity or Albion dwelt at peace in its Paradise or Atlantis. The Fall produced a chaotic world and the central symbol of chaos is water. The Platonic story that Atlantis was overwhelmed by a flood gets the meaning of this clearer. The Atlantic Ocean, then, symbolizes the fallen world in Blake; he calls it the "Sea of Time and Space." The rise of a new civilization of English origin in America indicates the reintegrating of Atlantis, the disappearance of the Atlantic Ocean, and the return of the Golden Age. For the revolution does not stop with the political independence of America: it plunges on into the sources of tyranny in the human mind. The poem ends with a vision of the imagination bursting through the senses until the chaos of earth and water that we see begins to dissolve in fire.[2]

Certainly *America* is not a fully successful poem; Blake had not yet mastered the art of integrating historical and mythical symbols, but there can be little doubt that the poem testifies to the hope inspired in Blake by the American Revolution that the Apocalypse had finally dawned. When Damon says that in *America* Blake embarked upon a new and final step in his career as a symbolist by attempting to describe Eternity as it is symbolized by history,[3] we might more properly remark that *America* records a vision of an Eternity that is manifest solely upon the plane of time.

The hero of *America* is Orc, a symbolical figure embodying the primordial and now revolutionary fire of passion, a cosmic rebel who will later be transposed into the figure of Los. As the poem opens, morning comes, the night decays, the grave is burst, the bones of death awake, and the suddenly-released souls of enchained men sing:

> "The Sun has left his blackness & has found a fresher morning,
> And the fair Moon rejoices in the clear & cloudless night;
> For Empire is no more, and now the Lion & Wolf shall cease."
> (6:13–15)

Orc appears, and is greeted by the agents of tyranny as a blasphemous demon, Antichrist, lover of wild rebellion, and transgressor of God's Law.

> The Terror answer'd: "I am Orc, wreath'd round the accursed tree:
> The times are ended; shadows pass, the morning 'gins to break;
> The fiery joy, that Urizen perverted to ten commands,
> What night he led the starry hosts thro' the wide wilderness,
> That stony law I stamp to dust; and scatter religion abroad
> To the four winds as a torn book, & none shall gather the leaves;

But they shall rot on desart sands, & consume in bottomless deeps,
To make the desarts blossom, & the deeps shrink to their fountains,
And to renew the fiery joy, and burst the stony roof;
That pale religious letchery, seeking Virginity,
May find it in a harlot, and in course-clad honesty
The undefil'd, tho' ravish'd in her cradle night and morn;
For everything that lives is holy, life delights in life;
Because the soul of sweet delight can never be defil'd."

(8:1–14)

In this poem, Orc *is* America, for the true America is a resurrected passion that awakes to reverse the sleep of history and to annihilate the iron laws of repression. The red fires of America's rebellion rage with fury upon Albion's evil "angels," reducing tyranny's armies to a naked multitude, deforming the ancient heavens, opening the doors of marriage, and driving the priests into "reptile coverts" where they hide from the fires of Orc, thereby leaving the females naked and glowing with the "lusts of youth."

For the female spirits of the dead, pining in bonds of religion,
Run from their fetters reddening, & in long drawn arches sitting,
They feel the nerves of youth renew, and desires of ancient times
Over their pale limbs, as a vine when the tender grape appears.

(15:23–26)

If Orc and America are "ruddy"—red being the color of the fiery joy of passion and revolution—then Urizen now appears in a white and icy form as:

Over the hills, the vales, the cities, rage the red flames fierce:
The Heavens melted from north to south: and Urizen, who sat
Above all heavens, in thunders wrap'd, emerg'd his leprous head
From out his holy shrine, his tears in deluge piteous
Falling into the deep sublime; flag'd with grey-brow'd snows
And thunderous visages, his jealous wings wav'd over the deep;
Weeping in dismal howling woe, he dark descended, howling
Around the smitten bands, clothed in tears & trembling, shudd'ring cold.
His stored snows he poured forth, and his icy magazines
He open'd on the deep, and on the Atlantic sea white shiv'ring
Leprous his limbs, all over white, and hoary was his visage,
Weeping in dismal howlings before the stern Americans,

Hiding the Demon red with clouds & cold mists from the earth;
Till Angels & weak men twelve years should govern o'er the strong;
And then their end should come, when France reciev'd the Demon's light.

(16:1–15)

France, alas, will be darkened by the "Demon's light," and Blake
will come to abandon the political hopes instilled in him by the
American Revolution, but he will never abandon the symbolical figure
of America even if he will never again associate the historical birth
of America with an apocalyptic death of God.

Notice that the fires of Orc or America renew the fiery joy that
Urizen perverted to the Decalogue; this very renewal consumes all
laws and religion, resurrects the holy life of youthful "lust," and
melts the heavens that hide Urizen from earth. Only as a consequence
of this cosmic reversal does Urizen appear in his white and icy form;
weeping and trembling he descends to earth, and pours forth his
"stored snows" upon the sea of time and space. Blake directs his
apocalyptic imagery to a vision of the dissolution of that chaos which
is the seer's name for a fallen cosmos, and, fragmentary as that vision
is in this its initial form, it succeeds marvelously in unveiling the
polar union between the distant Urizen and an inverted world. But
the "Mystery" of Urizen is here revealed in the context of an
eschatological end; only through a final reversal of a fallen time and
space does Urizen lose His numinous and transcendent form and
return to a now liberated humanity in the naked condition of His
dying state. It must be confessed that the prophecy of *America* was
premature for a prophet who had yet to undergo his deepest encounter with Urizen or the Christian God. At this point Blake had
only taken his first real step in the direction of "naming" Satan, a
"naming" that would transform both Blake and his work. Nevertheless, Blake already sees that the death of God is an eschatological
event which cannot be dissociated from the triumphant dawning of
the Apocalypse. While America virtually disappeared from his vision
throughout Blake's Job-like wrestling with the Christian God, it
returns still bearing an apocalyptic identity in the final stages of his
work. Blake wrote the following note in prose in the margin of a
page of *The Four Zoas* devoted to Vala and Urizen: "Albion clos'd

the Western Gate, & shut America out by the Atlantic, for a curse, and hidden horror, and an altar of victims to Sin and Repentance" (III, 105). This note may well have been derived from *Jerusalem* where America is identified as the closed "Western Gate" of Albion (43:6, 45:3); it is hidden "for a Curse, an Altar of Victims & a Holy Place" (82:29); for the tribes of America must hide until "sweet Jerusalem emanates again into Eternity" (83:60). May we surmise that Blake refrained from employing the symbolic name of America in any vision that fell short of the totality of the new Eden? In any case, it is clear that the late Blake simultaneously associated America with a dark altar of suffering humanity and a place destined for a cosmic renewal by an apocalyptic Light.

Blake might well have rejoiced that destiny was soon to give the world its most awesome vision of the Christian God, and he certainly would have expressed no surprise if he could have known that an American artist and seer would create Moby Dick. If *Moby Dick* is the first symbolical novel, then Ahab must be acknowledged as the first hero of modern literature who fully plays a dual historical and mythological role. Ahab is at once an embodiment of the dark altar of America—he has made the full transition from Innocence to Experience, and his Innocence reappears in the novel in the form of Pip only to be driven mad by Ahab's God—and a hero who plays the Orcian role of striking through the mask of God. When Starbuck accuses Ahab of madness for seeking vengeance on a dumb beast, Ahab replies with the never-to-be-forgotten words:

"All visible objects, man, are but as pasteboard masks. But in each event —in the living act, the undoubted deed—there, some unknown but still reasoning thing puts forth the mouldings of its features from behind the unreasoning mask. If man will strike, strike through the mask! How can the prisoner reach outside except by thrusting through the wall? To me, the white whale is that wall, shoved near to me. Sometimes I think there's naught beyond. But 'tis enough. He tasks me; he heaps me; I see in him outrageous strength, with an inscrutable malice sinewing it. That inscrutable thing is chiefly what I hate; and be the white whale agent, or be the white whale principal, I will wreak that hate upon him. Talk not to me of blasphemy, man; I'd strike the sun if it insulted me. . . ." (Ch. 36)

Ahab's Promethean pride is directed to striking off all the fetters that bind a suffering humanity to an unknown fate, and he passionately seeks the destruction of the face behind the mask of Moby Dick, knowing full well that this very quest has made of him a "Curse" and an "Altar." Denying that he is mad, Ahab insists that he is demoniac: "I am madness maddened! That wild madness that's only calm to comprehend itself!" (Ch. 37). Ahab the "grand, ungodly, godlike man" (Captain Peleg's words in Ch. 16) must surely have been Melville's personification of the tragic destiny of America; but the America who is Ahab destroys itself in its hatred of evil.

The White Whale swam before him as the monomaniac incarnation of all those malicious agencies which some deep men feel eating in them, till they are left living on with half a heart and half a lung. That intangible malignity which had been from the beginning; . . . Ahab did not worship it . . . but deliriously transferring its idea to the abhored White Whale, he pitted himself, all mutilated, against it. All that most maddens and torments; all that stirs up the lees of things; all truth with malice in it; all that cracks the sinews and cakes the brain; all the subtle demonisms of life and thought; all evil, to crazy Ahab, were visibly personified, and made practically assailable in Moby Dick. He piled upon the whale's white hump the sum of all the general rage and hate felt by his whole race from Adam down; and then, as if his chest had been a mortar, he burst his hot heart's shell upon it. (Ch. 41)

Melville's Moby Dick is a strange yet compelling counterpoint to Blake's Urizen. For Blake was incapable of a tragic vision; his comprehensive vision of fallenness, while unique in the world's literature, is never dissociated from both the possibility and the reality of regeneration; and the Urizen who is transposed into Satan, although a grand and overwhelming figure, never embodies the profound ambivalence of a Moby Dick. True, the God-Satan of the Job illustrations stands alone in Western art as a portrait of the full paradoxical union of the demonic and the sacred—perhaps its grander rival is the Jehovah of Blake's master, Michelangelo, but a theological analysis of Michelangelo's work has yet to be written —nevertheless, the very "exuberance" of Blake's prophetic poetry forecloses the possibility of concretely envisioning a light that is wholly light and darkness at once. When Urizen falls weeping from heaven at the end of *America,* he reveals his white and icy form and pours his snows on the "deep": but this is an apocalyptic act of cataclysmic destruction; the whiteness of Urizen is the death shroud of the now naked Creator. Moby Dick's whiteness is not only the color of sacred purity and the Holy Spirit but also of the cosmic evil which lies behind and beneath the creation: "yet for all these accumulated associations, with whatever is sweet, and honorable, and sublime, there yet lurks an elusive something in the innermost idea of this hue, which strikes more of panic to the soul than that redness which affrights in blood" (Ch. 42). The whiteness that is "the very veil of the Christian's Deity" is simultaneously the most powerful symbol of the Spirit and the "intensifying agent" in things the most appalling to mankind.

Is it that by its indefiniteness it shadows forth the heartless voids and immensities of the universe, and thus stabs us from behind with the thought of annihilation, when beholding the white depths of the milky way? Or is it, that as in essence whiteness is not so much a color as the visible absence of color, and at the same time the concrete of all colors; is it for these reasons that there is such a dumb blankness, full of meaning, in a wide landscape of snows—a colorless, all-color of atheism from which we shrink? And when we consider that . . . . all other earthly hues . . . . are but subtle deceits, not actually inherent in substances, but only laid on from without; so that all deified Nature absolutely paints like the harlot, whose allurements cover nothing but the charnel-house within; and when we proceed further, and consider that the mystical cosmetic which produces every one of her hues, the great principle of light, for ever remains white or colorless in itself, and if operating without medium upon matter, would touch all objects, even tulips and roses, with its own blank tinge—pondering all this the palsied universe lies before us as a leper . . . . (Ch. 42)

Ahab's fiery hunt unveils the whiteness of the whale, and through his monomaniac quest we know that: "Though in many of its aspects this visible world seems formed in love, the invisible spheres were formed in fright" (Ch. 42).

Can we accept Ahab as a personification of the eschatological destiny of America? *Moby Dick* has no apocalyptic imagery, and significantly enough it is a novel with neither a resolution nor a conclusion, yet its mythical center is set in the context of modern Western realism, and its nihilistic evocation of a faceless but cosmic evil makes the primordial chaos incarnate in the God who is present upon our horizon. Ahab, who has been burned and scarred by a sacramental worship of the God of fire, knows that "right worship is defiance."

"I own thy speechless, placeless power; but to the last gasp of my earth-quake life will dispute its unconditional, unintegral mastery in me. In the midst of the personified impersonal, a personality stands here. Though but a point at best; whencesoe'ver I came, whereso'ever I go; yet while I earthly live, the queenly personality lives in me, and feels her royal rights. But war is pain, and hate is woe. Come in thy lowest form of love, and I will kneel and kiss thee; but at thy highest, come as mere supernal power; and though thou launchest navies of full-freighted worlds, there's that in here that still remains indifferent. Oh, thou clear spirit, of thy fire thou mades me, and like a true child of fire, I breathe it back to thee" (Ch. 119).

Like America, Ahab has no history, except insofar as he has been burned by the chaos of history; by standing in the midst of "the personified impersonal" he anticipates a later destiny of America; and, although madness maddened, he greets the dawning apocalyptic "Mystery" of God with the true worship of defiance. As a tragic hero, Ahab has no "choice," he must seek out and kill Moby Dick —whether he succeeds or not is, of course, another matter. His tragic conflict with the white whale brings upon himself the death that he would inflict upon the whale, and by dying while lashed upon the whale's back he plunges into the sea of chaos and is swallowed up by the sepulcher of Moby Dick. Ahab himself freely accepts the death of the white God and passes into the chaos into which the God of our history has vanished. While *Moby Dick* fails to culminate in an apocalypse, if we incorporate this most prophetic of American novels into the world of Blake's vision we must be prepared to see that an America which can become the murderer of God will enact the initial victory of the Apocalypse. Blake believed that Europe was hopelessly bound to a history that is past, and, to the true European, America must appear as a desert, and a desert shorn of the vegetation of history. But a desert can also be a gateway to the future; ascetic virtues can arise from the nausea and the *ennui* of life in the desert, and a new ascetic may arise whose very weakness will give him the strength to say no to history. William Blake was such an ascetic, and if our destiny is truly one of chaos, or if we must pass through chaos to reach our destiny, then we must follow Blake in wholly abandoning the cosmos of the past, and pass with him through the agony and the triumph of the death of God.

II. Dialectic and Apocalypse

WILLIAM Blake is the only poet ever to have created an apocalypse or a fully apocalyptic form of art, and, when we reflect that the original message of Jesus was an eschatological proclamation of the dawning of the Kingdom of God, that the patristic Church transformed this message by a dissolution and elimination of its apocalyptic ground, that ever since, the dogmatic and ritual foundations of the orthodox Church have been non-apocalyptic, and that it has been only in the non-verbal arts that Christendom has produced an apocalyptic imagery, then on this ground alone we would be fully justified in pronouncing Blake to be a revolutionary artist and seer. To understand the theological significance of this fact, we must first draw together those points at which Blake is a unique Christian visionary. There are at least ten such points within the horizon of this study: (1) Blake alone among Christian artists has created a whole mythology; (2) he was the first to discover the final loss of paradise, the first to acknowledge that Innocence has been wholly swallowed up by Experience; (3) no other Christian artist or seer has so fully directed his vision to history and experience; (4) to this day his is the only Christian vision that has openly or consistently accepted a totally fallen time and space as the paradoxical presence of Eternity; (5) he stands alone among Christians in identifying the actual passion of sex as the most immediate epiphany of either a demonic or a redemptive "Energy," just as he is the only Christian visionary who has envisioned the universal role of the female as both a redemptive and a destructive power; (6) his is the only Christian vision of the total kenotic movement of God or the Godhead; (7) he was the first Christian "atheist," the first to unveil God as Satan; (8) he is the most Christocentric of Christian seers and artists; (9) only Blake has created a Christian vision of the full identity of Jesus with the individual human being (the "minute particular"); and (10) as the sole creator of a post-biblical Christian apocalypse, he has given Christendom its only vision of a total cosmic reversal of history. Each one of these points is integrally related to the foundations of Blake's apocalyptic work, and, although this study cannot hope to set forth the full theological ground of Blake's apocalypse, we must search for whatever light may be at hand.

We must proceed with caution in attempting to enter the center of the strange new world of Blake's vision; indeed, if possible, we should adopt the dialectical rule of disabusing ourselves of every idea or image that we must initially bring to his text. Let us therefore follow a circuitous path to our goal, and begin by examining the core of Northrop Frye's *Anatomy of Criticism*. This book is surely the most important comprehensive theory or "science" (Frye's own term) of literature to be produced in our generation; it was written after Frye's great study of Blake, and it is largely grounded in a Blakean mode of vision. Although Frye says that no importance is to be attached to the schematic form of this book, he insists upon the necessity of a systematic study of literature, and divides his own study in accordance with his theory of the four modes of literary criticism (historical, ethical, archetypal, and rhetorical). For our purpose, the center of Frye's study is what he terms "ethical" criticism or the theory of symbols, where he classifies literary symbols according to what he believes are their three phases: (1) formal, the symbol as image, (2) mythical, the symbol as archetype, and (3) anagogic, the symbol as monad. These phases are intended to correspond to the phases of literature itself, thus the anagogic phase is the culmination of literature: "In the greatest moments of Dante and Shakespeare, in, say *The Tempest* or the climax of the *Purga-*

torio, we have a feeling of converging significance, the feeling that here we are close to seeing what our whole literary experience has been about, the feeling that we have moved into the still center of the order of words."[4]

In the anagogic phase, literature imitates the total dream of man, and so imitates the thought of a human mind which is at the circumference and not at the center of its reality. We see here the completion of the imaginative revolution begun when we passed from the descriptive to the formal phase of symbolism. There, the imitation of nature shifted from a reflection of external nature to a formal organization of which nature was the content. But in the formal phase the poem is still contained by nature, and in the archetypal phase the whole of poetry is still contained within the limits of the natural, or plausible. When we pass into anagogy, nature becomes, not the container, but the thing contained, and the archetypal universal symbols, the city, the garden, the quest, the marriage, are no longer the desirable forms that man constructs inside nature, but are themselves the forms of nature. Nature is now inside the mind of an infinite man who builds his cities out of the Milky Way. This is not reality, but it is the conceivable or imaginative limit of desire, which is infinite, eternal, and hence apocalyptic. By an apocalypse I mean primarily the imaginative conception of the whole of nature as the content of an infinite and eternal living body which, if not human, is closer to being human than to being inaninate. "The desire of man being infinite," said Blake, "the possession is infinite and himself infinite."[5]

Frye freely confesses that the form of literature most deeply influenced by the anagogic phase is the "scripture" or apocalyptic revelation. However, the anagogic perspective may be found in any poem, for any genuine literary work may be read as microcosm of all literature: "Anagogically, then, the symbol is a monad, all symbols being united in a single infinite and eternal verbal symbol which is, as *dianoia* [the meaning of a work of literature], the Logos, and, as *mythos* [the narrative of a work of literature], total creative act."[6] Consequently, all poetry proceeds as though all poetic images were contained within a single universal body.

Frye believes that the Bible is a "definitive myth" having a single archetypal structure extending from creation to apocalypse, and that the Book of Revelation is the grammar of Western apocalyptic imagery. Actually, he reads the Bible through Blake, and, when he says that the Book of Revelation has been carefully designed to form an undisplaced mythical conclusion for the Bible as a whole, he might more accurately say, as he does in his book on Blake,[7] that *Jerusalem* is a re-creation of the Bible—yet it is a re-creation directed to inverting the literal and symbolical meaning of the Bible itself. Moreover, Frye's whole theory of the anagogic phase of literature is obviously derived from Blake, and he has great difficulty in citing concrete examples of anagogic literature which conform to his description. If we accept his definition of an apocalypse, then surely the *Purgatorio* and *The Tempest* can be judged to be apocalyptic works in only a very limited sense, for certainly neither Dante nor Shakespeare envisioned nature as the content of "an infinite and eternal living body." The body to which Frye refers is Blake's Albion, for Albion is the first literary symbol in the West of a cosmic totality which is human and natural at once, and Albion's movement embodies the kenotic fall and epiphany of the God who "only Acts & Is, in existing beings or Men." From our point of view, the great virtue of Frye's *Anatomy of Criticism* is its demonstration of the illumination that can be brought to the whole body of Western literature by Blake's apocalypse, and, when Frye says that the "point of epiphany" is the symbolic presentation of the point at which the undisplaced apocalyptic world and the cyclical world of nature come into alignment,[8] we might be tempted to say that Blake's work is the point at which the Western cycle of history is first unveiled.

What does Frye mean when he says that in anagogy nature becomes not the container but the thing contained? This language sounds suspiciously like that of Mahayana Buddhist philosophy, and when Frye remarks that in the apocalyptic world of total metaphor everything is potentially identical with everything else, as though it were all inside a single infinite body,[9] our suspicions must be deepened. These formulations of the meaning of anagogy and apocalypse abandon an eschatological form; they lose that definitive and absolute end which is the center of both scriptural and Blakean apocalyptic, and fall back upon the language of Indian mysticism, as Frye does in his book on Blake when he asserts that apocalyptic imagery depicts the world as disappearing because it is unreal[10] (Frye has actually said that Blake has the same conception of identity as the Buddhist[11]). Nevertheless, Frye's analysis of the poetic apocalypse is as close as our time has come to the meaning of Blake's apocalypse, and we must continue to bear it in mind as we press along our way.

Certainly Blake's vision is directed to effecting a coincidence of the opposites, a drawing together of all or most of those antinomies which our history has established, and at this point we must draw upon the work of the most effective dialectical thinker of recent years, Herbert Marcuse, whose latest book is the first dialectical assault upon the political reality of our totalitarian era. *One-Dimensional Man* carries forward the central motif of Marcuse's work, dialectical negation, an idea or method or movement of thought derived from Hegel; and this study is primarily directed to an attack upon the idea of reason in the modern West, an idea embodying an ideological transmutation of an originally free and dialectical reason into the logic of domination.

". . . that which is cannot be true." To our well-trained ears and eyes, this statement is flippant and ridiculous, or as outrageous as that other statement which seems to say the opposite: "what is real is rational." And yet, in the tradition of Western thought, both reveal, in provocatively abridged formulation, the idea of Reason which has guided its logic. Moreover, both express the same concept, namely, the antagonistic structure of reality, and of thought trying to understand reality. The world of immediate experience—the world in which we find ourselves living—must be comprehended, transformed, even subverted in order to become that which it really is.[12]

This dialectical equation of reason, truth, and reality joins the subjective and the objective worlds into one antagonistic unity: here, reason is the subversive power, the "power of the negative" that establishes the conditions in which men and things become what they really are.

Marcuse believes that Western thought and logic first came into existence as a mode of thought appropriate for comprehending the real as rational. Grounding itself in the assumption that men and things immediately exist as other than what they truly are, Western logic began by opposing its truth to that of the given reality. Consequently, thought assumes a subversive character; it opposes its truth to that which immediately or apparently is, and therefore contradicts the "given" reality. This subversive or negative character of truth inflicts upon thought an *imperative* quality: "Logic centers on judgements which are, as demonstrative propositions, imperatives —the predicative 'is' implies an 'ought.' "

This contradictory, two-dimensional style of thought is the inner form not only of dialectical logic, but of all philosophy which comes to grip with reality. The propositions which define reality affirm as true something that is *not* (immediately) the case; thus they contradict that which is the case, and they deny its truth.[13]

Yet today we are confronted with a whole mode of thought which accepts the given; our new "scientific" and "objective" thought does not contain in itself a judgment that condemns an established reality.

In contrast, dialectical thought is and remains unscientific to the extent to which it *is* such judgement, and the judgement is imposed upon dialectical thought by the nature of its *object*—its objectivity. This object is the reality in its true concreteness; dialectical logic precludes all abstraction which leaves the concrete content alone and behind, uncomprehended. . . . Dialectical logic cannot be formal because it is determined by the real, which is concrete.[14]

Dialectical logic understands contradiction as belonging by necessity to the very nature of thought because "contradiction belongs to the very nature of the *object* of thought, to reality, where Reason is still Unreason, and the irrational still the rational."[15]

While Marcuse ignores the whole tradition of Indian thought and logic, which at so many points is apparently identical with the dialectical logic of the West, his emphasis upon the necessity of dialectical logic's comprehending its world as an *historical* universe and thereby understanding how the established facts are the work of the historical practice of man, clearly sets his conception of dialectical thinking apart from its Indian counterpart. Western dialectical thought only attains its truth if it has freed itself from the "deceptive objectivity" which conceals the historical factors behind the established facts.

When historical content enters into the dialectical concept and determines methodologically its development and function, dialectical thought attains the concreteness which links the structure of thought to that of reality. Logical truth becomes historical truth. The ontological tension between essence and appearance, between "is" and "ought" becomes historical tension, and the "inner negativity" of the object-world is understood as the work of the historical subject—man in his struggle with nature and society. Reason becomes historical Reason.[16]

When "Reason" becomes historical reason, it loses its formal and ideological character, and directs itself to unveiling the reality behind and beyond the immediately given. Classical Marxism demonstrates all too clearly how a dialectical and historical reason can disclose the reality lying behind the established "facts"; but, liberating as Marx's vision has been, it remains a partial—and let it be said a demonically partial—vision. None of Hegel's disciples has even approached Blake's cosmic vision of history (nor did Hegel himself: if we were to judge his lectures on the philosophy of history by the dialectical criteria set forth in his *Logic* and *Phenomenology,* we could only judge the late Hegel to be a bad disciple). Furthermore, Hegelianism has thus far been successful only in its dialectical probing of the present and the past; it has yet to envision a non-utopian and non-ideological future. True, the Hegelian knows that "history" is the negation of "nature,"[17] but this—perhaps the most fundamental of all negations—has never occurred in the dialectical systems, and thus these systems have never been able to rise to a vision of an apocalyptic end or reversal of history.

What can it mean when so penetrating a scholar as Karl Löwith can identify Hegel's thought as an "eschatological system," asserting that its ultimate basis lies in Hegel's absolute evaluation of Christianity, according to which the eschatological end and fullness occurred with the Incarnation?[18]

If Hegel causes the eternal to be manifest in the temporal, this is not the result of any formal dialectics, but an intrinsic metaphysics of the Christian logos. In fact . . . his philosophy includes within itself the Christian consciousness of the "end of all things," because Hegel does all his thinking conscious of the absolute significance of the historical appearance of Christ.[19]

We might rather say that the history of the "idea" comes to an eschatological end with Hegel's system because his system unveils the absolute "idea" as the kenotic epiphany of the Christ who is both the beginning and the consummation of the history of Spirit. Lying at the heart of Hegel's system is a transposition of an apocalyptic end of time into a dialectical movement of pure negativity or absolute negation. Thus, time itself is the necessary vehicle of the Concept or Notion (*Begriff*), as Hegel says at the end of *The Phenomenology of Spirit*:

Time is just the Notion definitely existent, and presented to consciousness in the form of empty intuition. Hence Spirit necessarily appears in time, and it appears in time so long as it does not grasp its pure Notion, i.e., so long as it does not annul time. Time is the pure self in external form, apprehended in intuition, and not grasped and understood by the self, it is the Notion apprehended only through intuition. When this Notion grasps itself, it supersedes its time character, (conceptually) comprehends intuition, and is intuition comprehended and comprehending.[20]

If it were not for the fact that Spirit "necessarily" appears in time, his system could not be distinguished from those abstract forms of Brahmanic pantheism which Hegel so fiercely attacked; and, while time is Spirit's destiny and necessity only when Spirit is not yet complete within itself, it is only in time that Spirit becomes self-conscious and certain of itself.

There can be no doubt that for Hegel, history is both the way to and the way of the Christ whom he knew as Absolute Spirit; hence in the famous sentence which closes the *Phenomenology* he could say that the dialectical comprehension of history is: "at once the recollection and the Golgotha of Absolute Spirit, the reality, the truth, the certainty of its throne, without which it were lifeless, solitary, and alone." We have already seen that Hegel understands Spirit as a kenotic process of absolute negativity: Spirit empties or externalizes itself and becomes incarnate in its own Other. In the *Phenomenology*, each mode of consciousness passes over into a higher mode by abolishing itself, and thus its goal is its own negation. These modes of consciousness become abstract forms of the Notion in the *Science of Logic*, where the activity of the Notion is wholly negative: "it is negative as against itself, restraining itself in face of the given and making itself passive, so that the given may be able to show itself as it is in itself and not as determined by the subject."[21] Only by means of such negative passivity on the part of the Notion, can the "given" become or be a forward-moving process. Yet, paradoxically, the given is the "other" of the Notion, and Hegel calls the "*dialectic* moment" that act by which the original universal determines itself out of itself to be its own Other.[22] Gradually, Hegel's *Logic* reveals the dialectical method as the Notion which in knowing itself creates the objective and subjective forms of the Absolute.

Accordingly, what must now be considered as method is no more than the movement of the Notion itself, whose nature has already been understood. This meaning, however, is now added, that the Notion is everything and that its movement is the universal and absolute activity, the self-determining and self-realizing movement. Hence the method must be recognized to be universal without restriction, to be a mode both internal and external, and the force which is utterably infinite. . . .[23]

Indeed, the Notion is All: like Brahman-Atman, the Notion is both the knower and the known, both the knowing subject and the object known, and its process of knowing or revealing itself is the underlying reality of the cosmos. Nevertheless, and unlike all forms of Indian pantheism, the Notion is truly real in both its objective and subjective forms: the negation by which it becomes its own Other and the process of absolute negativity by which it realizes itself in nature and history are absolutely real, so real, indeed, that apart from these processes of negation, the divine Notion would be "lifeless, solitary, and alone."

But if the Notion would be lifeless and solitary apart from the processes of its self-negation, how can Hegel maintain that Spirit appears in time only so long as it does not comprehend itself? What does it mean to imply so strongly that when the Notion or Spirit fully knows itself it will annul the reality of time? What is the meaning of a Spirit that has totally negated itself and reached full self-consciousness? Does this final or ultimate form of Spirit transcend the process of self-negation? When we recall that Hegel's is a dialectical method in which the finite and the infinite, time and Eternity, and the given and the Absolute all reciprocally determine each other—for, dialectically, every concept is a union of its opposite moments—then, must the dialectical process itself be judged to be an incomplete form of Spirit that has not yet arrived at full self-certainty? Is the kenotic process of absolute negativity simply a lower or descending movement of Spirit? If not, how can there be a total and eschatological fulfillment of the absolute activity of the Notion? These profound ambiguities lie at the very center of Hegel's system; so far from agreeing with Löwith that Hegel's is an "eschatological system," we might well wonder whether his system is even capable of being given an eschatological or theological form. No apocalyptic vision is present here; yet it cannot be denied that Hegel's whole dialectical understanding of the process of negation has profoundly and perhaps truly captured the previously uncomprehended power of apocalyptic faith. If Hegel was the last Christian philosopher, he was also, as John Findlay insists,[24] the most Christian of thinkers, for no other thinker has created a whole system of thinking whose innermost movement is the kenotic process of self-negation. No doubt Blake, like Kierkegaard, would have condemned a thinker whose very method makes impossible the act of faith or vision. But just as Kierkegaard employed Hegel's dialectical method to establish the existential reality of faith, we must employ that method as a mode of entry into the mystery of Blake's apocalyptic vision.

Hegel concludes his *Logic* by speaking of the "absolute liberation" which is effected by the divine Notion. Has Hegel transformed an apocalyptic form of faith into a conceptual expression of a dialectical movement of absolute negativity which is the true identity of his Notion? Now that modern New Testament scholarship has fully established that Jesus' ethical message was grounded in an eschatological proclamation of the dawning of the Kingdom of God, and hence of the advent of an apocalyptic end of the world, can it be that Hegel's understanding of dialectical negation is an authentic appropriation of an original act of faith that engages in an absolute reversal of the world? We must take up these questions by asking whether Blake's apocalyptic vision is an eschatological form of faith revolving about a dialectical movement of negation. Already in *The Marriage of Heaven and Hell,* immediately after having declared that a new heaven is begun, Blake set forth a dialectical ground of his vision which he never abandoned: "Without Contraries is no progression. Attraction and Repulsion, Reason and Energy, Love and Hate, are necessary to Human existence." An immediate consequence of this choice of a dialectical mode of vision is a rejection of all dualism and an attack upon those dualistic dichotomies that have plagued the life of Western history (body and soul, reason and energy, good and evil). Not until *Milton* and *Jerusalem* was Blake able to create a full vision on the basis of this initial discovery, but in these works he moved into a totally dialectical mode of creation and vision. First, let us take note of the actual categories which Blake employed when he attempted to set forth the meaning of his apocalyptic vision. Written at the top of the 30th plate of *Milton,* in reversed writing, we find these words: "Contraries are positive. A Negation is not a Contrary." Not until the closing lines of *Milton* does a passage occur which explicitly illuminates these cryptic words: here, the regenerate Milton is speaking:

> "All that can be annihilated must be annihilated
> That the Children of Jerusalem may be saved from slavery.
> There is a Negation, & there is a Contrary:
> The Negation must be destroy'd to redeem the Contraries.
> The Negation is the Spectre, the Reasoning Power in Man:
> This is a false Body, an Incrustation over my Immortal
> Spirit, a Selfhood which must be put off & annihilated alway.
> To cleanse the Face of my Spirit by Self-examination,
>
> To bathe in the Waters of Life, to wash off the Not Human,
> I come in Self-annihilation & the grandeur of Inspiration,

DIALECTIC AND APOCALYPSE

To cast off Rational Demonstration by Faith in the Saviour,
To cast off the rotten rags of Memory by Inspiration. . . ."
(40:30–41:4)

All too clearly we see that the "Contraries" can be redeemed only by the destruction of the "Negation," that this destruction seems to be equivalent to the process of "Self-annihilation," and that the "Negation" in turn is equivalent to the Spectre (the false "Body" of ratio and memory). But none of these terms takes on any real meaning apart from the total body of Blake's vision.

Our task at this point must be to grasp the dialectical movement of Blake's apocalypse, to see how the "Contraries" pass into one another by destroying the "Negation." This movement is openly present in its full form only in *Jerusalem* and the illustrations to the Book of Job; but first we must note the primary vision that establishes the ground for the necessity of a dialectical movement: "Man is born a Spectre or Satan & is altogether an Evil, & requires a New Selfhood continually, & must continually be changed into his direct Contrary" (J. 52:9). This affirmation seems to be very close to Paul's understanding of original sin, and perhaps it is, but it is not to be confused with the orthodox Christian doctrine of sin if only because that doctrine is non-dialectical; it refuses to envision the New Adam as the "direct Contrary" to man's sinful state, and this is so because it is bound to a moral and non-apocalyptic conception of sin. The New Selfhood to which Blake refers is both an historical and a cosmic reality, and it comes into being only by a reversal of that Spectre or Satan which is man's given or immediate existence; but the Spectre comprehends the totality of a fallen cosmos. Perhaps the most puzzling aspect of Blake's dialectical statements is the role that he assigns the "Reasoning Power": not only is it universal in its role and scope, but it also seems to be the very incarnate body of Satan. Thus we discover this vision of the Fall in the first part of *Jerusalem:*

And this is the manner of the Sons of Albion in their strength:
They take the Two Contraries which are call'd Qualities, with which
Every Substance is clothed: they name them Good & Evil;

175

From them they make an Abstract, which is a Negation
Not only of the Substance from which it is derived,
A murderer of its own Body, but also a murderer
Of every Divine Member: it is the Reasoning Power,
An Abstract objecting power that Negatives every thing.
This is the Spectre of Man, the Holy Reasoning Power,
And in its Holiness is closed the Abomination of Desolation.

(10:7–16)

According to these statements, reason arises as an abstract negation
of a primordial energy; it dualistically isolates the two original
contraries of every member of the Divine Body, and thereby it
murders or "Negatives" every living thing, and encloses the Antichrist in its own "Holiness." Surely this mode of understanding
parallels Hegel's conception of the objective Absolute or Being-in-
itself, that form of Spirit in which Spirit or the Notion is its own
Other, and which embodies that Given which must be annulled and
transcended by the dialectical movement of Spirit. Blake frequently
says that in Beulah contraries are equally true (M. 30:1, J. 48:14),
and we must conclude that life and movement arise in Albion when
the contraries are torn asunder by the Fall. However, it is an abstract
and non-dialectical reason or ratio (Hegel's *Verstand*) that first eats
the fruit from the tree of the knowledge of good and evil—indeed,
that eating creates "good" and "evil"—and consequently reason is
the Satan whose destructive negativity isolates the contraries from
one another.

Quite naturally the symbolic embodiment of abstract reason in
Blake's mythology is Urizen ("your reason"), but the Spectre is the
creature of this numinous and transcendent Creator, and, after the
Spectre has come into existence through the Fall, it enacts the role
of Job and condemns the God of righteousness Who has no compassion:

"O that I could cease to be! Despair! I am Despair,
Created to be the great example of horror & agony; also my
Prayer is vain. I called for compassion: compassion mock'd;
Mercy & pity threw the grave stone over me, & with lead
And iron bound it over me for ever. Life lives on my

Consuming, & the Almighty hath made me his Contrary
To be all evil, all reversed & for ever dead: knowing
And seeing life, yet living not; how can I then behold
And not tremble? how can I be beheld & not abhorr'd?"
(J. 10:51–59)

Dialectically, of course, Urizen and the Spectre are two poles of one reality; but this very coupling of abstract reason with the Christian God reveals the comprehensive and cosmic role of reason. If reason is a cosmic power, its very advent creates the cosmos that we know, a cosmos in which man is alienated from both God and nature, existing as "a little grovelling Root outside of Himself" (J. 17:32). It is this inhuman existence "outside of Himself" that is the product of an abstract and destructive negation, despite the fact that such acts of negation have no real or intrinsic existence.

"Negations are not Contraries: Contraries mutually Exist;
But Negations Exist Not. Exception & Objections & Unbeliefs
Exist not, nor shall they ever be Organized for ever & ever.
If thou separate from me, thou art a Negation, a meer
Reasoning & Derogation from me, an Objecting & cruel Spite
And Malice & Envy; . . . . never! shalt thou be Organized
But as a distorted & reversed Reflexion in the Darkness
And in the Non Entity: nor shall that which is above
Ever descend into thee, but thou shalt be a Non Entity for ever. . . ."
(J. 17:33–44)

Negations do not and cannot exist in the true sense because they can only assume a solitary and isolated form—as epitomized by Urizen Himself; enclosed in their own darkness and separated from the holy energy of life, they are Ulro-powers, lifeless but brutal abstracts that exist as voids between the fragments of life and energy which they separate. As reversed fragments of light, the negations comprise a Hell or Ulro that is an inversion of an apocalyptic Eden:

From every-one of the Four Regions of Human Majesty
There is an Outside spread Without & an Outside spread Within,
Beyond the Outline of Identity both ways, which meet in One,
An orbed Void of doubt, despair, hunger & thirst & sorrow.
(J. 18:1–4)

177

In this "Outside" spread within and without, the Satanic "Wheels" turn upon one another into non-entity, and, murdering their own souls, they build a kingdom of the dead.

When the transfigured Milton declares that he has come to wash off the "Not Human," he is speaking of the fallen cosmos created by the negations, and this cosmos is unreal because it is inhuman. Simply by naming the inhuman, by unveiling the darkness of our Ulro-world, Blake created the most comprehensive and overwhelming vision of the Fall in literature, and discovered the reality—or, more precisely, the unreality!—of fallenness in every sphere in which the unregenerate man dares speak of life and light. Yet his very vision of the Fall is finally inseparable from his vision of Apocalypse: to know the fallen reality of the negations is to know the possibility of their apocalyptic reversal, to know the kingdom of death as a humanity turned inside out is to envision the hope of the resurrection of the dead, to know an inhuman cosmos and a solitary God as products of the Fall is to unveil an Apocalypse that will reverse the negations and redeem the now separated contraries. Do we have any choice but to acknowledge that Blake's vision of the destruction of the "Negation" is the first imaginative re-creation of an apocalyptic faith in the end of the world? Like the sacred apocalypses, both Jewish and Christian, Blake's apocalypse celebrates the dark terrors of a totally fallen world as signs of the advent of the end; his vision, too, calls for a total reversal of the Old Aeon of history. But, unlike its antecedents, his apocalypse transforms darkness into light, its symbolic re-creation of the apocalyptic drama draws all the separated contraries into a new unity; no longer do the contraries exist in dualistic opposition, for now man's infinite senses expand and behold the All as one: "As One Man all the Universal Family, and that One Man we call Jesus the Christ" (J. 38:19). If a comprehensive vision of the Fall unveils the universality and totality of fallenness, then a comprehensive vision of Apocalypse must discover an inversion and reversal of the Fall that obliterates every void separating the fallen life of the contraries. The dialectical movement of Blake's Apocalypse is surely a reversal of the Fall, a reversal that initially proceeds by unveiling the negations; this unveiling inevitably envisions a new and final rejoining of the contraries, an eschatological *coincidentia op-positorum*, culminating in a vision of the absolute and definitive end of that Satan who is the cosmos of nothingness separating "The Eternal Great Humanity Divine" from its union with itself. Blake's apocalyptic vision of the destruction of the "Negation" must then be judged to be an imaginative antecedent of Hegel's dialectical under-standing of the negation of negation: both simultaneously reveal and negate a history created by an abstract and destructive negation, both proceed by establishing the contraries in their true opposition and then move to a dialectical coincidence of the opposites, and, as we shall see, Blake's "Self-annihilation" fully parallels Hegel's abso-lute negativity in that both reveal that every opposite creates itself as its own Other, and can only be united with that Other by negating itself.

III. Mysticism and Eschatology

THROUGHOUT this study we have frequently had occasion to ob-serve that many of Blake's most scholarly interpreters maintain that Blake's mature work is a modern Western expression of a universal mystical vision, and, whether they have found the closest parallels to his prophetic poetry to lie in Western mysticism and Gnosticism or Oriental philosophy, they are agreed that Blake's vision is neither uniquely his own nor uniquely Christian. Bernard Blackstone, who has written the clearest and perhaps the most responsible book on Blake, while noting that from the Western point of view, Indian philosophy is static and passive, insists that Blake's conception of energy as the last significance of things both anticipates contemporary Western science and establishes the first vital link between the cul-tures of East and West: "His supreme achievement on the practical plane is the *energizing* of Oriental wisdom so as to make it accessible to the Western mind."[25] In his analysis of Blake's vision of nature, Blackstone quotes Blake's famous words from his second letter to the Rev. Dr. Trusler—"To the Eyes of the Man of Imagination,

Nature is Imagination itself"—and joins Frye by saying that this conception of the ultimate identity of all things exactly corresponds with the Mahayana Buddhist identification of *nirvana* and *samsara*.[26] Now that it is increasingly becoming apparent that Blake's vision both transcends and inverts the Western mystical tradition, we are confronted with the challenge that the true analogue to his vision lies in the world of Oriental mysticism, although no historical argument to this effect has yet been published. Blake himself could not possibly have had any knowledge of Buddhist philosophy, but that fact is irrelevant to the thesis at hand, for unquestionably the later expressions of Buddhist mysticism, with their nihilistic ontological ground and their profoundly ethical thrust, lie closer to Blake's vision than any other mystical systems of the Orient. Furthermore, no other mystical way has carried "Self-negation" so far as Buddhism, and, as we have previously noted, there is a clear parallel between the Buddhist path of self-dissolution and the apocalyptic form of Blake's vision.

Before approaching the problem of Blake's relation to Buddhism, it is necessary to speak briefly about the Mahayana Buddhist category of *sunya*, which in one way or another is the mystical ground of all the later forms of Buddhism. At about the time of the beginning of the Christian era, the Madhyamika school of Mahayana Buddhism arose with its proclamation of the ultimate oneness of reality, its denial that causal, conceptual, or differentiated thought can grasp the real, and its paradoxical identification of *nirvana* (the radical sacred) and *samsara* (the radical profane). Lying at the foundation of this school is a revolutionary teaching to the effect that the mystical Reality known in contemplation is of such a nature as to demand that the reality known in cognitive thought and conscious experience be judged to be an absolute Nothing or Void (*sunya*). Yet to the Madhyamika Buddhist, the voidness of "reality" (*samsara*) is simply the hither side of ultimate Reality (*nirvana*) itself; when known through consciousness and craving (*tanha*), reality appears as *samsara;* but, when known through mystical intuition (*prajna*) and self-giving compassion (*karuna*), reality appears as *nirvana*. Th. Stcherbatsky's *The Conception of Buddhist Nirvana*—which along with T. R. V. Murti's *The Central Conception of Buddhism* is one of the two most enlightening books on the Madhyamika school—describes the meaning of *sunya* as follows:

In Mahayana all parts or elements are unreal (*sunya*), and only the whole, i.e., the Whole of the wholes, is real. The definition of reality (*tattva*) in Mahayana is the following one: "uncognizable from without, quiescent, undifferentiated in words, unrealizable in concepts, non-plural—this is the essence of reality.". . . Since we use the term "relative" to describe the fact that a thing can be identified only by mentioning its relations to something else, and becomes meaningless without these relations, implying at the same time that the thing in question is unreal, we safely, for want of a better solution, can translate the word *sunya* by relative or contingent, and the term *sunyata* by relativity or contingency. . . . That the term *sunya* is in Mahayana a synonym of dependent existence and means not something void, but something "devoid" of independent reality, with the implication that nothing short of the whole possesses independent reality, and with the further implication that the whole forbids every formulation by concept or speech, since they can only bifurcate reality and never directly seize it—this is attested by an overwhelming mass of evidence in all the Mahayana literature.[27]

While the heart of Mahayana Buddhism is a new form of negative contemplation that discovers a Real that is the negation of all positive reals (including *nirvana* and *samsara* as presumed "existing" realities), it is accompanied by a new form of dialectical "thinking" that is directed to the dissolution of the cognitive or conceptual process itself. Not until this negative dialectic has destroyed all the categories of thought is it possible to make a positive dialectical affirmation of the ultimately Real. Thus there is a negative and a positive pole of the Madhyamika dialectic, and the two must be held in even balance, for the intuitive vision of the seer is impossible apart from the continuous negation of the thought world of the mind.

Most Buddhist philosophers resist the idea that the Madhyamika is a nihilistic philosophy, and it is not so in the popular Western sense, but the *sunyata* that it proclaims as the sole Reality must inevitably appear to the Western mind in the form of a mystical Void. Although the Mahayana Buddhist knows this Absolute as both the norm and the identity of all things whatsoever, it possesses no attributes of its own, and can appear only by means of the disappearance of the phenomena and the experience created by our knowing minds and our grasping wills. Silence is the only appropriate language for *sunyata*, for it is open neither to thought nor experience. Moreover, it is precisely this negative spirit of the Madhyamika that made possible a wholly new form of transcendence and immanence. As Murti interprets Nagarjuna, the great founder of the Madhyamika school:

> The transcendence of the absolute [*nirvana*] must not be understood to mean that it is an other that lies outside the world of phenomena [*samsara*]. There are not two sets of the real. The Absolute [*nirvana*] is the *reality* of the apparent; it is their real nature. Conversely, phenomena [*samsara*] are the veiled form or false appearance of the Absolute [*nirvana*]. . . . The absolute is the only real; it is identical with the phenomena. The difference between the two is epistemic—subjective and not real. In full accordance with this, Nagarjuna declares that there is not the least difference between the Absolute and the universe: "The Universe [*samsara*] viewed as a whole is the Absolute [*nirvana*], viewed as a process it is the phenomenal [*samsara*]—having regard to causes and conditions (constituting all phenomena; we call this world) . . . This same world, when causes and conditions are disregarded, i.e. the world as whole (*sub specie aeternitatis*), is called the Absolute."[28]

Unlike all forms of Brahmanic idealism, the Madhyamika repudiates every suggestion of the "isness" of the Absolute—Hegel appropriately speaks of the soulless word "is"[29]—and celebrates *sunyata* as an emptiness embracing the totality of the All. However, if this emptiness is all, it is a totality with neither motion nor energy, without process or direction, and with neither a beginning nor an end. Consequently, *sunyata* can undergo neither fall nor redemption; thus Murti says:

> There has been no initial fall, and there is no need for retransformation. *Nirvana*, says Nagarjuna, is non-ceasing, unachieved. There is only the dissolution of false views, but no becoming in the real. The Absolute has always been of one uniform nature (*tathata*). In the last resort, the consciousness of achievement too is subjective.[30]

The Madhyamika dialectic is ultimately directed to the dissolution of a false or illusory selfhood; it accompanies a self-giving compassion and a mystical contemplation of the Nothing, and it can in no way affect *sunyata*. Finally, its dialectic itself is unreal: it simply makes possible the unveiling of a total quiescence, the epiphany of an emptiness that is all in all.

We must rejoice that Blake had no knowledge of Buddhism and no real acquaintance with any kind of Oriental philosophy. For the sheer, naked, religious power of Oriental mysticism is simply unrivaled in the West. No Western expression of faith has either the subtlety or the depth of the great Indian mystical systems, nor the spontaneity and grace of their Far Eastern counterparts, and the Western seer who opens himself to the East must be prepared either for paralysis or for transformation. Yet our glance at the East should in no way uproot our confidence in the uniqueness of Blake's vision; it should rather prepare us for a fuller assessment of the theological meaning of his apocalypse. Allowing Madhyamika Buddhism to stand as a representative example of the higher forms of Oriental mysticism, we find these salient characteristics of the Oriental vision: (1) an absolute negation of both the internal and the external reality that is present in thought, consciousness, experience, and sensation; (2) a consequent and total affirmation of the oneness or the identity of all things whatsoever, leading to (3) an interior realization in a total and cosmic experience—or in a complete dissolution of individual experience—of an absolutely quiescent Totality. No Western mystic has gone so far in any of these directions, for Western mysticism, whether in its Jewish or Christian expressions, is closed to a vision of absolute quiescence.

Rudolf Otto, who has written the one distinguished study of mysticism in East and West, a comparison of Meister Eckhart with Sankara, the most influential master of the Hindu Vedanta, has discovered the uniqueness of Western mysticism to lie in its vision of the eternal "life-process" of the Godhead. Believing that Eckhart's God becomes a mystical God because He is a stream of "glowing vitality," Otto finds that the eternal repose of Eckhart's Godhead has a different meaning from that of the resting *Sat* or *Brahman* in India:

It is both the principle and the conclusion of a mighty inward *movement*, of an eternal process of ever-flowing life. "A wheel rolling out of itself," "a stream flowing into itself": these are metaphors which would be quite impossible for the One of Sankara. The Deity of Eckhart is *causa sui*, but this not in the merely exclusive sense, that every foreign *causa* is shut out, but in the most positive sense of a ceaseless self-production of Himself.[31]

While for Sankara it can only be through a great cosmic ignorance that God and the world can be known as moving and existing out of the depths of Brahman-Atman, Eckhart's God is in Himself a living *process*, not a static Being, who moves forward out of the Godhead:

God is the wheel rolling out of itself, which, rolling on, not rolling back, reaches its first position again. That it rolls from inward, outward and inward again is of deep significance. God is, in Himself, tremendous life movement. Out of undifferentiated unity He enters into the multiplicity of personal life and persons, in whom the world and therewith the multiplicity of the world is contained. Out of this He returns, back into the eternal original unity. "The river flows into itself." But it is not an error to be corrected in Him, that He is eternally going out from and entering "into" Himself; it is a fact that has meaning and value—as the expression of life manifesting its potentiality and fullness. The issuing forth becomes itself the goal again of that process enriched by the course of its circuit.[32]

Therefore, Eckhart's is a dynamic, as opposed to a static, mysticism; it celebrates the living process of God as a manifestation of ultimate Reality, and consequently it culminates in an active ethical life that engages in a positive confrontation with the world. But the ground of this deeply Christian form of mysticism is an eschatological vision of the final manifestation of God as the end and goal of an eternal cosmic process—and Otto quotes these words from Eckhart to substantiate his point:

Indeed, God Himself does not rest there where He is merely the first beginning of being. Rather: He rests there where He is the end and goal of all being. Not that being comes to nought there; rather it becomes perfected there to its highest perfection.[33]

Throughout history the circle has been the primary symbol of eternity in both East and West, and it should not surprise us that it was reborn in Nietzsche's vision of Eternal Recurrence, just as it had previously come to occupy the center of the "systems" of Blake and Hegel. When Albion contracts his infinite senses, he beholds multitude, or, expanding, he beholds as one: "As One Man all the Universal Family, and that One Man we call Jesus the Christ" (J. 38:17 ff.). And this cosmic movement of Albion is an expression of a forward if circular movement of Eternity:

> What is Above is Within, for every-thing in Eternity is translucent:
> The Circumference is Within, Without is formed the Selfish Center,
> And the Circumference still expands going forward to Eternity . . .
> (J. 71:6–8)

These cryptic words are illuminated by comparing them with their analogue in Hegel. In the preface to the *Phenomenology*—the best précis of his system Hegel ever wrote—and, in the context of saying that everything depends upon grasping the ultimate truth not only as substance but as subject as well, Hegel speaks from the very heart of his dialectical system:

> The living substance, further, is that being which is truly subject, or, what is the same thing, is truly realized and actual (*wirklich*) solely in the process of positing itself, or in mediating with its own self its transitions from one state or position to the opposite. As subject it is pure and simple negativity, and just on that account a process of splitting up what is simple and undifferentiated, a process of duplicating and setting factors in opposition, which [process] in turn is the negation of this indifferent diversity and of the opposition of factors it entails. True reality is merely this process of reinstating self-identity, of reflecting into its own self in and from its other, and is not an original and primal unity as such, not an immediate unity as such. It is the process of its own becoming, the circle which presupposes its end as its purpose, and has its end for its beginning; it becomes concrete and actual only by being carried out, and by the end it involves.[34]

Hegel even goes so far as to adopt the seemingly Indian idea that the life of the Godhead is love disporting with itself; but this is a

185

Christian vision of the Godhead, for Hegel insists that the life of the Godhead must never be dissociated from "the seriousness, the suffering, the patience, and the labor of the negative." Apart from the negative, and the process of self-negation, the Godhead would be neither realized nor actual, and hence would not *be*. Whereas in the *Phenomenology* this circular and negative process is the self-evolution of Spirit in consciousness, in the *Science of Logic* Spirit is transposed into the abstract Notion, but the form of its movement remains exactly the same:

. . . Absolute Spirit, which is found to be the concrete, last, and highest truth of all Being, at the end of its evolution freely passes beyond itself and lapses into the shape of an immediate Being; it resolves itself to the creation of a world which contains everything included in the evolution preceding that result; all of which, by reason of this inverted position, is changed, together with its beginning, into something dependent on the result, for the result is the principle. What is essential for the Science is not so much that a pure immediate is the beginning, but that itself in its totality forms a cycle returning upon itself, wherein the first is also last, and the last first.[35]

It certainly is not accidental that Hegel was able to absorb these eschatological words of Jesus into his own system, although he has transformed their original apocalyptic meaning into a dialectical movement that moves only by inverting itself. Nevertheless, this dialectical movement is a Christian process of self-negation, a self-negation that moves by continually ceasing to be itself, and therefore a kenotic self-negation that evolves by eternally becoming its own Other.

Seen in this perspective, the distinctive motif of Christian mysticism is its celebration of the Godhead as a living process, a process that moves *forward* to Eternity, and therefore authentic Christian mysticism retains an eschatological religious ground because it knows a final Reality whose end transcends its beginning. Christian mysticism must know the Godhead as a living and forward-moving process if only because a vision of ultimate Reality as absolute quiescence forecloses the possibility of the final reality of the essential being and the decisive acts of Jesus Christ. Yet at this point we have done no more than make an initial movement in the direction of understanding the uniqueness of the Christian faith, and, rather than turning to those innumerable theologians who have discovered the distinctiveness of Christianity to lie in its exaltation of those profane realities that have progressively immersed the Christian world in a sea of darkness, let us seek guidance from a theologian who was also an historian of religions, Archbishop Nathan Söderblom. Quite naturally, Söderblom entitled his Gifford lectures, *The Living God,* and these lectures remain one of the few competent comparisons of the prophetic faith of the Bible with the higher religions of the world. Finding the most striking feature of Old Testament faith to be its belief in the "activity" of God, Söderblom sets forth these five distinctive characteristics of biblical prophetic religion: (1) communion with God in Israel is expressed entirely in ethical action rather than in mystical states; (2) God appears as an omnipotent but gracious Will; (3) God demands love rather than sacrifice; (4) history is now brought into the sphere of religion, and thus the duration of time becomes invested with a hitherto unsuspected religious significance; and (5) prophetic religion in Israel is a founded religion and not a culture-religion.[36] He then goes on to speak of Christianity and asserts that: "The first and last originality and uniqueness of Christianity consists in this, that unique and absolute truth has in Christianity the form not of a rule, a law, Dharma, nor of ideas or theologies; Christian revelation has the form of a *man.*"[37] Consequently, the uniqueness of Christianity derives from the uniqueness of Christ, whose Incarnation and Atonement must be known as decisive and historical events.

Men had been seeking for God. The cross is the strongest testimony that *God has been seeking man.* God's way is as non-human as possible. But it is no mere idea; it is an historic fact which has proved to be stronger than any other fact or conception in Religion.[38]

However, if Christian revelation has the form of a man, it can scarcely give witness to a non-human God. Rather we must follow Blake and come to see that a Christian vision which unveils God as a man must culminate in an apocalyptic vision of "The Great Humanity Divine."

Writing before the impact upon religious scholarship of the historical discovery of the original eschatological form of the proclamation of Jesus, Söderblom inevitably failed to direct his attention to Christianity as an apocalyptic faith. Rudolf Otto is the only historian of religions who has critically examined the eschatological ground of Christianity, and it must first be noted that Otto believes that the hidden mainspring of eschatology is "the idea that righteousness is not possible in an earthly form of existence but only in the wholly other form of existence that God will give, not possible in this age but only in a new age."[39] This accords well with Otto's belief that the holy is an utterly supramundane value, and requires for its realization a supramundane existence[40]—thus, genuine eschatology invariably envisions a new creation, a new and final Kingdom of God which is coming in the immediate future. While the prophetic oracles of the Old Testament are grounded in an expectation of the immediate coming of a final judgment or renewal, these oracles fail to move from a prophetic to a fully eschatological form insofar as they proclaim an End or Eschaton that is only a promise and not yet a present reality. Not until the ministry of Jesus did a fully eschatological form of faith appear in Israel, and Otto maintains that the proclamation which was entirely unique and peculiar to Jesus was "that the kingdom—supramundane, future, and belonging to a new era—penetrated from the future into the present, from its place in the beyond into this order, and was operative redemptively as a divine power, as an inbreaking realm of salvation."[41] The message of Jesus confronts his hearer with the mystery of a Kingdom that is future and yet already dawning: the salvation of the new age is visible to him who can see the mystery of the Kingdom as already present. God's Kingdom is present, but not yet present in power: it is not yet disclosed or revealed; it is only latent, a hidden reality that still awaits its manifestation.[42] Whether the hidden reality of the Kingdom has yet become manifest Otto fails to say, but he demonstrates all too convincingly that Jesus' original teaching that the Kingdom is already "dawning" first fell into the background of early Christianity and then disappeared from the historic Church.

With the disappearance of the original form of Jesus' message, Christianity itself soon ceased to be an apocalyptic form of faith and became the first higher religion to embark upon a path of world-affirmation. The historical course of this process of transformation and its ultimate consequences have yet to be unravelled, but in abandoning its eschatological form Christianity was forced into a non-dialectical path. Now it could greet the world either with abject submission or with Gnostic defiance; or the Church could become Christendom and thereby attempt to Christianize the world. Unfortunately, the world triumphed over the Church, or seemingly so, and, while the Church now exists only as a flickering reflection or receding echo of its ancient self, the world created by modern Western history has triumphed with such power as to transform the very light of the gospel into darkness. We can pierce that darkness only by recovering some sense of the original power of Jesus' message, a message revolving about an eschatological proclamation of the dawning of the Kingdom of God, and therefore a triumphant message celebrating the dawning victory of a New Aeon that even now is destroying the powers of darkness. Jesus proclaimed a God who is dawning here and now in the reality of His Kingdom: He is not a distant or transcendent God, but rather a God whose presence is annulling or reversing the old order of history, and bringing to an end the very reality of the world. By opening himself to the immediate reality of Jesus' Word, his hearer could be led into a repentance that shatters the claims and the values of "Selfhood," thus making possible a participation even now in the eschatological work of God's Kingdom, a "work" that must finally culminate in God's Kingdom becoming all in all. Only in the transfiguring and apocalyptic power of the Kingdom of God does Israel's prophetic faith in the "activity" of God reach its consummation, but a true apocalyptic consummation must annihilate every distance separating man from God, and ultimately bring to an end the very reality of the "Satanic Wheels" of history and the cosmos.

When we examine what little we know of Christianity's original faith and proclamation with the intention of ascertaining its presumed uniqueness, particularly when we do so with the purpose of relating the inner faith of Christianity with the higher expressions of Oriental mysticism, we must first react with dismay and fore-

boding at the striking similarities presented by the religious worlds
of mysticism and eschatology. Of course, both are "higher" expressions of religion, and this means, among other things, that both
transcend their mythical and traditional roots, interiorizing the
archaic forms of religion, and thus abolishing any way to the sacred
that is truly susceptible to cultic, legal, or dogmatic expression. But
beyond this we discover that an eschatological faith shares with the
purer forms of contemplation a path of world- or self-reversal: both
must suspend or dissolve all awareness of or participation in the
profane reality of the world, just as both must dissolve or reverse
all individual selfhood, leading to an abrogation of the "reality"
of the world. True, the mystical way leads to an inner realization
of the ultimate voidness of history and the cosmos; while eschatological faith participates in an apocalyptic transfiguration of reality
that must culminate in the "end" of the world. Yet both are directed
to the total dissolution of the being of the world, the one by unveiling its intrinsic nothingness, and the other by engaging in an ultimate
transformation of its forms and structures. Consequently, both share
a dialectical movement of absolute negation: neither can reach its
goal apart from a total shattering or dissolution of selfhood, history,
and the cosmos. This negation is dialectical because it does not simply
annihilate all profane reality but rather negates it in such a way as
to lead to a total reversal of the apparent or the given existence of
an external cosmos and an autonomous selfhood. Therefore, this
negation leads inevitably to an immediate and total participation in
ultimate Reality, whether *nirvana* or Kingdom of God, and expresses
itself in an ethical life of self-dissolution or self-negation. Indeed,
by comparing eschatological faith with its counterpart in Oriental
mysticism, we can discover the dialectical ground of Christianity's
original proclamation, a ground that disappeared from the historic
form of the Church.

Fundamentally, the purer expressions of mysticism effect an interior dissolution of all that experience which has accrued to man
in the course of his history, abolishing both his autonomous selfhood
and his attachment to all exterior reality, leading simultaneously
to a total identification with and an immediate participation in an
all-encompassing ultimate Reality. Oriental mysticism, particularly

in its Indian forms, knows this Reality as an absolute quiescence, although this quiescence is a cosmic Totality. Moreover, this Totality is a primordial Reality; it is both the underlying identity of all reality and the original form of the cosmos. Therefore, the way of Oriental mysticism is a way *backward* to the primordial Beginning, and, while this Totality comprehends and in fact unifies all those antinomies that have evolved in the course of the history or the movement of the cosmos, it remains an eternal and unmoving Totality which at bottom has never ceased to be itself. It could even be said that Oriental mysticism must identify movement as the source of the "fall"; only through the advent of motion, process, and energy does the cosmos assume a fallen form, despite the fact that neither movement nor the "fall" can be judged to be ultimately real. Now it is precisely at this point that we must acknowledge the existence of a seemingly unbridgeable gulf between the worlds of Oriental mysticism and biblical eschatology. Eschatological faith is the expression of an immediate participation in the Kingdom of God, but that Kingdom is a dynamic epiphany of a Godhead in process of realizing itself; far from existing as a static and timeless Totality, here the Godhead appears and is real only insofar as it is an active process of negating the fallen form of history and the cosmos. A faith which celebrates the "dawning" of the Kingdom of God cannot know the God who alone is God, just as it cannot know an inactive and quiescent Godhead, for the God whom it proclaims is present solely in His Kingdom, and that Kingdom is a forward-moving process effecting an absolute transformation of the world. Consequently, the way of eschatological faith is a way *forward* to an ultimate and final Eschaton, that Eschaton is a once-and-for-all decisive events; it will happen only once, and its occurrence will be both a fulfillment of the total movement of the Godhead, and a realization of that final paradise which must wholly transcend the paradise of the Beginning.

At last we are in a position to ascertain the meaning both of an apocalyptic faith and of an apocalypse which embodies that faith in a concrete expression. Such a faith revolves about a response to the advent of the Eschaton: it must be a total response to reflect the all-encompassing finality of the Eschaton, for it knows God's final acts as being already present, and these acts are present solely in a dynamic and forward-moving process that even now is reversing the totality of history and the cosmos, and therefore effecting an absolute transformation of a Totality that is both human and divine. Only by abandoning its original faith in the dawning Kingdom of God which is in process of realizing itself could Christianity arrive at its belief in the transcendent and solitary God who is the Wholly Other. When the reality of God is eschatologically identified with His dawning Kingdom, then God can only be known as an active and apocalyptic process that even now is becoming all in all. Apocalyptic faith is the inevitable expression of an immediate and total participation in the dawning Kingdom; it must reflect a cosmic reversal that is bringing an "end" to the world, and thus it must give witness to a forward-moving process that is transforming the foundations of the cosmos. An authentic witness to the meaning of this process—and we can say nothing here of a life which would embody it—must incorporate a vision of a world that is ceasing to be itself, of a Godhead that is kenotically becoming its own Other, and of a transfigured humanity that is passing into the final paradise. This is precisely the function of an apocalypse. Accordingly, an apocalypse is an imaginative disclosure of a universal and kenotic process that moves through an absolute and total negation to reach the epiphany of a divine and human Totality that thereby becomes all in all.

IV.   Self-annihilation

IF OUR voyage through the world of Blake's vision has enabled us to recover something of the meaning of an apocalyptic faith, then not only should we be open to Jesus' eschatological proclamation, but we should also be in a position to understand the genuine distinctiveness of Christianity. Allowing Blake's apocalyptic vision to stand witness to an authentic Christian faith, there are at least seven points from within this perspective at which we can discern the uniqueness of

Christianity: (1) a realization of the centrality of the Fall and of
the totality of fallenness throughout the cosmos; (2) but the Fall
is not simply a negative or finally illusory reality, for it is a process
or movement that is absolutely real, yet is paradoxically identical
with the process of redemption; and this is so because (3) faith,
in its Christian expression, must finally know the cosmos as a
kenotic and historical process of the Godhead becoming incarnate
in the concrete contingency of time and space; (4) insofar as this
kenotic process becomes consummated in death, Christianity must
celebrate death as the path to regeneration; (5) so likewise the
ultimate salvation that will be effected by the triumph of the Kingdom of God can take place only through a final cosmic reversal;
(6) nevertheless, the future Eschaton that is promised by Christianity is not a repetition of the Beginning, but is a new and final
paradise in which God will have become all in all; and (7) faith,
in this apocalyptic sense, knows that God's Kingdom is already
dawning, that it is present in the words and person of Jesus, and
that only Jesus is the "Universal Humanity," the full coming together of God and man. Now if we were further to accept Hegel's
dialectical language as a philosophical translation of apocalyptic
faith, we could also see that a process of absolute negativity underlies the Christian proclamation, a kenotic process of Spirit's becoming
its own Other. This process is absolutely negative because here
negativity negates itself—"the negation of negation"—and to participate in this process is to pass through "Self-annihilation" and
become one with that Jesus whose proclamation reflects the inaugura-
tion of the Kingdom of God.

Apocalyptic imagery is essential to the original Christian proclamation if only because its message is a celebration of the dawning of
God's Kingdom: only in the Eschaton is God now manifest and real,
but the "new" reality of the Eschaton is inseparable from the end
which it is bringing to the "old" reality of the world. When the
faith of the Church abandoned an eschatological ground, it separated
God and the world, banishing God to a transcendent realm, and
affirming the world as God's creation only to the extent that it dissociated its reality from the transfiguring power of God's eschato-

logical acts. Orthodox Christianity from that time to the present
has proclaimed an individual redemption that takes place without
affecting the reality of the world; but radical Christianity refuses a
redemption which is confined to individual selfhood, and seeks an
apocalyptic transformation of the world. Blake's prophetic poetry
inevitably culminates in an apocalyptic vision: this is true of the
ninth night of *The Four Zoas,* the second book of *Milton,* and the
last part of *Jerusalem;* and Blake alone among Christian poets
dares to employ an apocalyptic imagery to depict the advent of
judgment and salvation.

Then fell the fires of Eternity with loud & shrill
Sound of Loud Trumpet thundering along from heaven to heaven
A might sound articulate: "Awake, ye dead, & come
To Judgment from the four winds! Awake & Come away!"
Folding like scrolls of the Enormous volume of Heaven & Earth,
With thunderous noise & dreadful shakings, rocking to & fro,
The heavens are shaken & the Earth removed from its place,
The foundations of the Eternal hills discover'd:
The thrones of Kings are shaken, they have lost their robes & crowns,
The poor smite their oppressors, they awake up to the harvest,
The naked warriors rush together down to the sea shore
Trembling before the multitudes of slaves now set at liberty:
They are become like wintry flocks, like forests strip'd of leaves:
The oppressed pursue like the wind; there is no room for escape.

(F.Z. IX, 10–23)

While a disciple of Jesus might have looked upon these lines as a
spontaneous expression of faith, a Christian who is bound to the
eternal reality of history and the cosmos must be dismayed at their
literal employment of biblical language, and react with condescen-
sion or rejection to a cosmic vision of the Eschaton. Yet it is precisely the totality of the apocalyptic vision which makes possible its
expression of a universal process of redemption.

Deeply embedded within the apocalyptic vision is the post-exilic,
prophetic hope in a coming cosmic reversal—cf. Isaiah 40:3–5, a
passage so dear to the early Church that it is repeated in one form
or another in the opening sections of all four of the Gospels—and,

when Blake writes of the explosion of the "bursting Universe," he says: "All things revers'd flew from their centers" (F.Z. IX, 231). These words are followed by a description of the coming resurrection and judgment of the dead, and, after the flames of judgment have rolled on, the "Cloud" of the Son of Man appears, descending from Jerusalem with power and glory.

The Cloud is Blood, dazling upon the heavens, & in the cloud,
Above upon its volumes, is beheld a throne & a pavement
Of precious stones surrounded by twenty-four venerable patriarchs,
And these again surrounded by four Wonders of the Almighty,
Incomprehensible, pervading all, amidst & round about,
Fourfold, each in the other reflected; they are named Life's—in Eternity—
Four Starry Universes going forward from Eternity to Eternity.
And the Fall'n Man who was arisen upon the Rock of Ages
Beheld the Vision of God, & he arose up from the Rock,
And Urizen arose up with him, walking thro' the flames
To meet the Lord coming to Judgment; but the flames repell'd them
Still to the Rock; in vain they strove to Enter the Consummation
Together, for the Redeem'd Man could not enter the Consummation.
(F.Z. IX, 278–290)

Once again Blake tries but fails in this epic to bring together an artificial mythology of the four Zoas—a mythology that he later in effect discarded—with the symbols of the Christian revelation; but he does succeed in dialectically inverting the imagery of the Book of Revelation by directing it to a seemingly anti-Christian theme. Thus when the Christian God and the redeemed Christian attempt to approach the apocalyptic Jesus they are repelled by the flames of judgment; and this occurs because they cannot enter the Kingdom of God "together." Just prior to this passage, Urizen had come under judgment and wept in the "deep dark" at his inability to reassume a human form, and then repented that He had ever looked into "futurity."

"Then Go, O dark futurity! I will cast thee forth from these
Heavens of my brain, nor will I look upon futurity more.
I cast futurity away, & turn my back upon that void
Which I have made; for lo! futurity is in this moment."
(180–183)

195

The word "futurity" is doubly significant in these lines, for it replaces the word "remembrance" which was used in the first version of the poem and is indicative of the regenerate Blake's faith in the presence of the new Jerusalem. Nevertheless, the figure of Urizen remains a static one as He continues to embody His own primordial "Error." For He continues to view the infinite and unbounded while His eyes are situated in the heavens (225 ff.), and therefore He cannot know that "futurity" is in the present moment.

Only after Urizen has ceased to be Himself by passing through an apocalyptic judgment, a cosmic judgment annihilating all that distance lying between a fallen man and a solitary God, can He enter the consummation of the Kingdom. Blake's symbol of this ultimate judgment is the "wine presses" of Luvah, whose action effects a Dionysian reversal of history and the cosmos, abolishes the "Mystery" of God and religion, and leads the "Human Grapes" through an eternal death.

> But in the Wine presses is wailing, terror & despair.
> Forsaken of their Elements they vanish & are no more,
> No more but a desire of Being, a distracted, ravening desire,
> Desiring like the hungry worm & like the gaping grave.
> They plunge into the Elements; and the Elements cast them forth
> Or else consume their shadowy semblance. Yet they, obstinate
> Tho' pained to distraction, cry, "O let us Exist! for
> This dreadful Non Existence is worse than pains of Eternal Birth:
> Eternal death who can Endure? let us consume in fires,
> In waters stifling, or in air corroding, or in earth shut up.
> The Pangs of Eternal birth are better than the Pangs of Eternal
>   death."
>   (F.Z. IX, 732–742)

An apocalyptic consummation is reached only by means of a passage through eternal death. But an eternal death is both universal and absolute: it brings to a definitive and final end the cosmic history created by the eternal Man's contracting senses, and ushers in a new Eden that abolishes all those spaces separating an external nature, an autonomous selfhood, and a transcendent God.

The Sun has left his blackness & has found a fresher morning,
And the mild moon rejoices in the clear & cloudless night,
And Man walks forth from midst of the fires: the evil is all consum'd.
His eyes behold the Angelic spheres arising night & day;
The stars consum'd like a lamp blown out, & in their stead, behold
The Expanding Eyes of Man behold the depths of wondrous worlds!
(F.Z. IX, 825–830)

If the ninth night of *The Four Zoas* fails to reach the totality of a full apocalyptic vision, this must be because it finally fails to transcend the Christian imagery that is its source, and consequently it fails to comprehend a redemptive movement in the Godhead, a dialectical movement of absolute negation which Blake will soon know as "Self-annihilation."

Blake's most luminous vision of "Self-annihilation" is contained in the second book of *Milton* where Milton, or a reborn Christianity, undergoes regeneration by transforming Satan into "The Great Humanity Divine." Urizen has now wholly been transposed into Satan, the Spectre of Albion, who made Himself a God and destroyed the "Human Form Divine" (32:12). As we have seen, this new and deeper vision of the mature Blake is accompanied by a new conception of the relation between human individuals and their changing states.

"Distinguish therefore States from Individuals in those States.
States Change, but Individual Identities never change nor cease.
You cannot go to Eternal Death in that which can never Die.
Satan & Adam are States Created into Twenty-seven Churches,
And thou, O Milton, art a State about to be Created,
Called Eternal Annihilation, that none but the Living shall
Dare to enter, & they shall enter triumphant over Death
And Hell & the Grave: States that are not, but ah! Seem to be."
(32:22–29)

While individual identities never die, all that which they become in the course of history must pass through an "eternal death," and it is precisely this passage through death that effects a cosmic and total regeneration. After Satan appears within the deadly Selfhood of Milton's "Shadow," Milton addresses Him with these words:

"Satan! my Spectre! I know my power thee to annihilate
And be a greater in thy place & be thy Tabernacle,
A covering for thee to do thy will, till one greater comes
And smites me as I smote thee & becomes my covering.
Such are the Laws of thy false Heav'ns; but Laws of Eternity
Are not such; know thou, I come to Self Annihilation.
Such are the Laws of Eternity, that each shall mutually
Annihilate himself for others' good, as I for thee."

(38:29–36)

Milton, the human state called "Eternal Annihilation," has, in his own state of self-negation, the power to annihilate Satan; but following the "Laws of Eternity" he annihilates himself for Satan's good. Repudiating the fear and dread inspired in men by Satan and His Churches—an *Angst* deriving from an abject and selfish terror of death (38:38 f.)—Milton's purpose is to teach men to despise death and to go on,

"In fearless majesty annihilating Self, laughing to scorn
Thy Laws & terrors, shaking down thy Synagogues as webs.
I come to discover before Heav'n & Hell the Self righteousness
In all its Hypocritic turpitude, opening to every eye
These wonders of Satan's holiness, shewing to the Earth
The Idol Virtues of the Natural Heart, & Satan's Seat
Explore in all its Selfish Natural Virtue, & put off
In Self annihilation all that is not of God alone,
To put off Self & all I have, ever & ever. Amen."

(38:41–49)

When self-righteousness is revealed as Satan's holiness, we are once again confronting a transcendence and inversion of the Western moral and theological tradition, an inversion that unveils the natural virtue of Selfhood as the inevitable expression of the Self-alienation of a fallen Albion. So long as self-righteousness is judged to be a moral phenomenon deriving from an isolated and autonomous self, there lies no way to a comprehension of its ultimate ground and its cosmic consequences. A self-righteousness that is simply the particular state of an individual selfhood—or, for that matter, the universal state of a fallen Adam—is closed to the possibility of either a cosmic origin or an apocalyptic end. The regenerate Milton discovers self-righteousness to be the totality of an unregenerate and fallen Selfhood, a totality comprehending the human, the cosmic, and the divine; and that totality has its origin in the initial movement of Albion's fall. Thus Percival concludes that the consequences of self-righteousness, as Blake conceives them, are the "externalization" of both God and the universe.[43] Only through a primordial act of absolute Self-affirmation, an act isolating individual identities from one another and creating the God who alone is God, does self-righteousness come into existence. Understood in this sense, self-righteousness can be seen to be identical with Selfhood; and the process of "Self-annihilation" must culminate with a reversal of the original act of Self-affirmation, thereby leading to an annihilation of Satan and the apocalyptic triumph of "The Great Humanity Divine." The process of "Self-annihilation" will not be complete until the distant and omnipotent God, whom Blake names Satan, has ceased to exist in His transcendent solitude and has become all in all in the new Eden of the "Human Imagination." Accordingly, H. M. Margoliouth can say: "To Humanize Urizen and to annihilate the Selfhood are two aspects of the same activity."[44]

Once Satan has ceased to exist as the transcendent and numinous Lord, there perishes with Him every moral imperative that is addressed to man from without, and humanity ceases to be imprisoned by an obedience to an external will or authority. In *The Everlasting Gospel* Blake presents a simple but powerful evocation of this antinomian theme, as can be seen in these lines recounting Jesus' reaction to the woman taken in adultery (who is blasphemously identified with Mary):

> What was the sound of Jesus' breath?
> He laid His hand on Moses' Law:
> The Ancient Heavens, in Silent Awe
> Writ with Curses from Pole to Pole,
> All away began to roll:
> The Earth trembling & Naked lay
> In secret bed of Mortal Clay,
> On Sinai felt the hand divine

Putting back the bloody shrine,
And she heard the breath of God
As she heard by Eden's flood:
"Good & Evil are no more!
Sinai's trumpets, cease to roar!
Cease, finger of God, to write!
The Heavens are not clean in thy Sight,
Thou art Good, and thou Alone;
Nor may the sinner cast one stone.
To be Good only, is to be
A God or else a Pharisee."

(e, 10–28)

Good and evil cease to be when man is delivered from Selfhood, when his solitary and autonomous ego is abolished, and he ceases to be aware of a distance separating himself from others. That very distance is solidified by the demands of a distant Lord, and apart from a fallen confinement in an isolated selfhood there could be no awareness of God as the Wholly Other. Yet only Jesus can save a fallen Albion from his cosmic Selfhood:

"In Selfhood, we are nothing, but fade away in morning's breath.
Our mildness is nothing: the greatest mildness we can use
Is incapable and nothing: none but the Lamb of God can heal
This dread disease, none but Jesus. O Lord, descend and save!"

(J. 45:13–16)

Max Plowman makes the telling point that ultimately *Jerusalem* is about nothing else but the forgiveness of sin; and he goes on to say: "The forgiveness of sin is a continual death in the Divine Image."[45] This statement would be more in accord with the paradoxical meaning of the poetry to which it is directed if it were to say that the forgiveness of sin is a continual death both *in* and *of* the "Divine Image." Only through God's death in Jesus, and through the repetition of that death in the "Minute Particular" who is united with Jesus, does that annihilation of Selfhood take place whose consequence is the forgiveness of sin.

Before examining Blake's celebration of the forgiveness of sin in *Jerusalem* we should take note of its roots in the Bible, and it is particularly significant that the biblical words lying closest to Blake's vision are contained in a post-exilic prophecy recorded in the Book of Jeremiah, a joyous prophecy embodying the initial promise of a New Covenant:

Behold, the days come, saith the Lord, that I will make a new covenant with the house of Israel, and with the house of Judah: Not according to the covenant that I made with their fathers . . . But this shall be the covenant that I will make with the house of Israel . . . I will put my law in their inward parts, and write it in their hearts; and will be their God, and they shall be my people. And they shall teach no more every man his neighbor, and every man his brother, saying, Know the Lord: for they shall all know me, from the least of them unto the greatest of them, saith the Lord: for I will forgive their iniquity, and I will remember their sin no more.

(31:31–34)

These words must have delighted the Blake who believed that every man may converse with God and be king and priest in his own house, but it is the final phrase of the prophecy that supplies a crucial key to *Jerusalem:* "I will remember their sin no more." Remarkably enough, these words have no clear analogue in the New Testament, but Blake was to join the greatest reformers of the Christian faith in discovering that the forgiveness of sin must culminate in an abolition of the memory of sin. If we know anything at all about the ministry of Jesus, we know that no action of that ministry brought a greater offense to his hearer than his forgiveness of sin; and no theme of his sayings or parables overshadows the proclamation of forgiveness, although we must recognize that this forgiveness is inseparable from the eschatological situation of the dawning of the Kingdom of God. Only through the advent of a new and glorious Kingdom that seeks out the sinner in the depths of darkness can the forgiveness of sin cease to be a promise and become instead a present and immediate reality.

Apparently the earliest form of the Christian tradition associated the atoning blood of Jesus with a New Testament or New Covenant, a tradition recorded by both Paul and the synoptic Gospels in their accounts of the institution of the Lord's Supper: "This cup is the new testament in my blood: this do ye, as oft as ye drink it, in remembrance of me" (I Cor. 11:25). Paul himself came to believe that the New Covenant was a covenant of Spirit and life, as opposed to an old covenant of death and the literal letter:

> But if the ministration of death, written and engraven in stones, was glorious, so that the children of Israel could not steadfastly behold the face of Moses for the glory of his countenance; which glory was to be done away; How shall not the ministration of the spirit be rather glorious?

He goes on to say that Moses placed a veil over his face, and thus hid the divine radiance, so that the children of Israel would not know how temporary the old covenant was to be.

> But their minds were blinded: for until this day remaineth the same veil untaken away in the reading of the old testament; which veil is done away in Christ. But even unto this day, when Moses is read, the veil is upon their heart. Nevertheless, when it shall turn to the Lord, the veil shall be taken away. Now the Lord is that Spirit: and where the Spirit of the Lord is, there is liberty. But we all, with open face beholding as in a glass the glory of the Lord, are changed into the same image from glory to glory, even as by the Spirit of the Lord.
> (II Cor. 3:4–18)

A radical Christian might well read Paul to mean that the glory of the God of the old covenant is to be abolished, for apart from this abolition of the God of judgment there remains no possibility of transforming the Christian into the "same image" as the glory of the Lord Jesus. Certainly such Christians have believed that the demands of the God of wrath and Law are annulled in the grace of the God who died on Calvary. Yet this grace cannot be fulfilled until it culminates in the cessation of the very memory of sin: indeed, a generation after Blake's death, Kierkegaard underwent his second conversion or "metamorphosis" when he finally came to realize that God had *forgotten* his sin, and then wrote *The Sickness Unto Death*, whose dialectical thesis is that sin is the opposite not of virtue but of faith.

A faith that recognizes itself as existing in opposition to the state of sin must give itself both to a negation of guilt and the Law and to a continual process of abolishing the consciousness of sin: "Come, O thou Lamb of God, and take away the remembrance of Sin" (J. 50:24). Seen in this perspective, guilt is the product of self-alienation; and it is not simply an alienation from an individual and private self, but rather a cosmic state of alienation from a universal and human Eternity.

> In Great Eternity every particular Form gives forth or Emanates
> Its own peculiar Light, & the Form is the Divine Vision
> And the Light is his Garment. This is Jerusalem in every Man,
> A Tent & Tabernacle of Mutual Forgiveness, Male & Female Clothings.
> And Jerusalem is called Liberty among the Children of Albion.
> (J. 54:1–5)

While Jerusalem is present in every "Man" as a tabernacle of mutual forgiveness, that tabernacle has been shattered by the Fall, as fallen man is sealed in the isolation of his individual selfhood:

> But Albion fell down, a Rocky fragment from Eternity hurl'd
> By his own Spectre, who is the Reasoning Power in every Man,
> Into his own Chaos, which is the Memory between Man & Man.
> (J. 54:6–8)

To name chaos as the memory separating man from man is to recognize that sin is a state of solitude, with the consequence that the forgiveness of sin is a cosmic process of "Self-annihilation." Furthermore, the forgiveness of sin is a universal and therefore an apocalyptic process of redemption: all those spaces separating a fallen Albion from his isolated parts must be annulled by a temporal process which draws the futurity of Eden into the present moment and thereby makes possible the final triumph of Jerusalem.

One of Blake's more cryptic symbols of the new Jerusalem that is breaking into time and space is Golgonooza, a symbol that first appears in the late additions to *The Four Zoas*. In *Milton,* after Ololon has lamented that the piteous female forms are compelled to weave the dreadful "Loom of Death" whereby the divine members of humanity are slain in offerings for sin, Blake comments:

So spake Ololon in reminiscence astonish'd, but they
Could not behold Golgonooza without passing the Polypus,
A wondrous journey not passable by Immortal feet, & none
But the Divine Saviour can pass it without annihilation.
For Golgonooza cannot be seen till having pass'd the Polypus
It is viewed on all sides round by a Four-fold Vision,
Or till you become Mortal & Vegetable in Sexuality,
Then you behold its mighty Spires & Domes of ivory & gold.
(35:18–25)

It is clear that Golgonooza can only be reached by the way of Experience, a passage through generation, sexuality, and death; thus the human traveler cannot see Golgonooza until he has passed the "Polypus" of an apocalyptic Satan. Golgonooza appears frequently in *Jerusalem* where it is identified as the labor of Los or the "Human Imagination":

Here, on the banks of the Thames, Los builded Golgonooza,
Outside of the Gates of the Human Heart beneath Beulah
In the midst of the rocks of the Altars of Albion. In fears
He builded it, in rage & in fury. It is the Spiritual Fourfold
London, continually building & continually decaying desolate.
(53:15–19)

While this passage clearly refers to Blake's prophetic and imaginative work, it is also intended to comprehend the vision of the total human Imagination, a vision that is not simply present in art, but is found wherever there is suffering and life.

Blake's commentators have been prone to identify Golgonooza as the City of Art; thus Frye asserts: "Complete awareness on the part of the poet that the tradition of poetry behind him is not a purely linear sequence but an evolution of a single archetypal form is thus the same thing as a vision of Golgonooza, the whole of human life seen in the framework of fall and redemption outlined by the poets."[46] However, this interpretation can be sustained only if we recognize that the word "art" here bears a peculiarly Blakean meaning, for it is both an imaginative and a redemptive reality. As Damon points out,[47] the root of the name "Golgonooza" seems to be "Golgotha," and this is but further testimony to Blake's belief that all true art is self-sacrifice. Golgonooza, moreover, is a new Golgotha; it is an apocalyptic repetition of Calvary drawing together the totality of suffering and passion into an ultimate act of "Self-annihilation." Therefore, we must beware of translating Golgonooza as the City of God—St. Augustine's *The City of God* marks the point at which the orthodox Church finally abandoned an eschatological ground, for Augustine understands the City of God as being already embodied in the Catholic Church—and recognize that Golgonooza is an apocalyptic symbol uniting the self-sacrifice of the "Universal Humanity" in Jesus with the triumphant dawning of the Kingdom of God. So long as Christianity confines the Crucifixion to the sacrifice of the unique and individual Jesus and remains closed to a universal process of passion and redemption, it will perpetuate the sealing of Jesus in Luvah's sepulcher, and continue to be that Wheel of Religion whose dark current condemns both Jesus and every man to guilt and death. Only when the Crucifixion is accepted as the innermost reality of the "Human Imagination" will the Kingdom of God appear in its universal form as the God who is becoming all in all.

If a universal Selfhood isolates man from man and man from God, then sin is equivalent to this cosmic state of isolation, and the forgiveness of sin must be a cosmic and historical process that negates this estrangement by annihilating the solitude that is its source. "Self-annihilation" is this process of negating the negations created by the birth of Selfhood: therefore it is a negative process of reversing the Fall, of transposing the contraries evolved by the contraction of the "Human Form Divine." On the 96th plate of *Jerusalem,* there is an illustration of two majestic figures rising from earth while drawing closer together in an ecstatic embrace. The figure on the left can only be the divine Creator and Judge, or Albion in his Satanic manifestation, and contrariwise the figure on the right is a beautiful and naked female form who must be Jerusalem. Satan-Albion ("The Ancient of Days") looks to the right while baring his right foot, both of which symbolize a spiritual ascent; whereas Jerusalem, who unlike her divine counterpart is facing us, rises on her left foot and looks to her right and our left. We may surmise that this illustration is a vision of the universal process of Crucifixion if only because Satan and Jerusalem are engaged in a mutual negation of that Selfhood which isolates each from the other: Satan reverses his destructive Selfhood so as to become Spirit, and Jerusalem reverses her spiritual movement so as to become "flesh" (i.e., *sarx*, in the Pauline sense of existence outside of or apart from Spirit). The text on this plate is saturated with apocalyptic imagery; it opens with a vision of the sun and moon leading forward the "Visions of Heaven & Earth," which is immediately followed by an apocalyptic epiphany of Jesus as the Son of Man:

> Then Jesus appeared standing by Albion as the Good Shepherd
> By the lost Sheep that he hath found, & Albion knew that it
> Was the Lord, the Universal Humanity; & Albion saw his Form
> A Man, & they conversed as Man with Man in Ages of Eternity.
> And the Divine Appearance was the likeness & similitude of Los.
>
> (3–7)

However, the traditional apocalyptic symbol of the Son of Man is a symbol of a heavenly and divine Being; and His epiphany—which marks the advent of the final Eschaton—occurs in the heavens where He appears with legions of angels. Blake dialectically inverts this ancient symbol so as to transpose it into the kenotic Jesus: hence the Lord appears in the form of a "Man," and his appearance is in the likeness and similitude of Los or the temporal form of the "Human Imagination."

We must not dissociate the lines of the text from their accompanying illustration, for the Albion who experiences the epiphany of Jesus is the Satan-Albion who embraces Jerusalem. The Satan of the illustration has His back turned toward us, and, in the lines directly facing His awesome buttocks, Albion laments his cruel and deceitful Selfhood, recognizing that the God of Sinai has ensnared him in a deadly sleep of six thousand years: "I know it is my Self, O my Divine Creator & Redeemer." Notice that the God of Law and judgment is not fully recognized as the deadly Selfhood until the human Jesus appears as the divine Creator and Redeemer! Nothing less is occurring here than an apocalyptic *coincidentia oppositorum*, and, while such a radical dialectical inversion has never previously occurred in the apocalyptic tradition, when it occurs here it is accompanied by a vision of a total process of redemption that is effected by a divine passage through death. Thus Jesus responds to Albion's terror of his own Selfhood with these words: "Fear not Albion: unless I die thou canst not live; but if I die I shall arise again & thou with me. . . ."

> So Jesus spoke: the Covering Cherub coming on in darkness
> Overshadow'd them, & Jesus said: "Thus do Men in Eternity
> One for another to put off, by forgiveness, every sin."
> (14-19)

The Satan whose darkness engulfs Jesus and Albion is the Satan who undergoes a cosmic reversal by dying in Jesus' death:

> Jesus said: "Wouldest thou love one who never died
> For thee, or ever die for one who had not died for thee?
> And if God dieth not for Man & giveth not himself
> Eternally for Man, Man could not exist; for Man is Love
> As God is Love; every kindness to another is a little Death
> In the Divine Image, nor can Man exist but by Brotherhood."
> (23-28)

Satan finally becomes manifest as the "Human Form Divine" when He dies for man and thus becomes united with Jesus or Jerusalem. While Satan's embrace of Jerusalem can only be consummated in death, that death annihilates His Selfhood and effects the forgiveness of sin. The "Divine Image" dies in Jesus so as to abolish the solitary God who is the source of judgment and bring about an apocalyptic brotherhood that is a full coming together of God and man. Consequently, the Crucifixion embodies an apocalyptic or total movement of Satan from left to right, from "flesh" to Spirit; and it is accompanied by a corresponding movement of Jerusalem from right to left, the kenotic movement of the Incarnation. Only when we understand the Incarnation and the Atonement as dual symbols of a single kenotic process will we be prepared for a vision of the apocalyptic Jesus, whose life *and* death is an epiphany of the "Great Humanity Divine."

v. Christ and Antichrist

ALMOST the whole of the penultimate plate of *Jerusalem* is given to a magnificent illustration of the full and final coming together of God and man. This illustration is obviously a portrait of the consummation of the initial union between Satan-Albion and Jesus-Jerusalem which we have just examined; for the most part it lies below the final words of the epic, "The End of the Song of Jerusalem," and we must accept it as Blake's final depiction of a Christian and apocalyptic *coincidentia oppositorum*. Only four copies of *Jerusalem* are now extant, and of these only the latest copy was printed in color (on paper dated 1820), and painted with water-colors and gold. All of the black and white copies seemingly portray God in His Satanic form, but in the colored version He appears as Jesus the Saviour, as Blake's ecstatic vision finally transfigured the awesome Creator into the apocalyptic Son of Man. Despite its apparent simplicity, this illustration is charged with paradoxical meaning, and it must have been intended as a portrait of a final coincidence of all those opposing realities which are celebrated on the pages of this apocalypse. On the lower right-hand corner of the illustration are the fiery flames of Hell and the "Human Imagination," dark currents of passion or energy are ascending toward the left, and in the center we discover God and man locked in the final throes of what is all too clearly a sexual embrace. Even Indian art has never so decisively portrayed an orgiastic epiphany of the sacred, but here the flames of an apocalyptic judgment flow equally into and out of the white and sepulchrous form of God, as He embraces the seared flesh of a resurrected humanity. A vibrant energy flows through the illustration, for the luminous figures are both passing into one another, and becoming transposed into their respective opposites even as they unite with one another. Against a circular background of blue, the heads of God and Jerusalem merge into an icon of Jesus, as Jerusalem's upward glance fulfills the motion of her buttocks by enclosing the face of God in the human and triangular space created by her outstretched arms. At last we encounter that sexual Eden promised by an earlier passage in *Jerusalem:*

> For the Sanctuary of Eden is in the Camp, in the Outline,
> In the Circumference, & every Minute Particular is Holy:
> Embraces are Cominglings from the Head even to the Feet,
> And not a pompous High Priest entering by a Secret Place.
> (69:41-44)

The final pages of *Jerusalem* are devoted to an ecstatic celebration of an apocalyptic epiphany, a final coming together of the long estranged limbs of Albion's "Body." After Jesus has declared that man exists by the eternal death of God for man, Albion recoils in terror at the destiny of his "Friend Divine," and loses himself in contemplation of the faith and wonder of the divine mercy. Realizing that "Eternal Death" is abroad, Albion then calls upon his friends to awake from sleep, addressing his call to all his cities and countries.

> So Albion spoke & threw himself into the Furnaces of affliction.
> All was a Vision, all a Dream: the Furnaces became
> Fountains of Living Waters flowing from the Humanity Divine.
> And all the Cities of Albion rose from their Slumbers, and All
> The Sons & Daughters of Albion on soft clouds, waking from Sleep.
> Soon all around remote the Heavens burnt with flaming fires,
> And Urizen & Luvah & Tharmas & Urthona arose into
> Albion's Bosom. Then Albion stood before Jesus in the Clouds
> Of Heaven, Fourfold among the Visions of God in Eternity.
> (96:35-43)

Now we see that a fourfold vision occurs only through a cosmic reintegration of a fallen "Humanity Divine." The four Zoas are the broken and fallen forms of a primordial Godmanhood, and, while Blake only succeeded in portraying God (Urizen) and Energy (Luvah) with any degree of clarity, it is evident that each of the Zoas is an incomplete and even perverse manifestation of the Humanity Divine. But the Zoas lose their perverse and fallen form only by passing through the "Furnace of affliction," a furnace that, like the wine-presses of Luvah, makes possible an ultimate vision only by leading Albion through an eternal death. Albion must die to awake, and his death is not simply a symbol of the dissolution of a cosmic *maya*, but is an actual and even historical event that transforms the constitution of the cosmos.

> "Awake, Awake, Jerusalem! O lovely Emanation of Albion,
> Awake and overspread all Nations as in Ancient Time;
> For lo! the Night of Death is past and the Eternal Day
> Appears upon our Hills. Awake, Jerusalem, and come away!"
> (97:1–4)

Albion awakes as Jerusalem only after the "Night of Death" is past; the "Eternal Day" can only appear when that night has come and gone: for Jerusalem will finally appear as the resurrected Albion, as the Albion who has passed through an eternal death.

When we recall that Albion both symbolizes and personifies a Totality that is human, cosmic, and divine, and that this Totality is not a timeless and quiescent Eternity but rather a dynamic and moving Eternity that becomes kenotically incarnate in concrete time and space, then we must realize that the historical Albion is a product of the absolute self-negation of Spirit and therefore is the historically realized consequence of the "Self-annihilation" of the primordial Totality. Contrariwise, the "Self-annihilation" of the historical Albion is equivalent to the eschatological process of absolute world-negation, an ultimate and decisive negation that leads not to the primordial paradise of Beulah but rather to the apocalyptic and final paradise of Eden. Only by means of a passage through an "Eternal Death" can Albion undergo that dialectical metamorphosis that will issue in the triumphant appearance of Jerusalem, for finally Jerusalem is the product of the absolute self-negation of the fallen Albion. Consequently, Jerusalem must be recognized as Blake's symbol of the resurrected and apocalyptic Jesus, a Christ who will be fully manifest only by the occurrence of a "Fourfold Annihilation." After the "Vision of Albion" has called upon Jerusalem to awake, the fourfold Albion takes up a loving bow of male and female, and wages wars of love and mutual benevolence by shooting a fourfold arrow of love:

Murmuring the Bowstring breathes with ardor. Clouds roll round the horns
Of the wide Bow; loud sounding Winds sport on the Mountains' brows.
The Druid Spectre was Annihilate, loud thund'ring, rejoicing terrific,
    vanishing,
Fourfold Annihilation; & at the clangor of the Arrows of Intellect
The innumerable Chariots of the Almighty appear'd in Heaven,
And Bacon & Newton & Locke, & Milton & Shakspear & Chaucer,
A Sun of blood red wrath surrounding heaven, on all sides around,
Glorious, incomprehensible by Mortal Man, & each Chariot was Sexual
    Threefold.

(98:4–11)

At points such as these, Blake's vision bursts the frames of his art,
and we may only dimly surmise its meaning. Nonetheless it is apparent that a fourfold annihilation will shatter the heavens, totally
annihilate the God who is the Wholly Other, and transform the
structure of the cosmos. While such a total annihilation reveals that
the chariots of the Almighty are sexually threefold, every "Man"
now stands fourfold:

The Four Living Creatures, Chariots of Humanity Divine Incomprehen-
    sible,
In beautiful Paradises expand. These are the Four Rivers of Paradise
And the Four Faces of Humanity, fronting the Four Cardinal Points
Of Heaven, going forward, forward irresistible from Eternity to Eternity.

(98:24–27)

If the Christ who is Jerusalem will only fully appear at the end of
time, then likewise it is only by means of a fourfold annihilation that
the Antichrist will be revealed, that final Antichrist who is associated
with the images of the red dragon and the hidden harlot in the Book
of Revelation. In the closing lines of *Jerusalem*, Blake goes so far
as to identify the forgiveness of sins or self-annihilation as the
"Covenant of Jehovah" (98:23). Yet, like Paul and Jeremiah, Blake
is here speaking of a New Covenant which abolishes the old covenant
of Law and sacrifice:

"Where is the Covenant of Priam, the Moral Virtues of the Heathen?
Where is the Tree of Good & Evil that rooted beneath the cruel heel
Of Albion's Spectre, the Patriarch Druid? where are all his Human Sacrifice

For Sin in War & in the Druid Temples of the Accuser of Sin, beneath
The Oak Groves of Albion that cover'd the whole Earth beneath his
   Spectre?"

(98:46–50)

Paradoxically, the Covenant of Jehovah effects a total negation of
God's Law. Thus Blake dares to cry: "Humanize in the Forgiveness
of Sins according to thy Covenant, Jehovah" (98:44 f.). Notice that
these lines come after the announcement that Albion has annihilated
the Druid Spectre, and they also follow the heavenly epiphany of
the sun of blood-red wrath. Only after the occurrence of these events
of apocalyptic judgment can the forgiveness of sins be named the
Covenant of Jehovah: now God has passed through an eternal death,
His identity as Satan has been fully and finally revealed, and thereby
He has lost that numinous power by which He judged and lorded over
a broken and humble man. Indeed, the very death of the "Divine
Image" reveals that God is love. His death makes possible the forgiveness of sins—for the forgiveness of sin is ultimately grounded in the
self-annihilation of God—thus, the Blake who continually celebrated
the glory of Satan finally came to grasp the eschatological necessity
of the death and therefore of the life of God. The God who finally
appears as Antichrist does so only by passing through an eternal
death, but that death effects the forgiveness of sin, and thereby makes
possible the final triumph of "The Great Humanity Divine."

God or Satan appears in His final form as Antichrist only after
He has died eternally for man; then He undergoes an apocalyptic
epiphany as the red dragon and the Whore of Babylon, revealing
that He has become that "Mystery" who will be vanquished at the
end of time: "And the beast that was, and is not, even he is the
eighth, and is of the seven, and goeth into perdition" (Rev. 17:11).
By reversing the imagery of the Book of Revelation, Blake unveils
the Antichrist as the eighth Eye of God who is dialectically coincident
with the apocalyptic Jesus or the resurrected "Humanity Divine."
In the Book of Revelation, the new Jerusalem descends to a new
earth only after Satan, death, and Hell have been cast into the lake
of fire:

And I saw a new heaven and a new earth: for the first heaven and the first earth were passed away; and there was no more sea. And I John saw the holy city, new Jerusalem, coming down from God out of heaven, prepared as a bride adorned for her husband. And I heard a great voice out of heaven saying, Behold, the tabernacle of God is with men, and he will dwell with them, and they shall be his people, and God himself shall be with them, and be their God. And God shall wipe away all tears from their eyes; and there shall be no more death, neither sorrow, nor crying, neither shall there be any more pain; for the former things are passed away.

And he that sat upon the throne said, Behold, I make all things new. And he said unto me, Write: for these words are true and faithful. And he said unto me, It is done. I am Alpha and Omega, the beginning and the end. I will give unto him that is athirst of the fountain of the water of life freely. He that overcometh shall inherit all things; and I will be his God, and he shall be my son. But the fearful, and unbelieving, and the abominable, and murderers, and whoremongers, and sorcerers, and idolaters, and all liars, shall have their part in the lake which burneth with fire and brimstone: which is the second death.

(21:1–8)

Going far beyond the Book of Revelation, Blake identifies the "second death" as a total Self-annihilation, an annihilation that in destroying Satan resurrects Him as the new Jerusalem, the universal Body of Jesus. Now the tabernacle of God appears as the apocalyptic Covenant of Jehovah; God's satanic Law has dialectically passed into the forgiveness of sin; the beastly body of Satan has become the human flesh of Jerusalem, His bride.

An apocalyptic and dialectical coincidence that unites Christ and Antichrist can be nothing less than a total process of cosmic regeneration, a process that in reversing the opposites of a fallen history makes possible their final reintegration. Thus the "Eternal Circle" that culminates in the union of Satan and Jerusalem is a moving and eschatological circle that evolves the opposites only to collapse them into one another by an ultimate reversal which dissolves the very reality of the circle itself. Eden dawns as the "Four Faces of Humanity" go forward from Eternity to Eternity:

And they conversed together in Visionary forms dramatic which bright
Redounded from their Tongues in thunderous majesty, in Visions

213

In new Expanses, creating exemplars of Memory and of Intellect,
Creating Space, Creating Time, according to the wonders Divine
Of Human Imagination throughout all the Three Regions immense
Of Childhood, Manhood & Old Age; & the all tremendous unfathomable
    Non Ens
Of Death was seen in regenerations terrific or complacent, varying
According to the subject of discourse; & every Word & Every Character
Was Human according to the Expansion or Contraction, the Translucence
    or
Opakeness of Nervous fibres: such was the variation of Time & Space
Which vary according as the Organs of Perception vary; & they walked
To & fro in Eternity as One Man, reflecting each in each & clearly seen
And seeing, according to fitness & order.

(J. 98:28–40)

Finally, Eden is the total epiphany of "One Man." Space and time will be totally humanized in an Apocalypse annihilating the non-human—the "Non Ens" of death—as the primordial Totality has finally come to an eschatological End and is thence resurrected as the apocalyptic Body of Man. The circle created by the fall from the primordial Totality is now broken; but the very passage of Albion through an "Eternal Circle" has foreclosed the possibility of a return to his unfallen beginning. Consequently, the Christ who is the resurrected Albion is not Alpha and Omega: He is the Alpha that has become Omega, the Beginning which has passed into the End, the Jerusalem who is Adam and Satan at once.

While the highest reaches of Vision transcend all that we can know or experience insofar as we remain bound to "Selfhood," they nevertheless give promise of an ultimate liberation, a liberation that will not simply dissolve but will wholly transform all that which we immediately and naturally are. Blake and every seer tells us that as a man is, so he sees; and, as the desire of man is infinite, so, finally, "Man" himself is infinite. Through faith the Christian knows that every man is called to an apocalyptic destiny, and through Vision we may know that the Apocalypse will reverse every opposite which has evolved in history. Once the primordial Totality has passed through an eternal death, the ground of alienation and estrangement will have been annihilated: an apocalyptic Totality will become all in all, and the glorious Body of Jerusalem will draw into itself every fragment of energy which has passed through pain and joy. Faith celebrates the eschatological triumph of the Kingdom of God or the mystical oneness of Brahman-Atman, Nirvana, or Tao; but an apocalyptic and spiritual Vision reverses the reality of faith, celebrating the final reversal of the sacred and profane, and thereby unveiling a "fearful symmetry" between Christ and Antichrist, Hell and Eden, Vala and Jerusalem. Only Vision in this radically apocalyptic sense is fully and finally dialectical, for only Vision in this final sense effects a true reversal of the opposites, a Vision that, in negating the opposites, unites them by making possible their transition into one another, thus effecting not an abolition of the opposites but a genuine *coincidentia oppositorum*. Both the higher forms of mysticism and the primitive forms of Christian eschatology proclaim an abolition of the opposites: the overwhelming reality of Nirvana becomes manifest as reality itself; the final epiphany of the Kingdom of God must bring an end to the reality of the world. Here, the opposites are negated only to be annulled; an absolute affirmation of the sacred is inseparable from an absolute negation of the profane. Neither Mahayana Buddhism nor biblical eschatology can know what Hegel termed the "negation of negation"—a dialectical negation that inevitably passes into affirmation. A final Yes-saying to the sacred reality lies at the center of faith, a Yes-saying that is total and all-inclusive, and which must therefore pass into an ultimate No-saying to the profanity or the worldliness of the world. Yet a radical and apocalyptic Vision embodies both a Yes-saying and a No-saying to the sacred—it unveils God as Satan only to embrace Him as Jerusalem—and therefore it necessarily passes into an ultimate affirmation and negation of the profane.

If the Fall is all, it must be present in Eden, for only through the dismemberment of the primordial Totality, and the advent of a progressively falling cosmos and history, does the apocalyptic Eden become a possibility. The movment from Fall to Apocalypse is a dialectical movement through an "Eternal Circle" demanding a full participation in every turn of the wheel. Just as Jesus is present in every pain and sorrow, so likewise every sorrow will be present in a transfigured form in Eden: indeed, Jerusalem is the transfigured body of Jesus and hence the true body of every man. Apart from the joy and horror of our fallen history, there could be neither a real nor a dialectical movement culminating in the Apocalypse. Therefore, every moment not only opens into Eden, but also the actual reality of Eden is inseparable from a fallen time and space; the sleeping Albion of our contracted senses is inseparable from the "One Man" whom our expanded senses know as Jesus the Christ. Finally, the Apocalypse is inseparable from Creation, Incarnation, and Crucifixion. Fall, Redemption, History, and Apocalypse are dialectical movements that both affirm and negate each other; each movement is necessary to the other, and only by means of the opposites which their movements evolve does a total dialectical movement derive the energy that makes possible both its motion and its culmination. A radical and apocalyptic Vision knows the necessity of the opposites and out of that necessity arises the reality of the *coincidentia oppositorum*. If the Apocalypse is to be all-embracing in a total and dialectical sense, then the opposites must pass into one another; they must coincide in a total union, as every movement of the falling Albion must culminate in the apocalyptic Jesus who is the full epiphany of Jerusalem, and every limb of Albion's dismembered body must reveal itself as being a kenotic form of the Christ who is Christ and Antichrist at once.

Living as we do in a time and space that is radically profane, in a wholly immanent mode of existence which has collapsed Eternity into time and disclosed the pure exteriority and total otherness of a fallen cosmos, we must remain closed to a positive vision of the sacred insofar as we accept the destiny of our history. Never before has man been so totally immersed in a profane consciousness; neither classical Confucianism nor the Olympian religion of ancient Greece was so decisively turned away from the transcendent and the holy, and today we can only wonder at the natural piety of the Stoic and Epicurean schools, to say nothing of the dismay and scepticism with which the contemporary sensibility must inevitably react to the call of the higher expressions of mystical sanctity for an identification with the finitude and the transiency of the world. Not until our time did the meaning and the reality of a radical finitude become embedded in human consciousness, for ours is the first form of human consciousness to have evolved after the historical event of the death of God. Even Blake was never fully immersed in a profane sensibility, and, while Blake prophetically foresaw the deeper reaches of Albion's "sleep," he apparently never immediately or actually participated in an Ulro-vision. Nevertheless, Blake succeeded in creating a magnificent vision of the deeper meaning of Ulro or Hell; he clearly delineated the necessary relation between the advent of a final form of the Ulro-vision and the death of Urizen, and his apocalyptic vision reveals that the transposition of Urizen into Satan can be nothing less than the initial dawning of the Apocalypse. If the Antichrist has appeared on our horizon, and is destined to become yet more fully incarnate in our world, then we can learn through Blake to greet His epiphany not only with horror but also with joy. For the Antichrist is the final kenotic manifestation of Christ, His white and alien body must pass into the ecstatic form of Jerusalem, His demonic energy must become consummated in the bliss of Jerusalem's total embrace. Apocalyptic imagery has always depicted the last age of history as the reign of Satan or Antichrist; it has known that the Kingdom of God cannot triumph until the world becomes swallowed up in darkness, but only the radical apocalyptic seer has unveiled that darkness as light. Realizing as we must that every original symbol of the sacred has disappeared in our darkness, we must be open to a dialectical metamorphosis of the sacred, a kenotic transformation of the sacred into the profane, an historical epiphany of the broken but triumphant Body of Jesus in a totally fallen human hand and face.

A genuine dialectical metamorphosis or kenotic transformation of the sacred into the profane can only occur by means of a passage through death: God must eternally die for man, a primordial Totality must pass through Self-annihilation, Christ must become Antichrist before He can be resurrected as Jerusalem. Accordingly, an apocalyptic and dialectical regeneration must transpose every opposite into its own other. When the opposites move through the finality of death they will be resurrected in reverse form: Spirit will die as Spirit and become fully incarnate in flesh, Eternity will wholly dissolve its transcendent form and become solely present in the immediate moment, the Jesus who descends into Hell will appear as the body of Satan in the initial epiphany of the Apocalypse. By moving through an actual death of its original form, every opposite will dialectically pass into its other: this self-annihilation will wholly dissolve the original identity of each opposite, and this process of the negation of negation will draw all the estranged contraries of a fallen Totality into a final coincidence of the opposites. The penultimate design in *Jerusalem* of this final coincidence reveals how the apocalyptic union of God and man will annihilate the God who alone is God by resurrecting Him as "The Great Humanity Divine." Every fragment of ecstatic joy and bodily delight foreshadows this apocalyptic union, every momentary death of Selfhood negates a barrier to this apocalyptic consummation, every affirmation of an opposing other sanctifies that Satan who will ultimately be transfigured into Jerusalem. Finally, Albion will become a radiant Jerusalem, a glorious "Humanity Divine" who will embody a cosmic Totality. Thus the final lines of *Jerusalem* prophetically proclaim the promise of an Eden who is "One Man":

All Human Forms identified, even Tree, Metal, Earth & Stone: all
Human Forms identified, living, going forth & returning wearied
Into the Planetary lives of Years, Months, Days & Hours; reposing,
And then Awaking into his Bosom in the Life of Immortality.

And I heard the Name of their Emanations: they are named Jerusalem.

NOTES

SECTION ONE

1. G. W. F. Hegel, *Science of Logic,* tr. by W. H. Johnston and L. G. Struthers (The Macmillan Co., New York, 1929), I, p. 168.

2. Joseph H. Wicksteed, *Blake's Innocence and Experience* (E. P. Dutton & Co., New York, 1928), p. 246.

3. H. M. Margoliouth, *William Blake's Vala* (Clarendon Press, Oxford, 1956), p. 111.

4. Joseph H. Wicksteed, *Blake's Vision of the Book of Job,* Second Edition (E. P. Dutton & Co., New York, 1924), pp. 114 ff., 145 ff., 161 f., 166.

5. Hegel, p. 155.

6. *Ibid.,* p. 153.

7. *Ibid.,* p. 155.

8. *Ibid.,* pp. 166 f.

9. Arthur Symons, *William Blake* (E. P. Dutton & Co., New York, 1907), p. 274. An appendix in this book is the most convenient source for Crabb Robinson's writings about Blake; it also contains other contemporary accounts of Blake.

10. Cf. Albert S. Roe, *Blake's Illustrations to the Divine Comedy* (Princeton University Press, Princeton, N.J., 1953), esp. pp. 30–38.

11. Milton O. Percival, *William Blake's Circle of Destiny* (Columbia University Press, New York, 1938), p. 80.

12. Northrop Frye, *Fearful Symmetry: A Study of William Blake* (Princeton University Press, Princeton, N.J., 1947), p. 349.

13. *Ibid.,* p. 258.

14. Cf. *Ibid.,* pp. 14–23.

15. Alfred N. Whitehead, *Process and Reality* (The Social Science Book Store, New York, no date), p. 239.

16. Blake's annotations to *Reynold's Discourses.*

17. Whitehead, p. 252.

18. *Ibid.*

19. *Ibid.,* p. 254.

20. M. Merleau-Ponty, *The Phenomenology of Perception,* tr. by Colin Smith (Routledge & Kegan Paul, London, 1962), p. 37.

21. *Ibid.,* p. 36.

22. *Ibid.,* p. xi.

23. *Ibid.,* p. 430.

24. Cf. Ruthven Todd, *Tracks in the Snow* (Charles Scribner's Sons, New York, 1947), pp. 29 f.

NOTES

25. Gershom G. Scholem, *Major Trends in Jewish Mysticism* (Schocken Books, New York, 1954), p. 215. Although it was published too late to be employed in this study, Désirée Hirst's *Hidden Riches: Traditional Symbolism from the Renaissance to Blake* (Barnes and Noble, New York, 1964) deserves citation at this point. Once again we find an attempt to demonstrate that Blake's was a traditional mystical symbolism, but, unlike Damon and Percival, Miss Hirst has neither a critical understanding of Blake nor a very intimate acquaintance with the phenomena of mysticism. However, the book does succeed in clearly presenting the major esoteric movements of Europe between the fifteenth and nineteenth centuries; and, contrary to Miss Hirst's intention, her data shows all too clearly the chasm that separates Blake's vision from that of his forebears.

26. *Ibid.*, p. 227.

27. Hegel, pp. 64 f.

28. *Ibid.*, p. 65.

29. *Ibid.*, p. 36.

30. *Ibid.*, p. 117.

31. *Ibid.*, p. 124.

32. *Ibid.*, p. 125.

33. *Ibid.*, p. 185.

34. *Ibid.*, II, pp. 167–172.

35. *Ibid.*, pp. 66 f.

36. *Ibid.*, p. 68.

37. Blake's marginalia on Spurzheim's *Observations on Insanity*.

38. Percival, p. 232.

39. Wicksteed, *Blake's Innocence and Experience*, pp. 248 f.

40. Frye, p. 135.

41. Bernard Blackstone, *English Blake* (Cambridge University Press, Cambridge, 1949), p. 230.

42. Whitehead, p. 519.

43. *Ibid.*, p. 520.

44. G. W. F. Hegel, *The Phenomenology of Mind,* tr. by J. B. Baillie (The Macmillan Co., New York, 1949), pp. 752 f.

45. *Ibid.*, p. 251.

46. *Ibid.*, p. 369.

47. *Ibid.*, p. 257.

48. J. N. Findlay, *Hegel: A Re-Examination* (Collier Books, New York, 1962), p. 348.

49. Hegel, *Phenomenology*, p. 513.

50. *Ibid.*, p. 551.

51. *Ibid.*, p. 553.

52. *Ibid.*, p. 768.

53. *Ibid.*

54. G. E. Bentley, Jr., *Willam Blake's Vala or The Four Zoas* (Clarendon Press, Oxford, 1963), pp. 162–166.

SECTION TWO

1. Emanuel Swedenborg, *Angelic Wisdom Concerning the Divine Love and the Divine Wisdom* (Swedenborg Foundation, New York, 1962), No. 11, p. 7.

2. Blake's annotations to Watson's *Apology for the Bible.*

3. A. L. Morton, *The Everlasting Gospel* (Lawrence and Wishart, London, 1958), pp. 36 f. The writings of the Ranters have been censored in our time almost as effectively as they were in their own; but a representative selection is available in an appendix to Norman Cohn's *The Pursuit of the Millennium* (Harper Torchbooks, New York, 1961), pp. 321–378.

4. *The Prophetic Writings of William Blake*, edited by D. J. Sloss and J. P. R. Wallis (Clarendon Press, Oxford, 1926), II, pp. 6 ff., 81 ff., 90 ff.

5. S. Foster Damon, *William Blake: His Philosophy and Symbols* (Houghton Mifflin Co., Boston and New York, 1924), p. 194.

6. Bentley, pp. 171–175.

7. Hegel, *Phenomenology*, p. 75.

8. *Ibid.*, pp. 559 f.

9. *Ibid.*, p. 561.

10. *Ibid.*, p. 588.

11. Joseph Wicksteed, *William Blake's Jerusalem* (The Trianon Press, London, 1954), p. 244.

12. Frye, pp. 250 f.

13. Rudolf Otto, *Mysticism East and West,* tr. by Bertha L. Bracey and Richenda C. Payne (Collier Books, New York, 1962), pp. 187–206.

14. *Meister Eckhart: A Modern Translation,* by Raymond Bernard Blakney (Harper Torchbooks, New York, 1957), pp. 203 f.

15. *Ibid.*, p. 181.

16. *Ibid.*, p. 280.

17. *Ibid.*, p. 180.

18. G. W. F. Hegel, *Early Theological Writings,* tr. by T. M. Knox and Richard Kroner (The University of Chicago Press, Chicago, 1948), p. 316.

19. Hegel, *Phenomenology*, p. 81.

20. *Ibid.*, p. 766.

21. Eckhart, p. 247.

22. Hegel, *Phenomenology*, p. 86.

23. *Ibid.*, p. 556.

24. *Ibid.*, p. 722.

25. *Ibid.*, pp. 755 f.

26. *Ibid.*, p. 782.
27. *Ibid.*, p. 758.
28. *Ibid.*, p. 776.
29. *Ibid.*, p. 767.
30. Frye, p. 401.
31. Percival, p. 29.
32. Wicksteed, *Jerusalem*, pp. 13, 250n.
33. Frye, pp. 342 f.
34. Hegel, *Phenomenology*, pp. 762 f.
35. *Ibid.*, pp. 774 f.
36. *Ibid.*, p. 781.
37. *Ibid.*, pp. 783 f.
38. *Ibid.*, pp. 784 f.
39. Margoliouth, p. 3.
40. Bentley, p. 163.
41. Wicksteed, *Jerusalem*, p. 219.
42. *The Way of Lao Tzu*, tr. by Wing-Tsit Chan (The Library of Liberal Arts, Bobbs Merrill Co., Indianapolis, Indiana, 1963), No. 6, p. 110.
43. Wicksteed, *Jerusalem*, p. 154.
44. *Ibid.*, p. 204.
45. Frye, p. 335.
46. Pervical, p. 186.
47. Wicksteed, *Jerusalem*, p. 122.
48. *Ibid.*, p. 245.

SECTION THREE

1. Percival, p. 47.
2. Frye, p. 299.
3. *Ibid.*, p. 320.
4. *Ibid.*, p. 340.
5. Blackstone, p. 200.
6. Peter F. Fisher, *The Valley of Vision:* "Blake as Prophet and Revolutionary," edited by Northrop Frye (University of Toronto Press, Toronto, 1961), pp. 212 f.
7. *Ibid.*, p. 52.
8. Mircea Eliade, *The Myth of the Eternal Return*, tr. by Willard R. Trask (Bollingen Series XLVI, Pantheon Books, Inc., New York, 1954), pp. 156 f.
9. Percival, p. 49.
10. Frye, p. 389.
11. Sloss and Wallis, pp. 203–209.
12. Wicksteed, *Blake's Vision of the Book of Job*, p. 174.

NOTES

13. For an excellent analysis of Blake as a biblical poet in this sense, cf. Frye, *Fearful Symmetry,* pp. 144, 337–346, 360–371.

14. Wicksteed, *Jerusalem,* pp. 86 f.

15. Cf. Hazard Adams, *William Blake: A Reading of the Shorter Poems* (University of Washington Press, 1963), pp. 180–200.

16. Sloss and Wallis, *Prophetic Writings of Blake,* I, p. 141.

17. Frye, p. 53.

18. Blake's Laocoon engraving.

19. Blake's annotations to Reynold's *Discourses.*

20. Th. Stcherbatsky, *Buddhist Logic* (Dover Publications, Inc., New York, 1962), I, pp. 181 ff.

21. Quoted by Henri de Lubac, *Aspects of Buddhism,* tr. by George Lamb (Sheed & Ward, Inc., New York, 1954), p. 28.

22. Hubert Benoit, *The Supreme Doctrine:* "Psychological Studies in Zen Thought" (Compass Books, New York, 1959), p. 25.

23. Frye, p. 449.

24. Wicksteed, *Jerusalem,* p. 81.

25. *Ibid.,* p. 165.

SECTION FOUR

1. David V. Erdman, *Blake, Prophet Against Empire* (Princeton University Press, Princeton, N.J., 1954), p. 235.

2. Frye, p. 206.

3. Damon, p. 109.

4. Northrop Frye, *Anatomy of Criticism* (Princeton University Press, Princeton, N.J., 1957), p. 117.

5. *Ibid.,* p. 119.

6. *Ibid.,* p. 121.

7. Frye, *Fearful Symmetry,* p. 360.

8. Frye, *Anatomy of Criticism,* p. 203.

9. *Ibid.,* p. 136.

10. Frye, *Fearful Symmetry,* p. 306.

11. Northrop Frye, "Notes for a Commentary on *Milton,*" *The Divine Vision,* edited by Vivian De Sola Pinto (Victor Gollancz, London, 1957), p. 111.

12. Herbert Marcuse, *One-Dimensional Man* (The Beacon Press, Boston, 1964), p. 123.

13. *Ibid.,* p. 132.

14. *Ibid.,* p. 140.

15. *Ibid.,* p. 142.

16. *Ibid.,* p. 141.

17. *Ibid.,* p. 236.

18. Karl Löwith, *From Hegel to Nietzsche:* "The Revolution in Nineteenth Century Thought," tr. by David E. Green (Holt, Rinehart and Winston, New York, 1964), p. 35.

19. *Ibid.*, pp. 127 f.

20. Hegel, *Phenomenology*, p. 800.

21. Hegel, *Logic*, II, pp. 427 f.

22. *Ibid.*, p. 473.

23. *Ibid.*, p. 468.

24. Findlay, p. 359.

25. Blackstone, p. xvii.

26. *Ibid.*, p. 249.

27. Th. Stcherbatsky, *The Conception of Buddhist Nirvana* (Leningrad, 1927), pp. 42 ff. Cf. *Buddhism*, edited by Richard Gard (Washington Square Press, Inc., New York, 1963), pp. 103–106.

28. T. R. V. Murti, *The Central Philosophy of Buddhism:* "A Study of the Madhyamika System" (George Allen and Unwin, Ltd., London, 1960), pp. 232 f.

29. Hegel, *Phenomenology*, p. 777.

30. Murti, p. 233.

31. Otto, p. 187.

32. *Ibid.*, p. 188.

33. *Ibid.*

34. Hegel, *Phenomenology*, pp. 80 f.

35. Hegel, *Logic*, I, p. 83.

36. Nathan Söderblom, *The Living God:* "Basal Forms of Personal Religion" (The Beacon Press, Boston, 1962), pp. 303–317.

37. *Ibid.*, p. 327.

38. *Ibid.*, p. 344.

39. Rudolf Otto, *The Kingdom of God and the Son of Man,* tr. by Floyd V. Filson and Bertram Lee-Woolf (Lutterworth Press, London, 1938), p. 49.

40. *Ibid.*, p. 59.

41. *Ibid.*, p. 72.

42. *Ibid.*, pp. 146 f.

43. Percival, p. 219.

44. H. M. Margoliouth, *William Blake,* (Oxford University Press, Oxford, 1951), p. 142.

45. Max Plowman, *An Introduction to the Study of Blake* (E. P. Dutton & Co., New York, 1927), pp. 178, 182.

46. Frye, *Fearful Symmetry*, p. 323.

47. Damon, p. 375.

INDEX

INDEX